BEETHOVEN
THE MAN WHO FREED MUSIC

VOLUME TWO

From the painting by Stieler, 1819

BEETHOVEN

THE MAN
WHO FREED MUSIC

BY

ROBERT HAVEN
SCHAUFFLER

VOLUME
TWO

GARDEN CITY   NEW YORK

DOUBLEDAY, DORAN & COMPANY, INC.
MCMXXIX

Contents of Volume Two

34 WHEN BEETHOVEN LAUGHED   329

Humour in Beethoven's Music — Becomes a Creative Force — Musical Slaps on the Back — False-Start Passages — Practical Jokes on Players — Baulked Expectations — Musical Puns — Elfin Fun — Infectious Verbal Felicity — Violoncello Humour — Pun Habit — "Ears on His Feet" — Fantastic Threats — Pun in C Sharp Minor — Horseplay with the Abbé Stadler — Laughs at Himself — Irony.

35 THE BEETHOVENATE SYMPHONY   340

"*Corkscrew*" Sonata, Finished 1812 — Shows Consideration for Rode — 1813, a Bad Year — Poverty — Maelzel's Panharmonicon — Battle Pieces in Fashion — The "*Battle*" Symphony — First Performance, December 8, 1813 — Celebrities in the Orchestra — Popular Success — Defrauds Maelzel — Repents of His Folly — His Forward-looking Mind — Interest in Invention : Fountain Pens, Aviation, Steam Cannons, Steamboats, Lifts — *The Glorious Moment* — Polonaise, Op. 89 — E Minor Piano Sonata, Op. 90 — Its Program — Last Revision of *Fidelio*, 1814 — The Germ-Motive — The Source-Motive — Marginalia — "The Mad Musician" — "Man, Help Thyself!"

36 "AS GOOD AS LOST"   350

Last Public Appearance as Pianist, 1814 — Growing Avarice — Kindness to Brother — Karl Dies, November 16, 1815 — Beethoven Joint Guardian of Nephew — Litigation with Sister-in-Law — Fervid Love for Nephew — The "van" in His Name — A Purely Musical Witticism

CONTENTS

— Receives Freedom of City, about December 1, 1815 —
Violoncello Sonatas, C Major and D Major, 1815 — Tenta-
tive Beginning of Third Period — Its Characteristics —
A Major Sonata, Op. 101 — Song Cycle, *To the Distant
Beloved*, 1816 — A Milestone in Musical History — Mar-
ginalia, 1816–1817 — Fish Suppers at Nussdorf — His
Favourite Symphony — Despair — Offer from London
Philharmonic — *Hammerklavier* Sonata, 1818–1819.

37 THE EMANCIPATOR EMANCIPATED   364
Present from Broadwood, 1818 — Progress of Deafness —
Suspicion and Violence — A Musical Bootjack — The
Conversation Books — Irregular Habits and Exposure —
Failing Health, 1818–1823 — "A Hearty, Free Word"
— Helplessness — Creative Freedom — Inertia in Starting
New Compositions — 1820, E Major Sonata, Op. 109 —
1821, A Flat Sonata, Op. 110 — A Memory Sonata —
Simultaneous Echoes of Haydn, Mozart, and Bach —
Souvenir of the *Eroica* — Fugue-Finale — "Imagination
Claims Its Rights" — 1822, C Minor Sonata, Op. 111 —
Its Difficulties for the Listener — Beethoven Arrested
as a Vagabond, 1820 — Present Intelligence of Vienna
Police — Beethoven's Concentration — Sir John Russell's
Description of Him, 1821 — Tricked into Improvising
— Rossini Calls, 1822 — *Fidelio* Revived, 1822 — Bee-
thoven Fails as Conductor — The Real Tragedy of His
Deafness.

38 HE FREES THE MASS   381
Mass in D, Begun 1818 — Intended for Rudolph's En-
thronization Ceremony, 1820 — But Not Finished Until
1823 — An Unecclesiastical and Unvocal Writer — His
Personal Creed — His Detachment from Earth, 1819
— *Missa* Begun as an Occasional Work — Music with a
Purpose — Handicaps to Composition — Comparative
Failure of *Kyrie, Gloria,* and Part of *Sanctus* — *Power*
and Beauty of *Credo, Benedictus,* and *Agnus Dei* — A
Barefaced Plagiarism — Hints of Military Music — The
Finest Melody in the *Missa* — Evaluation as a Whole —
Defensive Rationalization — Beethoven Frees the Mass.

CONTENTS

39 MR. HYDE AND THE HELL–HOUNDS   390
    Bad Faith with Publishers — Palliations — Did Beethoven
    Have a Higher Private Moral Code? — Weak Case for the
    Defense — Solicits Private Subscriptions for *Missa* — Mis-
    representations to Zelter — Letter to Goethe, February 8,
    1823, Unanswered — Schindler Established as Factotum,
    1822 — Liszt's Début, 1823 — Diabelli Variations, 1823.

40 THE *CHORAL* SYMPHONY   399
    Choral Symphony, Begun before 1817, Finished 1823 —
    Long Incubation Period — 1818, Memorandum for Ninth
    and Tenth Symphonies — Fusion of the Two Schemes —
    Echoes — Initial Difficulty in Composing — The Program
    Question — Beethoven's Three Most Original Contribu-
    tions — First Movement — *Scherzo* — The Kettledrum
    Joke — Origin of First Subject — *Adagio-Andante* —
    Choral Finale — Skill in Selecting Words — Merits and
    Defects of *Hymn to Joy*.

41 HE EMBRACES THE AMATEURS   416
    February, 1824, an Address to Beethoven — His Indecision
    — Conspiracy of Friends — Announcement of Concert —
    Rehearsal — Concert May 7, 1824 — Deaf to Applause —
    A Financial Failure — Accuses Supper Guests of Dishon-
    esty — Breaks Faith with London Philharmonic — Word
    Portrait by Rochlitz.

42 THE CREATIVE LISTENER AND THE LAST
        QUARTETS   423
    Project of English Trip Revived, 1824 — And Wrecked
    — Prince Galitzin Orders String Quartets — Preparation
    Necessary for Hearing Last Quartets — Alpine Blossoms
    of Experience — Anticipations of Man's Evolution — The
    Ineffable Residue of Reality — Our Debt to His Deafness
    — "Ditties of No Tone" — The String Quartet a Fit
    Vehicle — Invents New Forms — Aids for the Listener —
    How to Approach this Music.

43 "LA GAIETE"   430
    1824, First Galitzin Quartet, E Flat — Its Emotional
    Unity — Suggestion of the *Pathétique* — And of the *Missa*

[vii]

CONTENTS

— Inspires Schumann and Brahms — An Impish Passage — First Performance, 1825 — Two Shabby Tricks — Failure of Schuppanzigh — Replaced by Boehm — Holz Supplants Schindler — Domestic Troubles — Furious Letter to Copyist Wolanek — Minerva and the Sow — Beethoven Not to Be Judged by Ordinary Standards.

44 THE A MINOR QUARTET   438
Illness — 1825, Second Galitzin Quartet, A Minor — Mottos of Slow Movement — Programs — Echo of *Arioso Dolente* — Defect of First Movement — Economy in *Allegro ma non Tanto* — Harmonic Syncopation — High Lights.

45 LESS LACK OF FANCY   443
1825, Word Portrait by Rellstab — Beethoven Complains of Neglect — Relations with Nephew — Loneliness — Premonitions of Death — Karl Runs Away — 1825, Third Galitzin Quartet, B Flat — *"Quartetto Scherzoso"* — Beethoven's *"Leibquartett"* — *Cavatina* Cost Him Tears — Modesty — Contrapuntal Miracles in First Movement — Influences Wagner — Fairy Music in *Andante con moto* — The Great Fugue — Writes a New *Finale*.

46 "SPANGY" IN THE BLACK SPANIARD'S HOUSE   454
1825, Moves to Black Spaniard's House — Renews Intimacy with Von Breunings — "Trouser Button" — Relics — Frau von Breuning — An Embarrassing Escort — Unconsciousness of Discord.

47 THE MASTER'S MASTERPIECE   458
C Sharp Minor Quartet Completed, 1826 — Its Preëminence — Sketches — "Cribbed," yet "Spanking New" — The Author's Own Reaction — "Twenty Minutes of Reality" — From Heaven to Earth — The Opening Fugue — "Consciousness Surpassing Our Own" — An Expressionistic *Allegretto* — A Mighty Compensation.

48 THE "MADMAN" AT GNEIXENDORF   468
Karl Goes from Bad to Worse — Lays Hands on His Uncle — Attempts Suicide — Decides to Be a Soldier — Bee-

CONTENTS

thoven Takes Him to Gneixendorf, September, 1826 — A
Trying Guest — Homely Brother Johann — Beethoven's
Habits of Composition Too Much for Cook — The Vine-
Dresser Valet's Account — What the Natives Thought of
Him — *"A Bissel Stada!"* — Friction.

49   RETROSPECT IN F MAJOR   473

October 30, 1826, Last Quartet Finished — Reason for
Its Brevity — *The Merchant of Venice* — Op. 135, a Retrospect — *"The Midway"* Forecast — Origin of *"Muss es
sein?"* — The Housekeeper Theory — Dembscher and
the Canon.

50   THE DIVINE COMEDY IS FINISHED   478

Return to Vienna, December 2, 1826 — Last Illness —
Brave Wit During Operation — Sick-Room Conditions —
Enjoys Gift of Handel's Works — Confident of Pos-
terity's Verdict — Tries to Learn Arithmetic — Repre-
sentations of Poverty — Gift of £100 from Philharmonic,
February 28, 1827 — Was It Obtained Under False Pre-
tenses? — Rationalization — "A Stormy Flood" — Karl
Leaves Vienna — Mental Confusion — Schubert's Visit
— Last Handwriting, March 23 — "Applaud, Friends" —
Last Words, March 24 — Delirium — Death, March 26,
1827 — Cause of Death — Finding the Secret Drawer —
Philharmonic's Handsome Action — Burial, March 29 —
Reburial, 1872 — Tomb.

51   HOW BEETHOVEN FREED MUSIC   489

A Versatile Emancipator — Established Composer on
Professional Basis — Democratized and Universalized
Music — No Disparagement of Bach Implied — Culti-
vated Nuance — Developed the Continental Concert —
Matured the Art — Freed Form — Helped to Liberate
Harmony — Created New Technic for Keyboard Instru-
ments — Emancipated Modulation — Took Music Out-
of-Doors — Freed It from Cloistered Outlook — The
Luther of Church Music — And of the Dramatic Over-
ture — Rid Music of Exhibitionism — Fought Venality
— Developed Mechanism of Piano — And of Orchestra —

CONTENTS

Dissolved Time-honoured Identity of Composer and Inter-
preter — Made Music More Self-Contained — Encouraged
Rise of Creative Listening — Beethoven the Chief of
Many Liberators.

52 WHAT BEETHOVEN MEANS TO US   495
A Supreme Master of Construction — Novel Architec-
tonic Method — Made Forms "Internal" — Developed
Them — Closely Knit Structures — Lengthened Sonata
and Symphony — Multiplied Movements — The Germ-
Motive — The Source-Motive — Modified the Rondo —
And the Fugue — Three Greatest Contributions — The
Titanic *Allegro* — The *Scherzo* — The Mystical *Adagio*
— Treatment of Variation Form — Originality — Dra-
matic Power — Unexpectedness — Lavish Vitality —
Economy — Concentration — Large Calibre — The Bee-
thoven Religion — Beethoven as Physician — Conscien-
tious Idealism — Trough and Crest — Fluctuations of
Fashion — A Gift from Nature.

PART II — BEETHOVEN'S WORKSHOP

53 THE BORROWING ALCHEMIST   511
Prospecting Adventures in Beethoven — True Value of
Such Researches — Beauty in the Making — Plagiarism *vs.*
Genial Appropriation — Choice of Subject Matter for
Part II — Beethoven Borrows from Haydn — And Mozart
— From Himself — Foreign Folk Tunes — From Himself
— The Rust Imposture — Mozart Fathers the Joy Tune
— Echoes in the Last Quartets.

54 BEETHOVEN INVENTS THE GERM–MOTIVE   530
Germ-Motive *vs.* Source-Motive — New Meaning of the
Word "Idea" — Beethoven Feels His Way — A Con-
sciously Used Device — Treatment of Germ-Motive in
Part I — Progenitor of Leitmotif — Early Experimenta-
tion — First Elaborate Use in *Pathétique* — C Minor
Quartet — Violin Sonatas A Minor and F Major — Second
Symphony — *"Kreutzer"* Sonata — *Eroica* — *"Appas-*

CONTENTS

sionata" — C Minor Symphony — *Serioso* Quartet —
B Flat Trio — Eighth Symphony — A Masterpiece of
Camouflage — Beethoven Describes His Own Creative
Processes — Initial Germ-Motive in Last Sonatas —
Choral Symphony — Last Quartets.

55 SOME SOURCE–MOTIVES 566

Source-Motives in Part I — Thrift and Resource — "Cer-
tain Musical Pets" — *Pathétique* Source-Motive — Its
Modern Uses — Four Quarters and a Dotted Half — A
Motive from Op. 14, No. 2 — Joy Source-Motive —
Great Fugue Motive — *Adelaide* Motive — Triad Habit.

56 A CHIEF SOURCE–MOTIVE OF BEETHOVEN 578

Economy of Material — Variety in Unity — Originality
and Uniqueness Not Claimed for Motive — Fertility of
Creative Resources — Relative Frequency of Motive in
His Symphonies, Sonatas, Etc. — Was Its Use Conscious?
— Devices for Concealment — The Formula Stated —
Traced Through Entire Life Work — Its Protean Nature
— Conscious Employment — Beethoven as an Impro-
visator — Improvises on This Motive — Inter-Resemblance
of Certain Uses — Newman's Three Notes — His
Theory of Beethoven's Unconsciousness — Employment of
Source-Motive by Other Composers — Objects of This
Chapter — The Anagram Idea — Implications.

APPENDIX

1. How to Know Beethoven Through Automatic Instruments 615
2. Glossary: Some Technical Terms Every Music Lover Should 626
   Know
3. Bibliography 636
4. A List of Beethoven's Printed Works 642
   Index 663

List of Illustrations in Volume II

BEETHOVEN, FROM THE PAINTING BY STIELER
Frontispiece

BEETHOVEN'S LIFE MASK, FROM A PAINTING BY STANISLAV REMBSKI   332

BEETHOVEN IN 1812, AFTER THE BUST BY KLEIN   340

BEETHOVEN IN 1814, ENGRAVED BY HÖFEL, AFTER A CRAYON SKETCH BY LETRONNE   352

TWO PEN SKETCHES OF BEETHOVEN BY BOEHM   376

BEETHOVEN, FROM A CRAYON PORTRAIT BY KLOEBER   384

BEETHOVEN'S FACTOTUM, ANTON SCHINDLER   400

BEETHOVEN IN 1823, AFTER THE PAINTING BY WALDMÜLLER   408

PRINCE VON LICHNOWSKY   416

BEETHOVEN'S CHIEF PATRONS   424

BEETHOVEN'S NEPHEW KARL   448

GERHARD VON BREUNING   456

BEETHOVEN AT THE POINT OF DEATH, FROM DRAWINGS BY TELTSCHER   480

BEETHOVEN'S FIRST GRAVE   496

MOZART   528

[xiii]

BEETHOVEN
THE MAN WHO FREED MUSIC

VOLUME TWO

Chapter XXXIV

WHEN BEETHOVEN LAUGHED

*Humour in Beethoven's Music — Becomes a Creative Force
— Musical Slaps on the Back — False-Start Passages —
Practical Jokes on Players — Baulked Expectations —
Musical Puns — Elfin Fun — Infectious Verbal Felicity
— Violoncello Humour — Pun Habit — "Ears on His
Feet" — Fantastic Threats — Pun in C Sharp Minor —
Horseplay with the Abbé Stadler — Laughs at Himself —
Irony*

THE passage in the great coda of the Eighth symphony's
finale (at bar 372), where the huge D flat ruthlessly breaks
up the blameless fun, through the Gargantuan shoutings
and roarings of the ensuing tumult in F sharp where the
boisterous horns and trumpets strike in with F natural and
herd the mob unceremoniously into the key of F, is like the
unbridled wit of some Bernard Shaw born out of due time
and setting a classical world agog.

This passage is characteristic of much of the laughter
scattered through the Eighth and the *finale* of the Seventh
symphony. To the musical humour of the past it stands in
somewhat the relation of a freakish cyclone to a refined
simper.

Humour had heretofore been occasionally and sparingly
used in music as a kind of sauce consciously and skilfully
applied to a veal cutlet. Now, for the first time on a large

scale, this son of the laughing Rhineland made it one of the elemental inexhaustible forces of unconscious artistic creation. It held in solution all human emotion and lay deep as tears or wisdom.

In his able biography[1] Mr. Harvey Grace contends that "the chief ingredient" of Beethoven's humour consists of dynamic surprise—a sort of musical "slap on the back. . . . It seems a slender foundation on which to build a reputation as a humourist."

But to the mind of the present writer the obvious *Surprise* symphony kind of horseplay which he inherited from Papa Haydn seems a distinctly secondary feature of his repertory of laughs. Beethoven's choicest fun lies rather more in the roguery of *After-you!* false-start passages such as close the introduction of the First symphony's *finale;* such as grimace at bars 89 and 251 of the last movement of the E minor quartet[2] (Op. 59, No. 2), and delight us at the *listesso tempo* of the little *scherzo* in the B flat quartet (Op. 130).

It is found in such practical jokes as he played on his favourite butt, Zmeskall's instrument the violoncello. Think of the start of the *scherzo* in the First Rasoumowsky quartet (Op. 59, No. 1),[3] or of bar 147 in the first movement of the E minor quartet where, after a unison passage with the first violin, he makes the big fiddle seem to come half a measure tardy with his descending run. As we have

---

[1]*Beethoven*, 1927, p. 273 ff.
[2]See pp. 186–187.
[3]See Ex. 61, p. 183.

already mentioned, it is seen during the Trio of the Fifth symphony's *scherzo*, in the ludicrous apoplectic red dyeing the cheeks of the contra-bassists as they toil frantically at the musical washboard. It is seen in the kettledrum joke at bar 208 of the *Choral* symphony's *scherzo*.[4] It is found in the kindly caricature of peasant musicians in the *scherzo* of the *Pastoral*;[5] in the grotesquely contorted rhythms of the *scherzos* of the sixth quartet (Op. 18, No. 6)[6] and the G major sonata (Op. 14, No. 2).

We hear it in the development section of the Eighth symphony's opening movement, where the first subject is shooed away whenever it shows its face. And in the exasperating fashion in which a hasty Italian cadence hustles the little *Allegretto* out of doors just as the hearer is preparing to enjoy the longed-for repeat.

It is found, as Mr. Grace himself neatly brings out,[7] in the purely musical punning of enharmonic change. This is the sudden revelation of much in common between two apparently incongruous things, whereby a chord is taken in one relation and left in another. An excellent example of such a manœuvre occurs in the *finale* of this same Eighth symphony. The portentous, brazenly interrupting big C sharp[8] is taken as the leading tone of D minor. But as the movement is at once resumed in its normal key of F major, the C sharp changes in the listener's ear to D flat, the dominant

[4]See pp. 408–409.
[5]See pp. 266–268.
[6]See pp. 69–70.
[7]See p. 278.
[8]In the seventeenth measure. See last two bars of Ex. 132, p. 327.

minor ninth of F. These C sharp and D flat witticisms are more jokes of incongruous and punning tonalities than of startling dynamics. They represent the sort of humour that came, like Walt Whitman,

> . . . to spread a new gladness and a new roughness among men.

Later on, at bar 372, in the passage mentioned at the beginning of this chapter, the same sort of interruption is put down as D flat, the tonic of that key—carried on as C sharp, the tonic of C sharp minor, and, by a surprising and amusing juggling feat, left as the dominant of F sharp minor.

Some highly characteristic humour is found in the tender, infectious tonal skylarking that fills the *scherzos* of the F major violin sonata (Op. 24) and of the First Rasoumowsky quartet (Op. 59, No. 1). It is found in the elfin fun that sparkles all through the first part of the *scherzo* of the B flat quartet (Op. 130). Here is something that cannot be translated into words. It is heavens removed from the obvious slap-on-the-back drum crash of the *Surprise* symphony.

This new force of humour which Beethoven set free for the enrichment of his art was very much the sort to which he had always given play in word and deed and letter. The truth is that, notwithstanding his distaste for writing words, —he once declared to Simrock that he had "rather write 10,000 notes than one letter of the alphabet,"—he was capable of a more infectious kind of verbal felicity than is generally realized. A passage in his letter to Amenda, 1801,

BEETHOVEN'S LIFE MASK (1812)

From a painting by Stanislav Rembski

has often been cited as an instance of his absent-mindedness. But to the writer it seems a deliberate verbal parallel to the C sharp joke in the Eighth:

Of the two persons who possessed my entire love, and of whom one still lives, you are the third.

The epistles to his factotum Zmeskall, "The Music Count," are full of solemn Eighth symphony fooling—and often in connection with his henchman's instrument, the violoncello.

Presently I will forward to you my treatise on the four violoncello strings, very fundamentally written, first chapter on gut in general—second chapter on strings composed of gut—etc.

This gibe at the glacial agility of Teutonic scholarship might have been written by Mark Twain or Mr. Stephen Leacock.

The Master depended on Zmeskall to cut his goose-quill pens, and was never weary of varying the following formula.

Damned (former) music Countlet, where is the devil concealing you? . . . We entreat you to endow us with a few feathers, we will shortly send you a whole packet so that you need not pluck out your own.—It may well be that you will yet receive the great decoration of the order of the violoncello.

This half promise was apparently fulfilled. For these words to the same friend are dated two years later. "Most well-born one, eke Violoncellistic Greatcross" (*Violoncellität Grosskreuz*).

Even in other hands than Zmeskall's the "bull-fiddle" remained Beethoven's butt. When Countess Erdödy had an

[333]

ensemble house party at her country place Beethoven wrote:

The violoncello is ordered to betake himself to the left bank of the Danube and to keep on playing until everybody has crossed over from the right bank of the Danube. In this wise would your population soon increase.

One wonders whether this could have been a subtle allusion to that excess of brawn notoriously prevalent among amateur violoncellists.

Consider this note to Brauchle:

For the violoncellist let a *Guglhupfen* be baked in the form of a violoncello, that upon it he may practise, if not his fingers, at least his belly and his muzzle.

A *Guglhupfen*, be it remarked, is a Viennese raisin cake.

Beethoven's puns were most appreciated by himself. His supreme efforts in this minor department of fun were references to the *"Musikfreunde"* (Friends of Music) as *"Musikfeinde"* (Foes of Music); and to the *"Gelehrten"* (learnèd) as the *"Geleerten"* (emptied). But his verbal aptness was sometimes conspicuous; as when he called pay "metallic recognition."

Often he struck out compact characterizations, like this for inattention: "For me everywhere one has ears on his feet." Or this for a haughty valet: "To-day arrives the Duke who will be my servant." Or this for Zmeskall, who was striving to forestall Maelzel's Chronometer by inventing an armless metronome: "Extraordinary first oscillator of the world, and that without lever!!!!" About this contrivance

[334]

he let the fancy roam in an Einsteinian manner and wondered whether the machine could not be turned to vaster uses in measuring from time to eternity.

He signed a letter to Schindler:

From low C sharp to high F,

BEETHOVEN

Composers normally feel that their publishers are not all they should be. Beethoven's persecution mania and his vivid imagination resulted in some crisp lines to his own. He warned Steiner to let him know when to expect proofs— "otherwise he will have only himself to blame for all the misery which, seething like melted sealing-wax, will trickle down upon the evildoer."

To his publisher Haslinger he wrote that if a musical paper did not retract certain lies,

I will cause the editor, with his consumptive managing editor, to be harpooned in northern waters along with the whales.

To the same:

By virtue of my exclusive prerogatives, I decree that the gentleman who bears this is to tweak, shake etc. you, first by the right ear *cresc.* . . . then by the left ear *ff mo.* . . . From the post of janitor which I had for some time considered for you, you are now again promoted to be a manufacturer of *appoggiaturas.*

To the head of Breitkopf and Härtel:

It seems to me there is a whisper that you are looking out for a new wife. . . . I wish you a Xantippe such as fell to the lot of the holy Greek Socrates, so that I might see a German *Verleger,* which is saying a lot, *verlegen, ja, recht in Verlegenheit.*

[335]

This pun was one of Beethoven's stock favourites. *Verleger* means publisher, *verlegen,* to publish—also, embarrassed.

Beethoven sent his C sharp minor quartet (Op. 131) to the publisher Schott's Sons with an enigmatical phrase which has somewhat troubled the learned: "Do not be horror-stricken at the four crosses" (*vier Kreuze*). The learned realized, of course, that the *vier Kreuze* meant the four sharps of the key signature. But why should Beethoven placate Schott on account of four sharps? The difficulties presented by the key were as nothing compared with the difficulties of the music itself. We do not find the Master apologizing for the equally awkward four flats of the F minor quartet, nor for the pages in three consecutive movements of the great B flat quartet written in five or six flats. The commentators did not see that the word *Kreuze* which means crosses as well as sharps, may have been one of Beethoven's elaborate puns. In the traditional way of an artist with a publisher he may have been making a heavy-footed allusion to the three crosses of Christ and of the two thieves, and a spare cross ready for the thievish publisher.

This possibility of a bad joke is strengthened by Beethoven's letter to the quartet player Holz (a name which signifies "wood"), in which he threatened him with transformation into a block of real wood and being nailed upon another wood ("*Auf ein anderes Holz Genagelt*"). Sometimes he addressed this youth as "Best *lignum crucis*" or "Best splinter from the Cross of Christ." In a letter to

Nanette Streicher there occurs a similar reference, about a kitchenmaid who

pulled a rather crooked face as she carried wood; but I trust she will recall that our Saviour carried his cross on Golgotha.

And the Master's low opinion of the genus publisher may be inferred from his contemporary letter to Holz:

It is immaterial which hell-hound licks and gnaws my brains . . . he will soon be plucked by the ears by Beelzebub, the chief of devils.

Ex. 133

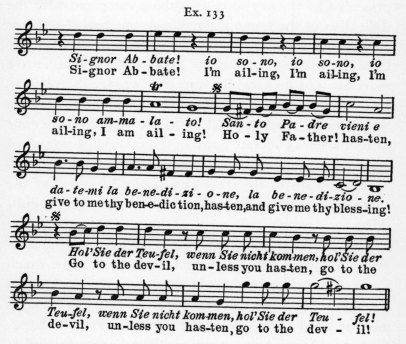

The Master's love of somewhat blasphemous horseplay is illustrated in this anecdote from the memoirs of Castelli.

In a piano store Beethoven once ran across his good friend the old Abbé Stadler. He knelt down and said: "Reverend Sir, your blessing!" Quite unembarrassed, Stadler made the sign of the cross over the suppliant and in Austrian dialect mumbled the semblance of a prayer: "*Hilft's nix, schadt's nix*" (If 'twon't help, 'twon't hurt). Then Beethoven kissed his hand and everybody roared with laughter. The canon (Ex. 133) was dashed off, if not for this, at least for a similar occasion.

Beethoven's strong love of practical joking was like an efficiently policed one-way street. By tolerating no return traffic it insured unobstructed progress towards his victim. Like Wilhelm II, he *verstand keinen Spass*. That is: he could not see a joke when it was directed towards himself. Witness the incident of poor Ries and the *"Andante Favori."*[8] If Goethe had ever embarrassed the Master half as much as he had Goethe when the court went by he would have snapped the old poet's head off.

But though he let nobody laugh at him he poked occasional fun at himself.

Yesterday [he wrote Zmeskall] I took a letter to the post-office, and they asked me where it was supposed to go.

Verbally the Master had much the same pretty turn for irony which found musical expression here and there in the symphonies. A stranger once sent him a weak arrangement for quintet, of the C minor trio (Op. 1, No. 3). In

---

[8]See p. 150.

self-defense Beethoven arranged it himself and affixed the following inscription:

Trio transcribed into a four-voiced quintet by Mr. Goodwill, and out of the illusion of five voices brought to the light of day with five real voices, as well as raised from the utmost miserability to a certain prestige by Mr. Benevolence. . . . N. B. The original three-voiced quintet score has been rendered as a solemn burnt-offering to the gods of the underworld.

Chapter XXXV

THE BEETHOVENATE SYMPHONY

"Cockcrow" Sonata, Finished 1812 — Shows Considera-
tion for Rode — 1813, a Bad Year — Poverty — Maelzel's
Panharmonicon — Battle Pieces in Fashion — The "Battle"
Symphony — First Performance, December 8, 1813 —
Celebrities in the Orchestra — Popular Success — Defrauds
Maelzel — Repents of His Folly — His Forward-looking
Mind — Interest in Invention: Fountain Pens, Aviation,
Steam Cannons, Steamboats, Lifts — The Glorious Mo-
ment — Polonaise, Op. 89 — E Minor Piano Sonata, Op. 90
— Its Program — Last Revision of Fidelio, *1814 — The*
Germ-Motive — The Source-Motive — Marginalia — "The
Mad Musician" — "Man, Help Thyself!"

LATE in 1812 the G major violin sonata (Op. 96) was finished. This work has been nicknamed *"The Cockcrow."*
It was written for the famous visiting violinist Rode, then
in the decline of his powers. The *Adagio* is one of the most
comely and satisfying among the slow movements. But the
three fast ones show a compromise Beethoven, trying to
adapt a second-period technic to third-period thoughts, and
—with unheard-of consideration—to Rode's somewhat
shaky execution.

In composing it [he wrote the Archduke, to whom it was
dedicated] I had to consider the playing of Rode; in our *finales*
we are fond of tempestuous passages, but these do not suit Rode
and this—embarrassed me somewhat.

[340]

BEETHOVEN IN 1812
After the bust by Klein

A surprising remark. Were advancing years making Beethoven less uncompromising? Was this the same man who had snapped Schuppanzigh up about his "puling little fiddle" when "Milord" had expostulated over certain difficulties in a quartet?[1]

Eighteen thirteen was a bad year for the composer. Little of value was added to his list. Material troubles preoccupied him. He sued Prince Lobkowitz and the widow of Prince Kinsky for arrears of his pension. And, influenced in part by his obsession against light women, he brought brother Karl's wife into court for the return of a loan of 1,500 gulden.

True, he needed the money. Nanette Streicher reported that he had no good coat and not a single whole shirt. To Spohr, who had missed him at the tavern for days, he confessed that he had suffered "house-arrest" on account of the failure of his only pair of shoes.

Poverty made him amenable to a far worse compromise than the G major violin sonata. At this psychological moment the devil, in the person of Maelzel the inventor, came and whispered, or rather shouted, into his ear. He promised to show him the kingdoms of the earth (i. e. France and England) and to fill his pockets with red gold if the Master would only write a certain piece of program music for an ingenious instrument of Maelzel's own invention.

The occasion was the Duke of Wellington's recent victory over the Napoleonic forces at Vittoria in Spain. The instrument was called the "Panharmonicon." This ancestor

[1]See p. 180.

of the automatic organ and piano was a sort of glorified music-box. According to Thayer it

combined the common instruments then employed in military bands, with a powerful bellows—the whole being enclosed in a case. The motive power was automatic and the keys were touched by pins affixed in a revolving cylinder.

We must bear in mind that in those days a proposal to write such compositions sounded more respectable than it would to-day. Battle pieces had long been popular. Koczwara's *Battle of Prague* was just then all the rage in Europe and America. Many suppose that the famous "grand battle piece for two flutes" was a mythical *reductio ad absurdum* of this idea. Not at all! It was actually published, as an arrangement of Fuch's *Battle of Jena*. And who can doubt its effectiveness in routing any possible enemy? Beethoven probably knew that Mozart had written an Eighteenth Century anticipation of the *Victory Ball* for Count Deym; and that Cherubini had concocted a tonal fight for Maelzel himself. With this branch of composition thus legitimized Beethoven gave ear to the tempter.

Money was needed for the proposed trip to London, where he was sure he could make tons of it. For the first time in his life he decided deliberately to prostitute his art. The result was a piece of startling crudity. Before *Wellington's Victory* was quite finished for Maelzel's machine, Beethoven arranged it, at the latter's suggestion, for orchestra. In this form it is known as the *"Battle"* symphony (Op. 91).

Among the immortal nine this so-called symphony cuts much the same figure that the *chef d'œuvre* of a sidewalk artist would cut in the main hall of the National Gallery. It consists of brisk business for drums and trumpets, with brilliant changes rung on "Rule, Britannia" and "Malbrook," the tune known to Americans as "We Won't Go Home Till Morning." The climax of this preposterous phantasmagoria is actually "God Save the King," tortured into a fast fugato,[2] with ingenious effects representing the huzzas of the populace.

Beethoven wrote this Beethovenate music in order to smite the groundlings upon the side of the head. He did. What an ironic commentary on mankind's present infinitesimal distance from the tree ape that such a man should have succumbed thus, and that his trashiest composition should have won his first overwhelming triumph!

On December 8 and 12, 1813, the Seventh symphony and the *"Battle"* symphony were performed upon the same program for charity. Still more horrible to relate, these numbers were separated by marches of Pleyel and Dussek, emanating from Maelzel's Mechanical Trumpeter.

The leading musicians gave their services and regarded the event as a huge professional joke. Spohr, Mayseder, and Dragonetti fiddled. Moscheles crashed the cymbals. Salieri conducted the battery from off stage. Hummel smote the big drum, in company with a young fellow of twenty-two named Beer, who pounded without the courage of his con-

---

[2] It is interesting to remember that when Brahms came to write his own essay at a celebration of victory, the *Triumphlied*, he also used "God Save the King." But, oh! the difference to us!

victions and got himself disgracefully scolded by the Master. This young fellow, owing to the terms of a legacy, changed his name to Meyerbeer and proved that a poor drummer might become a rich composer. The antics of these celebrities must have presented an amusing spectacle. But it would have been wise to do as all the prudent do who go to-day to see *Turandot,* and attend this show equipped with opera glasses—and ear muffs.

The popular success of the *"Battle"* symphony completely threw the Seventh into the shade. Its *éclat* was so shattering that, on January 2 and February 27, 1814, Beethoven gave the thing again, with the Seventh and Eighth symphonies, for his own exclusive benefit. Fate smiled upon the box office. With cash in hand he decided not to visit England after all.

Thus he defrauded Maelzel of his just profits. When the desperate inventor managed to collect the music, part by part, for his own eventual use, Beethoven called him a thief. "You're another," retorted Maelzel. And they went to court. Three years later the case was amicably settled.

The *"Battle"* symphony made Beethoven for the first time popular among the people. He was immensely pleased when, walking one day on the Kahlenberg, he was given some cherries by a couple of girls. They would take nothing in return and said adoringly: "We saw you in the Ridotto Room when we heard your lovely music."

Beethoven was now in cash and the man of the hour. But soon he came to realize that he had sold part of his birthright for a mess of pottage and gone back on the sound æsthetic principles which he had proclaimed with the *Pastoral* symphony. "*Wellington's Victory* was a piece of folly," he declared. "It was dear to my heart only because with it I gave the Viennese a sound drubbing."

His successful championship of the metronome shows one characteristic of the man who freed music. He was not a red revolutionary. Great creators seldom are. But he had a decidedly forward-looking mind. It was interested in the march of the world and in invention. He carefully noted the address of a goldsmith who made "fillable pens which may be transported"—ancestors of our fountain pen. Like Leonardo da Vinci, he was fascinated by the problem of human flight. Some of the first attempts at aviation, by the Viennese clock maker Jacob Degen, roused his lively interest. Degen used to try soaring near Baden, the scene of some of the Master's own loftiest flights above this workaday world.

The approach of the mechanical era thrilled him.

Let us thank God for the promised steam cannons and for the already realized steam navigation. What far swimmers shall we presently have, to bring us air and freedom?!

In a day when Austria was even less equipped with elevators than at present he dreamed of an engine for lifting the Falstaffian Schuppanzigh, "because the thick one mounts badly." In a letter floridly superscribed: "*Al Signore Milord stimatissimo nominato Scuppanzig* [note the Master's humorous realization of how an Italian would

[345]

pronounce the fiddler's name] *granduomo della citta da Vienna*," we read:

As soon as my machine is finished, whereby you can be transported with perfect ease up here to me on the fourth floor, I'll let you know.

Beethoven's worldly and cynical activities in connection with the Peace Congress of Vienna were many. Besides the "*Battle*" symphony there was *The Glorious Moment*, a deplorable potboiler cantata written as a timely act of homage to the rulers of Austria, Germany, and Russia. And there was the trashy Polonaise for piano (Op. 89) dedicated to the Empress Elizabeth Alexievna of Russia. Like nearly all of the compositions which did not come from inner impulse these things were quite unworthy of Beethoven's pen. But the crowned heads, and the many-headed crowd, came in such numbers as to provide the Master a snug nest egg. We shall see how tenaciously he clung to it.

The E minor piano sonata (Op. 90), with its tender intimacy, its brooding loveliness, and its lack of appeal to the virtuoso or to the standard concert audience, seemed to arrive as a token that the Master had done dallying with the brilliant world and come to himself. This quiet revelation of one of the most hidden and alluring chambers in the mansion called Beethoven seemed to indicate that he had turned from the crowned heads in order to crown his own head with the last sonatas and quartets.

The E minor was dedicated to his good friend Count Moritz Lichnowsky, who had been divorced and, after surmounting various difficulties, had recently married a beautiful young dancer. When the Count stupidly asked him the meaning of the music (*mille fois hélas!* as M. Arsène Alexandre exclaimed about an equally asinine question by Schindler), Beethoven, "with a boisterous laugh" gave him the stupid answer he deserved:

First movement: "a struggle between the head and heart."

Last movement: "a conversation with the beloved."

A composer with the authority of a Beethoven is like an Indian magician performing the legendary rope trick. He can hypnotize us into seeing anything he wishes us to see. He can tell us a sonata is a lovers' dialogue, or a leviathan swallowing its tail. This will force most of us to hear that, and that only, in music capable of a million equally plausible interpretations. And—another *mille fois hélas!*—sometimes as here, we take him literally when he is only trying to make a bad joke.

Late in 1814 Beethoven gave three more concerts, consisting of *The Glorious Moment* sandwiched between the Seventh and the *"Battle"* symphonies. They were liberally patronized by royalty.

But material success did not obscure his sense of values.

Of our monarchs etc., their realms etc., [he wrote Dr. Kanka] I write you nothing. . . . I prefer the spiritual realm and Him who stands above all spiritual and celestial monarchs.

This year Beethoven rebuilt, as he phrased it, "the devastated ruins of an old castle." In other words, building upon Treitschke's revision of the *Fidelio* libretto, he gave the opera its final form. It was produced with conspicuous success before the assembled potentates.

There is nothing of the Wagnerian leitmotif to be found in *Fidelio*. But the Master was hot on its trail. His ingenious idea of tying together his sonatas and symphonies by letting some germ-motive[3] appear at intervals throughout a work, either disguised or openly, gave a quite novel unity to such compositions as the *Pathétique,* the "*Appassionata*" and *Hammerklavier* sonatas, the C major violoncello and "*Kreutzer*" sonatas, the last quartets and the Third, Fifth, Eighth, and Ninth symphonies.

Indeed, in 1815 Beethoven almost anticipated the music dramatists of the future. In his notes for an afterwards abandoned music drama, *Bacchus,* one may read, under a motive for the words "*Gütiger Pan*": "It must be derived from the Bacchus-motif." In chapter LVI we shall see how one favourite source-motive recurs in the principal themes of his chief works.

Certain marginalia in the Sketch Books of 1814–1815 throw brief flashes of light on the Master's character:

Much to be done on this earth, do it soon!

. . . . .

No time rolls more quickly by than that in which we busy ourselves with our spirits or I with my muse.

Another entry hints at Beethoven's tremendous vitality.

Let everything that has life ("*Alles, was Leben heisst!*") be sacrificed to the sublime, and sacred to art. Let me live, even with artificial helps, if these can only be found.

---

[3]His use of the germ-motive will be studied in detail in chap. LIV.

And here is the Master's dream for his old age—his equivalent of

> The hairy gown, the mossy cell

of "Il Penseroso":

A little court—a little orchestra, its song written there by me, performed to the honour of the Almighty, the Eternal, the Unending. So may the last days flow by. . . . The portraits of Handel, Bach, Gluck, Mozart, Haidn in my room—they might help me to lay claim to submission.

. . . . . .

A peasant property, then will you escape your wretchedness.

Part of this wretchedness lay, no doubt, in being misunderstood by his fellow citizens. For about this time the Viennese began calling Beethoven *"der närrische Musiker"* (the mad musician).

It was then that he threw off what was destined to be his most famous *mot*. Young Ignaz Moscheles arranged the piano version of *Fidelio*. At the bottom of the manuscript he wrote: "Finished with God's help." The Master's instant reaction was to scrawl upon the page, "Man, help thyself!"

Chapter XXXVI

"AS GOOD AS LOST"

Last Public Appearance as Pianist, 1814 — Growing Avarice — Kindness to Brother — Karl Dies, November 16, 1815 — Beethoven Joint Guardian of Nephew — Litigation with Sister-in-Law — Fervid Love for Nephew — The "van" in His Name — A Purely Musical Witticism — Receives Freedom of City, about December 1, 1815 — Violoncello Sonatas, C Major and D Major, 1815 — Tentative Beginning of Third Period — Its Characteristics — A Major Sonata, Op. 101 — Song Cycle, To the Distant Beloved, 1816 *— A Milestone in Musical History — Marginalia, 1816–1817 — Fish Suppers at Nussdorf — His Favourite Symphony — Despair — Offer from London Philharmonic* — Hammerklavier *Sonata, 1818–1819*

BEFORE letting the world hear the great *"Archduke"* trio Beethoven had waited three years. In the spring of 1814 he himself performed its piano part at two concerts. Then he renounced public playing forever.

It was a distressing dénouement. Spohr, who was present at one of the rehearsals, has told us how Beethoven's mastery of his instrument had failed through deafness and lack of practice.

In *forte* passages the poor deaf man pounded on the keys until the strings jangled, and in *piano* he played so softly that whole groups of tones were omitted.

Perhaps the jealous Spohr exaggerated somewhat. In any case, the Master's public career as a pianist lamentably ended with the unresolved discord of an inadequate performance of the least adequate *finale* in all his chamber music.

Beethoven's avarice grew with his fortunes. During the years after he had put by the first considerable nest egg he slipped more and more into the way of misrepresenting his resources. To Ries he wrote about his chief benefactor and closest friend Rudolph: "My unlucky connection with the Archduke has brought me almost down to the beggar's staff."[1]

In 1814 he complained to Kanka, "The table of Zeus is no more where one might propose oneself for ambrosia." In a letter to Neate, May 18, 1816, he referred to "my almost indigent life."

There is a striking incongruity [says Thayer] between Beethoven's pleas of poverty in his letters to correspondents in England at this period and the facts drawn from official and other authentic sources.

But when we consider his kindness to his dying brother, presto change! Exit Hyde; enter Jekyll. He begged Brauchle to take a journey after a horse for Karl.

Stop at no expense, I'll gladly meet it. It is not worth while to let anyone suffer for the sake of a few miserable gulden.

---

[1]Beethoven's occasional designations of such kind friends remind one of Richard Wagner's *My Life,* with its unworthy remarks about avoiding his "skulking creditors"; and about Franz Liszt, his much abused benefactor, his warmest friend, and his father-in-law, with whom this great master singer confessed that he "never actually came to blows."

23768

He actually went so far as to ask a society woman, Antonie von Brentano, to peddle about Karl's old pipe-head among her friends: price: 10 louis d'or.[2] But, eight years after, he was royally to repay this favour by dedicating to her the *Diabelli Variations*.

Brother Karl died of tuberculosis November 16, 1815. The habit of suspicion had so grown upon Ludwig that he was sure the death had been caused by poison and would not be appeased until Dr. Bertolini had performed a post-mortem. Karl left his nine-year-old son of the same name under the joint guardianship of the widow and brother Ludwig. In a codicil to his will he enjoined upon the former of these ill-assorted guardians compliance, and upon the latter, moderation.

Appreciable amounts of neither compliance nor moderation were ever shown by either guardian. Driven by his hatred of the "Queen of the Night," as he called his sister-in-law, Beethoven took her into court and fought her for five years. At the end of this time he obtained full custody of the lad.

The long, tedious, sordid story need not be gone into. It is enough to say that Beethoven's own physical and temperamental limitations made him a preposterous guardian for any child; and all the worse for a lad who had inherited most of the weaknesses of the Beethovens with few of their stronger traits. The quarrels, lawsuits, anxieties, and annoyances of this affair cast a shadow, deepening

---

[2] "Never in my life," wrote Dr. Weissenbach, who knew Beethoven at this time, "have I met a more childlike nature paired with so powerful and defiant a will."

BEETHOVEN IN 1814
Engraved by Höfel after a crayon sketch by Letronne

to tragedy, over the rest of the Master's life, and sadly hampered his creative work. But even so, his natural kindness of heart often showed itself toward that "Queen of the Night," upon whom he looked as the chief cause of his woes. After he had decreed that she should never see her boy again he broke out: "Mother—even a bad one still remains a mother." He relented, let her see the boy, sent her money, paid her debts. This side of him moved Dr. Weissenbach to write:

If Heaven had endowed him with no other gift than his heart, that alone would make him one in whose presence many would have to rise and bow.

Beethoven's love for this nephew seems almost as morbidly exaggerated as his hatred of the boy's mother—that is, unless one were to go so far as to accept literally the Master's statement in his letter of September 6, 1816, to Dr. Kanka:

I am truly the bodily father [*Ich bin wirklich leiblicher Vater*] of my late brother's child.[3]

If these words, which have apparently escaped comment, should be taken at their face value they would turn the half-mad solicitude and almost ridiculously inflamed love of a bachelor uncle for a nephew into the natural love of a father for a son to whom, through his own fault, he had given an impossible mother.

But telling against any literal acceptation of this apparent

[3]Kasper Anton Karl van Beethoven married Johanna Reiss, May 25, 1806, and little Karl was born October 4, 1806.

[353]

confession of paternity is a marginal entry in a Sketch Book of 1816:

> *Karl betrachtest du als dein eigenes Kind* (You look upon Karl as your own child).

This is a much less flat-footed proposition than the former. One must also take into account a statement about Karl's mother in his letter to Bernard (1819):

> I hear that she gets 480 fl. W. W. annually from Hofbauer, for, as I hear, he holds her child to be his, it is probably true.

During the litigation, one of the courts discovered that, despite the "van" in his name, Beethoven was not of noble birth. So he was turned over to a plebeian court. An apocryphal tale runs that, when questioned, the Master pointed to his head and heart exclaiming: "My patent of nobility is here and here!" For this there is unfortunately no authority. But in a letter to Piuk he wrote:

> The talk turned on the little word *van*, and I had pride enough to declare that I had never bothered my head about my nobility (*"dass ich mich nie um meinen Adel bekümmert"*).

This was a somewhat disingenuous statement, seeing that there was no technical nobility for him to bother his head about. Over the change of venue he was furious and hotly protested against being forced to take his chances there. "I do not belong among these plebs!"

Schindler relates that when his noble friends learned about the little word "van," they were chilled and disillusioned. So that "Vienna became too small" for him. If true, this statement disengages as deep an irony as the incident of the Master's imprisonment for vagrancy when he was composing the *Missa*.[4]

But, however deeply such vexations struck in, they could not dry up the springs of his humour. He sent Steiner a note about something done by Tobias Haslinger (nicknamed "The Adjutant"), which is as purely musical a witticism as the wordless one which opens the Eighth symphony.[5]

The shameful performance of the Adjutant has been entered in the register (though not in the organ-register.) If it were, what a bad sound would issue thence?

Ex. 134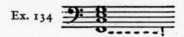

In these days of Stravinsky, Hindemith, and Carillo, it is hard to see how any musical joke could sound much more anachronistic.

A trifling compensation for his woes at this time was Vienna's graceful act, about December 1, 1815, in giving him the freedom of the city.

July and August had been devoted to the two sonatas for violoncello and piano in C and D major (Op. 102, Nos. 1 and 2). Certain of their traits mark the authentic, if still tentative, beginning of the third period.

(1) An uncompromising disregard of mere sensuous charm. A roughness verging at times on brutality. An indif-

[4]See p. 376.
[5]See pp. 321–322.

ference to practical concert effects, entailing on the listener many hearings and much strenuous good-will between first acquaintance and wholly appreciative enjoyment.

(2) A novel plasticity of form, especially in the C major, the manuscript of which was labelled *"Free Sonata."* This consists of two movements, each subdivided into slow and fast sections, with the dreamy *Andante* theme

Ex. 135

which opens the work as if it were a motto, reappearing later with refrain value.

(3) A fugal tendency, as shown in the *finale* of the D major. This is the first strict fugue in the forty-seven sonatas the Master had thus far written. And it is the first of the nine fugues which form such a gloriously characteristic feature of the third period. Thirty years' study of this rough-hewn movement, as violoncellist and critic, has never altered the writer's conviction that its brutality, inflexibility, and lack of poetic relief make the first fugue of the nine the worst of them.

(4) The *Adagio con molto sentimento d'affetto* of the D major, the deepest movement and the only full-sized *adagio* in all of the violoncello sonatas, is filled with the brooding religious exaltation so characteristic of the Master's final years.

The A major piano sonata (Op. 101), written at about

[356]

the same time, has little of the dry crabbedness of opus
102. Indeed, the sensuous lump-in-the-throat beauty of the
first movement has provided an inexhaustible inspiration
(and loan office) for a host of Romantic composers from
Schumann, Mendelssohn, and Brahms down. It even offers
us in this phrase

Ex. 136

The horns of elfland faintly blowing.

But the A major has in common with its violoncello
neighbours—among other things—a canon in the Trio of
the March, where sound is as ruthlessly sacrificed to bleak
sense as in the *finale* of the D major; also a fugue—a better
one; and a depth and nobility of feeling in the *Adagio,*
akin to that in the slow movement of the last violoncello
sonata.

Although the human voice was less adapted than any
other medium to the expression of Beethoven's genius, his
chief work in the unfruitful year 1816 was a group of
Lieder. An die ferne Geliebte (To the Distant Beloved)
(Op. 98) was destined to have a momentous effect on the
evolution of the art. It was Beethoven's loftiest flight in
lyric song.

True, in setting these lines, he was as iconoclastic towards
poetic rhythms and the delicacies and subtleties of the
fragile music of vowels and consonants, as musicians since
the dawn of song have almost invariably been. Nor were

[357]

his tones as expressive of the sense of the argument as those of many later song writers. Perhaps he felt that a good poem needs no musical bush; whereas, if the poem is bad, no composer can make it better. At any rate he did the natural thing for a great master of absolute music to do: instead of setting the lines he tried to set what was between them.

But other composers before him had done this too. What made *To the Distant Beloved* a red-lettered milestone in the history of music was the fact of its being the first real song cycle. Here the Master continued his work as emancipator by freeing the song tribe from solitary confinement in individual cells.

During this dark period, 1816–1817, Beethoven was plagued almost beyond endurance by the rapid approach of total deafness; by those questions of food and shelter which were always to him more recondite than triple counterpoint, concealed subjects, or reversible canons; and by the truly damnable business of getting young Karl away from his mother, the "Queen of the Night."

This is the fashion in which, on the margins of his Sketch Books, *Le Grand Sourd* communed with himself:

1816

Submission—submission! Thus may we win something even in the deepest misery, and make ourselves worthy to have God forgive our shortcomings.

Fate, show your force! We are not lords over ourselves. What is determined must be, and so let it be!

He who is burdened with an ill which he cannot alter, which

is bringing him closer and closer to death and without which his life would have lasted longer, must remember that he might have been killed even sooner by assassination or other causes.

Live in your art alone. Limited as you now are by your hearing, this is the only existence for you.

Follow the counsel of others only in the rarest instances. In a matter that has already been considered, to whom can all the circumstances be as clear in consciousness as to oneself?!

Just as the State must have a constitution, so must the individual have one of his own.

1817

Peace and freedom are the best of all things. True friendship can be founded only on the union of similar natures.

One of his friends, a poet named Kuffner, came this summer to live near him in Heiligenstadt. The two often went together to Nussdorf for fish suppers, either to the Sign of the Rose, or nearer the source of supplies. In a Conversation Book a year before the Master's death we find Kuffner's handwriting:

Do you remember the fisherman's house in Nussdorf, where we sat till midnight on the terrace under the full moon, before us the rushing brook and the swollen Danube? I was your guest.

During one of these suppers, the poet seized his opportunity when the Master was feeling at peace with the world to ask:

KUFFNER:—Tell me frankly, which is your favourite among your symphonies?
BEETHOVEN:—(In great good humour) Eh! Eh! The *Eroica*.
KUFFNER:—I should have guessed the C minor.
BEETHOVEN:—No; the *Eroica*.

On August 21, 1817, just as his hearing was at times near the vanishing point, the Master mailed this bitter cry to his sick friend Zmeskall:

I am often in despair and would like to end my life. . . . God have mercy on me, I regard myself as good as lost. . . . If the condition does not change I shall next year be not in London but in the grave.—Thank God the rôle will soon be played out.—

The reference to London meant that the Philharmonic Society had renewed its offer of 300 guineas if Beethoven would come across the Channel with two new symphonies. And he had accepted. If carried out, this plan might have solved his financial problems for the rest of his life. But, as he seldom did first-class work to order, the result might possibly have been a repetition of the unfortunate *"Battle"* symphony episode.

The event did honour to his artistic conscience. While his English friends impatiently awaited the promised works, he let the sketches of the D minor symphony lie in his desk while he sent this word to Czerny:

Just now I am writing at a sonata which shall be my greatest.

It was the one in B flat (Op. 106), known as the *Hammerklavier*. This enormous work occupied him, off and on, until March, 1819. It is as long as a symphony, as brilliant and difficult as a concerto. It makes more strenuous demands upon the instrument, the performer, and the listener than any other composition of the Master.

To clothe these gigantic limbs in such inadequate vesture as piano makers carry in stock is attempting to force Samson into rompers. This is ideal music, but "not for the

[360]

sensual ear," and fit only for a Brobdingnagian keyboard. It seems to ask of the interpreter more than is possible for human nerve and sinew, brain and emotion to supply. Among the scores of times the writer has heard the *Hammerklavier* sonata played he can recall but one performance which came within appreciable distance of adequacy, and that took place among the favouring conditions of a Beethoven festival at Bonn.

But even if some yet undreamed-of super-virtuoso were to give a perfect reading of this work upon the most superb instrument of a Twenty-first Century Steinway, and our spirits responded eagerly to the privilege, the flesh would still be weak.

We can savour to the full the heroic strength and noble tenderness of the opening movement. We can enjoy the puckish fantasy and Ariel-like winsomeness, the "nods and becks and wreathèd"—but somewhat wistful—"smiles" of the second movement; and are seized anew with the conviction that we are hearing the most luscious of Beethoven's piano *scherzos*.

Reverently we enter into the ethereally poignant tragedy of the *Adagio sostenuto*. The Master's just quoted remark to Zmeskall recurs to us:

God have mercy on me, I regard myself as good as lost.

Von Bülow has set a true word beneath the last page of this *Adagio:*

The pain that tears the heart no longer has the word here, but—as it were—tearless resignation rigid as death.

In this superhuman passage of the *Hammerklavier*, Beethoven triumphantly stands the test of the supreme artist—even in death we are in beauty. This corruption is swathed in the incorruption of loveliness.

But we have gone too fast. For only halfway through the immensity of this movement something happens. We have been too long under an intense strain. Exhausted nature baulks and begins to falsify beauty, just as it falsifies the miracle of sunset playing on the clouds that half fill the Grand Canyon, as observed after fourteen hours in the saddle. Though the movement is in strict form and every note has its unimpeachable reason for being, the listener is so weary by the time he reaches the middle that, from there on, much of the music sounds to him as though Beethoven, plunged into the depths of an amorphous daydream, had remained too long submerged.[6]

Then comes a titanic three-voiced fugue with a subject ten bars long. It involves the greatest effort Beethoven ever demanded of the listener to his sonatas. It is terribly stark, furiously bleak music. Mr. Sullivan calls it "the expression of the final refusal of annihilation, even if no hope and no object be left in life."[7]

By this time the hearer is too spent to appreciate much more than the immensity of the subject, the mastery with which the poet hides the scholar in its manipulation, the heavenly relief of the singing D major episode *sempre dolce*

---

[6]The tired hearer is reminded of the Master's notorious absent-mindedness and wonders whether he were composing these passages the afternoon when he asked the waiter for his bill without having ordered any food.

[7]*Beethoven: His Spiritual Development*, p. 209.

e cantabile following a terrific climax and after one of the most dramatic measure's pauses in all music.

As the monster fugue rages on and on, apparently intent on shattering to bits not only the piano and the struggling virtuoso, but the form of the sonata itself, the weary listener finds himself feebly resenting this brutal whirlwind, coming, as it does, after the ineffable poetic dream of the *Adagio*. But on the way home he asks himself what could have provided a more convincing close to this mighty work. Another piece in sonata-form? Variations? A rondo? No! A thousand times no! And he is driven to the conclusion that the Master was right as usual. Nothing besides a fugue, a ruthless hurricane of a fugue, could have said a fitting last word to such an *allegro,* such a *scherzo,* and such an *adagio.*[8]

During this life one does not expect to see the day when the *Hammerklavier* shall be adequately performed, on an adequate instrument, to adequate listeners. But if there be a next world, and if the report of its being a musical one be true, one hopes to hear the composer of this work, purged long since of Hydean dross, play it upon an instrument as far removed from the piano as the piano is now removed from its ancestor, the primitive harp of David.

---

[8]This work might perhaps be played, like *Parsifal*, with long intermissions for recuperation and an interval after the *scherzo* for dinner!

THE EMANCIPATOR EMANCIPATED

Present from Broadwood, 1818 — Progress of Deafness —
Suspicion and Violence — A Musical Bootjack — The
Conversation Books — Irregular Habits and Exposure —
Failing Health, 1818–1823 — "A Hearty, Free Word"
— Helplessness — Creative Freedom — Inertia in Starting
New Compositions — 1820, E Major Sonata, Op. 109 —
1821, A Flat Sonata, Op. 110 — A Memory Sonata —
Simultaneous Echoes of Haydn, Mozart, and Bach — Sou-
venir of the Eroica *— Fugue-Finale — "Imagination*
Claims Its Rights" — 1822, C Minor Sonata, Op. 111 — Its
Difficulties for the Listener — Beethoven Arrested as a
Vagabond, 1820 — Present Intelligence of Vienna Police
— Beethoven's Concentration — Sir John Russell's De-
scription of Him, 1821 — Tricked into Improvising —
Rossini Calls, 1822 — Fidelio Revived, 1822 — Beethoven
Fails as Conductor — The Real Tragedy of His Deafness

IN 1818, during his summer at Mödling, Beethoven received a present. It was a Broadwood pianoforte from the
English makers. Scratched beside the keyboard were the
names of England's leading virtuosi: Cramer, Knyvelt,
Kalkbrenner, Ferrari, and Ries. The instrument was admitted by the Austrian authorities free of duty.

Beethoven was delighted. In his most elegant French
he wrote a letter of thanks, promising to regard the piano
"as an altar on which I shall present to the divine Apollo

the highest offerings of my spirit" (*"Comme un autel, où je déposerai les plus belles offrandes de mon esprit au divin Apollon."*)

Unfortunately this gift came too late to be of much practical use to the Master, for his hearing was now almost entirely gone. When told that the Broadwood was out of tune he replied with the characteristic suspicion of the deaf: "That's what they all say. They would like to tune it and spoil it; but they shan't touch it." Woe, however, to any piano that Beethoven himself touched! A contemporary reports that at this period the Master attacked the keyboard so savagely he broke from twenty to thirty strings each time he played. And a few years later, to show Stein that certain strings needed replacing in this very instrument, he actually hammered its keys with a bootjack.[1]

The same suspicion and violence which he showed towards his pianos was often turned against his servants. In 1816 he gave Peter Simrock pencil and paper and told him to write down everything personal or confidential, as the servant was an eavesdropper. But when Simrock called again a few days later, the Master said: "Now we can talk, for I've given my servant five gulden, a kick in the rear, and sent him to the devil." In connection with one of these domestic dramas some unidentified hand wrote in one of the small tablets called Conversation Books the following

---

[1]This may have been the very utensil which Schuppanzigh saw put to another novel use in 1823. "Milord" came into the deaf man's room unobserved. Beethoven had his back to the door and was using a bootjack as if it were an enormous tuning fork, striking it against the wall and then holding it close to his ears to try and detect the after vibrations. It throws an unpleasant light on the fat man's character that he retailed this pathetic incident "with humour and sarcastic observations." (Frimmel, *Beethoven Handbuch*, Vol. II, p. 163.)

[365]

sage counsel: "Don't beat her! You might have trouble with the police."

Communication with the Master had now to be carried on by means of these Conversation Books, in which the deaf man's answers are, naturally, seldom found. A page transcribed from one of them (November–December, 1819) will give some idea of the intellectual quality of the usual talk that went on in his rooms.

Goethe says the spot on which a good man has set his foot remains consecrated for all time.
To-day he cut open his frozen toe.
Roast veal (Kälbernes) *with some ham and tongue.*
If only everyone could understand and appreciate your love for your nephew.
The dog is missing.
If you lose the book they'll lock me up.
For all eternity.
There are fresh oysters.

When inspiration seized him he would run out of doors, hatless and coatless, perhaps before dawn, and wander about the fields and woods in an oblivious frenzy of creation. Often he returned late at night, cold, wet, and famished. In 1820 Wilhelm Müller called on him at Mödling. The house-keeper said that Beethoven had gone out walking early and he might return that evening—or perhaps in three days. After such exposure he was capable of the incon-sistency of objecting to rooms opening upon a garden, because "garden air is precisely the worst sort for me"!

Small wonder his health suffered. In the years from 1818 to 1823 he complained of gout, rheumatism, jaundice, pain in the ears, and failing eyesight. It is sad to think how much torture, how many unborn masterpieces, and how many decades of life he might have saved by observing the most elementary physical prudence.

Small wonder that many thought the worst of his intelligence. In 1819 Zelter wrote Goethe:

Some say he is a fool. That is soon said: God forgive us all our trespasses!

The following year Beethoven, in all seriousness, invented a delightful euphemism for his own language when violent and abusive. It was a gem of rationalization. "Now and then," he remarked to Wilhelm Müller, "I let drop a hearty, free word. On that account people think me mad." Perhaps his often childlike impracticality may have influenced what people thought. On September 27, 1821, the author of "Man, help thyself!" wrote to an unknown correspondent in great distress for aid in selling one of his bank shares. But on the wrapper he scribbled:

You'll easily see what kind of commercial genius I am. After the enclosed letter was written, I talked over this matter of the share, with a friend. He showed me at once that one has only to cut off a coupon, and therewith the whole matter is at an end.

This helpless side of the man—the side which had to do with everything nonmusical—comes out vividly in his correspondence. Reading it, one thinks of him as a sort of Nineteenth Century Don Quixote, three parts sane, super-Sanchoed, first by Krumpholz, whom he nicknamed "My Fool"; then by poor faithful Zmeskall, the "Music Count,"

[367]

"Baron Greedygut," "Your Zmeskality"; then by "Papageno" Schindler, the "Samothracian ragamuffin"; then by Holz, that "Splinter of the True Cross."

Alas! Poor Knight! Alas! Poor soul possest!

He and his faithful Sanchos were almost never out of such troubles as normal common sense might easily have averted. He freed music. Himself he could not free from the bondage of his absent-mindedness, his lack of practical common sense, and his dangerous temperament.

But the writing was a different matter. In all his chief works from now to the premature end we find his faculties working with such a glorious freedom as scarcely any other artist has ever attained. This is not to say that he was fluent. Beethoven was never that on paper; least of all in these later years, when he was increasingly bothered by inertia in beginning a new composition. But once the momentum was up he found himself stimulated, not hampered, by the formal, technical side of his art. He could freely utter his profound mind and pour out his great heart, because he was now at last an emancipated artist, in full command of his medium.

The three sonatas which end the immortal series of thirty-two for piano are in remarkable contrast to that monumental concert piece, the *Hammerklavier*. They are intimate and personal, in a sort of string quartet style, with a tinge of improvisation. They have forgotten both the virtuoso and his ways, and the old strict outlines of sonata-form. In fact, they are called sonatas only by a somewhat liberal stretch of courteous imagination. All three were done in the intervals of toil upon the *Missa Solemnis*, which was begun in 1818. And they have much in common with that gigantic work.

The E major sonata (Op. 109) was written in 1820. It is a fantasia sonata, lyrical in mood. The passionate unrest of the sonata-form *prestissimo* which does duty as *scherzo* heightens the happy grace of the opening movement and the calm, serene, reassuring loveliness of the closing variations.[2]

Ex. 137

Andante molto cantabile ed espressivo.
mezza voce.

Behrend[3] calls the A flat (Op. 110, written in 1821) a "memory sonata." Sir George Grove pointed out the resemblance of measures 5—8 of the first movement

Ex. 138   1821

Sonata Op. 110

---

[2]The present writer's own feeling about the theme of these variations may be inferred from his selection of it to stand beside Bach's B flat *Choral Prelude* in the "Pure Beauty" section of *The Poetry Cure with Music and Pictures*, 1927.

[3]William Behrend, *Ludwig van Beethoven's Pianoforte Sonatas*, 1927, p. 182.

to themes from four of Beethoven's earlier works.

Ex. 139   1798
Sonata Op. 10. No 1

Ex. 140   1800
String Quartet Op. 18. No 5

Ex. 141   1802
Violin Sonata Op. 30. No 3

Ex. 142   1808
Trio Op. 70. No 2

He went farther and traced this theme back to Haydn's fifty-eighth sonata.

Riemann pointed out the resemblance of the beginning of the introductory measures

Ex. 143

to the start of the variation theme of the foregoing E major sonata.[4] And others have remarked that the second theme of the *Allegro molto* is like the old popular song *"Ich bin liederlich."*

But no one seems to have noticed two other curious resemblances. While the right hand, beginning at the fifth measure of the first movement, is calling up a flood of memories of Haydn and of Beethoven himself (Ex. 138), the left actually intones in the bass

Ex. 144

the four opening bars of the *finale* of the *"Jupiter"* symphony

Ex. 145

Allegro molto

(which Mozart derived from one of his five favourite Bach fugues, the E major). And Beethoven even goes so far as to imitate Mozart's six following notes, although transposing his own a semitone higher. Mozart to left of him, Haydn to right of him, Bach behind him! It is hard to look upon this meeting of the four masters as purely accidental.

---

[4]See Ex. 137, p. 369.

One shrewdly suspects that Beethoven's right hand knew what his left hand was doing.

The fugued *finale* contains an even more entertaining memory. If one takes the clarinet tune of the fugato of the *Eroica* Funeral March (bars 135–140), divests it of passing notes, and transposes it for purposes of comparison to the key of this *finale,* one has the following:

Ex. 146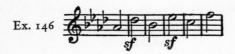

which is nearly the theme of the opus 110 fugue.

Ex. 147

Loans hidden thus artfully have as protective a colouration as that insect named the "walking-stick."[5]

The *Allegro molto* of the A flat sonata, despite its grimness, has gipsy-like gestures which point down the years to the Hungarian rhapsodies of Liszt and such movements of Brahms as the *finale* of the G minor piano quartet. Its first phrase

---

[5]At Munich in the summer of 1927 Herr Wilhelm Furtwängler conducted from memory a prodigious performance of the *Eroica*. Afterwards the writer asked him if he knew that the fugue of the A flat sonata was concealed there. In his forceful Rooseveltian way he swore that such a thing was impossible. Did he not know every note of the symphony by heart? But when the writer produced a pocket score and pointed out the place his surprise and delight were equally forceful.

Ex. 148

seems like a scherzification of the beginning of the short *Arioso dolente*.

Ex. 149

This *Arioso* is the grievously poignant utterance of a man on the downward slope, deaf, ailing, suspicious, mateless, who felt unjustly neglected as an artist and convinced that all the world was banded against him as a man.

The *finale* is one of the most satisfying contrapuntal pieces in all the sonatas. It is as if the monumental majesty

[373]

of Bach and the poetic magic of Brahms had met midway. Beethoven had remarked to Holz[6] not long before the composition of these last sonatas:

> There is no art in making a fugue. In my student years I made them by the dozen. But imagination also claims its rights. And nowadays into the time-honoured form there must enter a truly poetic element.

This element takes such masterly possession of the A flat fugue that it persists even while the theme is being eruditely stood on its head (in *L'inversione della Fuga*).

There could be no more fitting end for the great thirty-two than the C minor sonata (Op. 111). This two-movement work has no *scherzo*, but each movement offers a supreme example of its own type. Beethoven created both of these types, and his supremacy in them has never since been threatened.[7]

The principal theme of the *Allegro con brio ed appassionato*,[8]

> Thundering like ramping hosts of warrior horse,

is one of the most portentously powerful melodies in music. While the *Arietta*, with a naïve simplicity as of folk music, makes one think of those words of St. Paul:

> I will come to visions and revelations of the Lord. I knew a man in Christ above fourteen years ago, (whether in the body, I cannot tell; or whether out of the body, I cannot tell: God knoweth:) such an one caught up to the third heaven. And I

---

[6] See p. 27.
[7] See pp. 499–500.
[8] See the transposed Ex. 330, p. 593.

knew such a man . . . how that he was caught up into paradise, and heard unspeakable words, which it is not lawful for a man to utter. Of such an one will I glory.

Here is the opening portion of the sublime theme

Ex. 150

This movement brings the last sonata to a perfectly satisfying completion. Any addition is unthinkable. Yet poor Schindler is said to have asked Beethoven why he did not write a brilliant fast ending. And the publisher, too, made it clear that this was what he had expected.

Nobody can justly blame them. For even after the lapse of a century it remains true that the listener who can easily cope with the earliest piano sonatas at a first or second hearing requires literally years of persistence, good-will,

[375]

and sympathy in order to comprehend the thirty-second.

From the sublimities of the C minor to the ridiculous was but a step. Early one morning in 1820 Beethoven rose with his mind full of the sonatas and the *Missa*, slipped into a ragged old coat, and set out for a hatless walk. By evening he was famished and had lost his way. Still deep in thought, he was arrested as a vagabond.

"I am Beethoven," he declared.

"Sure, why not, indeed?" mocked the policeman. "You're a tramp, that's what. Beethoven doesn't look like that."[8a]

He was put in jail for the night, but made such a hullabaloo hour after hour that he forced them to get the police commissioner out of bed, who aroused the musical director of the Wiener Neustadt, who identified the turbulent jailbird as Beethoven. Whereupon the man who had not only received the freedom of the city but free lodging at the expense of the city was sent home in state by the burgomaster in the magisterial coach.

Perhaps as a salutary consequence of this farcical episode the Vienna policemen of to-day know more about musical celebrities than they did in 1820. One moonlight evening last year a Viennese lady undertook to show the writer Beethoven's famous place of residence, the Pasqualati House. But it did not look like the familiar pictures.

Recourse was had to one of Vienna's famously cultured and polite policemen. He smiled and said that the building

---

[8a]This idealist among policemen resembled such painters as Neugass, and such writers as M. Romain Rolland, who have insisted on attributing to the squat, ugly, and highly human little Master, a Jovian front, a Roman toga, and the character of a seraph.

BEETHOVEN
Two pen sketches of Beethoven, about seven years before his death, by Boehm

was Schubert's Dreimäderlhaus. Then he led the way around the corner to No. 8 Mölker Bastei. And with a gallant "Kiss the hand!" to the lady and "I have the honour to recommend myself" to her escort, left them to a study of the tablet commemorating the birth of the Fourth, Fifth, and Eighth symphonies, the Rasoumowsky quartets, and the Violin concerto.

Such is real fame. One tries to imagine what response would issue from a Parisian gendarme, a London bobby, or one of New York's "finest" if asked, respectively, about the home of César Franck, Milton's tomb, or Poe's cottage.

Ignaz von Seyfried reported at first hand, in the florid style of his day, the Master's intensely concentrated mode of life.

From the first sunbeam to dinner time, the whole morning was consecrated to mechanical toil, namely writing his music down. The rest of the day was given over to thought and the ordering of his ideas. The last mouthful had scarcely entered his lips when—in case he had no longer excursion in mind—he began his usual promenade. That is to say, he ran on the double-quick a couple of times round about the city as though he were being stung. Whether it rained, snowed, or hailed, whether the thermometer showed sixteen degrees of cold, whether the north wind puffed his cheeks out and blew his icy breath across Bohemia's frontiers, whether the thunder roared, the lightning's zigzag cut the air, a gale howled, or Phoebus' heat rays fell direct on the skull;—what difference did all this make to the consecrated one who carried his God in his own heart and for whose spirit, perhaps, in the very midst of the elements' uproar, the mild springtide of paradise was blooming?[9]

[9]Translated from A. Leitzmann, *Ludwig van Beethoven, Berichte der Zeitgenossen*, 1921, Vol. II, p. 47.

"Only the artist," Beethoven once wrote, "or the emancipated scholar carries his own happiness about inside himself."

In 1821 Sir John Russell visited Vienna, saw Beethoven, and wrote vividly about him:

His eye is full of turbulent energy. His hair which seems to have remained for years out of touch with comb or scissors, shades his broad brow in an abundance and disorder with which only the snakes about the Gorgon's head can be compared. . . . Friendliness and affability do not lie in his character except when in a circle of trusted intimates. . . . Even his oldest friends must always obey his will as though he were a spoiled child.

At this time, reported the Englishman, Beethoven never played the piano for people unless he were tricked into it. Sir John and Beethoven both dined one evening with a close friend of the latter. At a preconcerted signal everyone left the musician and his host alone together. Now the composer could hear music better than speech. While carrying on a written conversation with him about finance the clever friend touched the piano keys as if by accident, then began to play one of Beethoven's own compositions, intentionally making such glaring blunders that Beethoven finally condescended to stretch out his hand and correct one of them. Once on the keys his hand remained there. On some pretext his friend left the room. Beethoven absent-mindedly sat down at the piano, played a few desultory chords, and gradually lost himself in a half hour's improvisation. Of course the whole company listened breathlessly in the open doorway.

[378]

The enthusiasts were carried away [wrote Sir John]. For the uninitiated it was all the more interesting to notice how the music translated itself from the man's soul to his features. . . . His facial muscles swelled and his veins stood out; the doubly wild eye rolled in twice as fine a frenzy, the mouth twitched, and Beethoven looked like a sorcerer who feels himself overpowered by the very spirits whom he has conjured up.

In 1822 Rossini, the popular musical idol of the day, visited the Master whom his own reputation had thrown somewhat into the shade. Beethoven received him pleasantly enough, described himself as "*un infelice*" (an unhappy one), and advised Rossini that he would be doing violence to his destiny if he tried his hand "at anything but opera *buffa*."

Overcome by Beethoven's apparently wretched poverty the generous "Swan of Pesaro" tried to raise a subscription for him. But everyone declined with much the same remark: "He is a misanthrope, cranky, and can't keep friends."

After this call Beethoven remarked: "Rossini is a good scene-painter. . . . He would have been a great composer if . . ." and he roughly outlined the painful and humiliating discipline which the Italian's music teacher should have applied to an inconsidered portion of his anatomy. However, despite his low opinion of Rossini as an absolute musician, Beethoven occasionally condescended, as we have seen,[10] to imitate his cruder popular effects.

In November, 1822, *Fidelio* was revived; and soon conquered, and held a high place in the affections of the

[10]See pp. 173-174.

German-speaking peoples. Beethoven tried to conduct the dress rehearsal. But he was now so deaf that he repeatedly threw everything into confusion. No one dared approach him until Schindler ventured to hand him a note: "I beg you not to go on; will explain at home."

Like a flash Beethoven sprang into the parterre saying only, "Out quickly!" and fairly ran to his house. Schindler relates that

he threw himself upon the sofa, covered his face with both hands, and stayed so until we sat down at table. But not a sound did he utter during the meal. His whole figure was the image of deepest melancholy and despondency.

A tragic situation: his last direct *rapport* with his public roughly snapped. But he was suffering from something even less supportable. As Mr. Grace points out:

One cannot but feel that the real tragedy lay in the fact that at this period, when his powers were at their height, he was so beset with hindrances (many of them avoidable) as to be unable to make the most of his gifts. Probably he alone was fully aware of the discrepancy between his powers and the quantity of his output; and the knowledge must have been an added touch of bitterness to a cup already full.[11]

This knowledge it was that gave the agonizing poignancy to the *Arioso dolente* of the A flat sonata and to that music which was presently to cry to heaven from the opening movement of the *Choral* symphony.

[11]*Beethoven,* p. 142.

Chapter XXXVIII

HE FREES THE MASS

Mass in D, Begun 1818 — Intended for Rudolph's Enthronization Ceremony, 1820 — But not Finished Until 1823 — An Unecclesiastical and Unvocal Writer — His Personal Creed — His Detachment from Earth, 1819 — Missa Begun as an Occasional Work — Music with a Purpose — Handicaps to Composition — Comparative Failure of Kyrie, Gloria, *and part of* Sanctus *— Power and Beauty of* Credo, Benedictus, *and* Agnus Dei *— A Barefaced Plagiarism — Hints of Military Music — The Finest Melody in the* Missa *— Evaluation as a Whole — Defensive Rationalization — Beethoven Frees the Mass*

IN ORDER to write true church music, look up and go through all the church chorales of the monks etc.

Beethoven scribbled this reminder in a Sketch Book of 1818. He had just heard that the Archduke Rudolph was in a year or so to be made Archbishop of Olmütz. So he started his Mass in D (Op. 123) with a view to having it performed at the installation ceremony. This ceremony took place almost two years later, but the *Missa Solemnis,* as he called it, was far from ready. Beethoven toiled on it more or less continually for half a decade.

The delay was probably fortunate for the success of Rudolph's ceremonial. His composer friend was decidedly neither an ecclesiastical nor a vocal writer. When he wandered half a dozen paces into either of these fields he became as submerged in his own purely instrumental thoughts as the day he started to accompany the van of his furniture into the country and promptly forgot all about it.

For vans, voices, and churches his sympathies did not blaze brightly. The reason he made things so uncomfortable for all three was not lack of knowledge but lack of the love which breeds consideration. "Singers," he once remarked coldly, "ought to be able to do anything, except bite their own noses!" Hence the fatiguing length of the *Missa* and its loose adaptation to the precise time-table of the church service. Hence those ghastly difficulties for the wretched sopranos, there and in the *Choral* symphony, which made Fräulein Unger call him to his face "tyrant over all the vocal organs," and which made a perfect performance of these works almost unheard of—even in the days before our present high pitch came into fashion. In this connection there is much significance in Beethoven's casual remark: "When I think of a theme, it is always for some instrument."

It was unfortunate for this department of Beethoven's work [writes Mr. Grace] that he lived in a bad choral period when the idiom was secular and operatic, and the beauty of unaccompanied singing seems to have been unrealized.[1]

Beethoven was not as close to the Mass text as many suppose. In his ignorance of Latin he had to have the words translated for him into German. Though he was religious

---

[1] *Beethoven*, p. 287.

in the sense that he had constructed his own religion, his heart did not warm to the less spiritual aspects of ecclesiasticism. There were even affirmations in the *Credo* which he must have actively disbelieved. So it is hard to see how he could have entered into the composition of the *Missa* with that whole-hearted, enthusiastic conviction which is a necessary antecedent for the greatest works of art.

The leading items of Beethoven's personal credo were: self-reliant strength, goodness, beauty as shown in nature and art, and a supreme Being who exemplified and fostered all these. Through the finer parts of the *Missa* such a belief blazes forth in a personally Beethovenian way.

Realizing perhaps that a task like this presented peculiar difficulties to such a man as himself, he plunged into it with a kind of desperate abandon. In a Sketch Book he admonished himself: "Once more sacrifice to your art all the little things of social life. O God above all!" "When I am alone," he once remarked, "I am never alone." And these words apply peculiarly to this period. Schindler testified that never before or after had he seen the Master so detached from earth as in 1819.[2]

Towards the end of August, accompanied by the musician Johann Horsalka, still living in Vienna, I arrived at the master's home in Mödling. It was four o'clock in the afternoon. As soon as we entered we learned that in the morning both servants had gone away, and that there had been a quarrel after midnight which had disturbed all the neighbours, because as a consequence of a long vigil both had gone to sleep and the food which had been prepared had become unpalatable. In the living-room,

---

[2]Ed. of 1860, Vol. I, p. 270.

behind a locked door, we heard the master singing parts of the fugue in the *Credo*—singing, howling, stamping. After we had been listening a long time to this almost awful scene, and were about to go away, the door opened and Beethoven stood before us with distorted features, calculated to excite fear. He looked as if he had been in mortal combat with the whole host of contrapuntists, his everlasting enemies. His first utterances were confused, as if he had been disagreeably surprised at our having overheard him. Then he reached the day's happenings and with obvious restraint he remarked: "Good housekeeping, this! [*Saubere Wirthschaft!*] Everybody has run away and since noon yesterday I haven't had anything to eat!" I tried to calm him and helped him to make his toilet. My companion hurried on in advance to the restaurant of the bathing establishment to have something made ready for the famished master. Then he complained about the wretched state of his domestic affairs, but here, for reasons already stated, there was nothing to be done. Never, it may be said, did so great an art work as is the *Missa Solemnis* see its creation under more adverse circumstances.

Beethoven felt that this Mass was his best composition. And nearly all of his biographers have agreed with him and with one another in declaring it the crown, or something near it, of the Master's career—worthy to stand with Bach's B minor Mass at the summit of all choral compositions. It is time to forget what anyone has ever said about the *Missa*, to hear it with one's own ears and scrutinize it strictly on its own merits according to the light vouchsafed us to-day.

Judged by both outer and inner standards this was started as an occasional work. It was begun as a compliment to his rich patron the Archduke, a man to whom Beethoven in his letters often referred contemptuously as "the weak cardinal," and the like. Such outer incentives

BEETHOVEN
From a crayon portrait by Kloeber, 1817 or 1818

for composition almost never resulted in Beethoven's best. Think of the pedestrian triple concerto, written for this same Rudolph. Think of the *"Battle"* symphony, *King Stephen, The Ruins of Athens,* the Scotch Songs, and *The Glorious Moment.* All of these compositions give a Beethoven lover a gone feeling, and make him perhaps recall that comforting declaration of Mozart's: "He who judges me by my bad works is a knave!"

Subjectively, as well, much of the *Missa* suffers the blight of the occasional. Beethoven wrote Andreas Streicher, September 16, 1824:

During the work on this Grand Mass my main purpose was to evoke in both the singers and the auditors religious sentiments and to instil them permanently.

If this was true it goes far to explain the comparative failure of something like one half of the work. Can one possibly imagine Beethoven confessing that his main purpose in writing things like the *Eroica* or the C sharp minor quartet was ethical, philosophical, religious, or anything but purely musical?

Besides these handicaps the composer was sick much of the time between 1818 and 1823. He was distracted by the wretched business of Karl, and by hopeless domestic affairs which were aggravated *crescendo* by the morbid suspicions natural to almost total deafness. These circumstances may abundantly account for the comparatively commonplace *Kyrie,* and for the lack of spontaneity and magic in the *Gloria.* The culminating point of the latter, the *In gloria Dei patris,* is merely the work of a capable fugue-smith who

[385]

has, however, hammered the thing out cold. There are no sparks.

The only wonder is that, starting with these formidable handicaps, he should have been able, by the time he arrived at the *Credo*, to brush them all aside like so many midges. The *Crucifixus* and the *Et vitam venturi* fugue

Ex. 151

Allegretto ma non troppo

et vi-tam ven-tu-ri sae - - - cu li, a - -

are as gripping and overpowering as anything he ever did for the voice. For sixteen pages the *Sanctus* is undistinguished. Then it breaks into the *Benedictus* with its soaring violin obbligato—that unsurpassed progenitor of the most ethereal, celestial pages of Schubert, Wagner, Brahms, Franck, and Richard Strauss.

The *Agnus Dei* confronts us with an amazing barefaced plagiarism

Ex. 152

ff

pa - cem, do - - na no - bis pa -

from the *Hallelujah* Chorus of *The Messiah*.

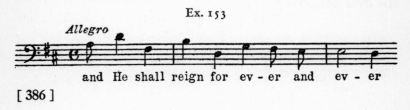

Ex. 153

Allegro

and He shall reign for ev - er and ev - er

[386]

This fact might lend comfort and countenance to the jazz pickpockets of a century later—especially to the writer of that best-selling popular song of a recent year, "Yes, We Have No Bananas," who likewise helped himself to part of the *Hallelujah* Chorus. Perhaps in this instance Beethoven was too much overpowered by his curious conviction that Handel was the greatest composer who had ever lived, to succeed in transmuting Ex. 153 into his own coin. And the result was an ugly rift in the unity of the Mass.

Yet this same *Agnus Dei* contains what is, in the writer's opinion, the loveliest music of all. Its most moving portion begins with the motto "Petition for Internal and External Peace." There are subtle hints of military music, delicate enough to suggest to those hearers who have poetry in their souls symbols of spiritual dangers, struggles, and triumphs. They are also plain enough to have shocked the horny-minded literalists into indignant protest against the impropriety of martial strains in a Mass.

But Beethoven's sense of propriety in the *Agnus Dei* was exquisite. He felt that an exciting close on a note of triumph or splendour would be inappropriate. So with his almost unerring instinct for endings he made an *"innig"* end, with the finest melody in the Mass. It is one of the most superbly beautiful and haunting tunes that he or anyone else ever conceived.

Ex. 154

do - - - na no - bis pa - cem,

M. D'Indy suggests that part of its penetrative force lies in the curious arrangement by which none of the nine notes stands on a degree previously heard. But it must be a small part, if one may judge from the many weak melodies of which the same is to be said.

Despite the marvellous qualities of its best portions, the *Missa Solemnis,* taken as a whole, stands in the author's opinion on a plane somewhat below its composer's best sonatas, quartets, and symphonies. It stands considerably below that choral Abou Ben Adhem, the B minor Mass of Bach, whose name leads all the rest. And it stands below Bach's *St. Matthew Passion,* and, yes, below *The Messiah.*

Those who have accepted the Master's own estimate of the *Missa* should take into account that this creation cost him more time and trouble than any of his other spiritual children; that artists are notoriously unreliable judges of their own productions; and that a cripple, reared with difficulty, is usually its mother's favourite child.

"From the heart—may it speak to the heart" are the unusual words which stand at the top of the score. The composer "doth protest too much." There is no need for any such statement with the *Eroica* Funeral March or the Violin concerto or the B flat trio or the two last sonatas or the ten last quartets. Perhaps Beethoven had some unformulated misgiving about the qualifications of half of his *Missa* to speak to the heart. Perhaps this motto represents a bit of what the psychologists would call defensive rationalization. Beethoven, as is well known, told Rudolph that having the *Missa* performed at his enthronement as Arch-

[388]

bishop would give the composer the happiest day of his life. This protestation should not be taken too literally. It should be collated with his letter to Franz von Brentano, November 28, 1820, about "the weak cardinal who has got me into this morass and does not know how to help himself." And it should be read in connection with the scores of polite but palpable fibs which he wrote over a period of three decades to this most generous and consistent of his patrons.

Though half of it was comparatively weak, the *Missa* continued that work of liberation which its creator had carried on in much of his instrumental music. The tardy appearance of a Bach cult, which delayed the publication of Bach's vocal works until the middle of the Nineteenth Century, conferred upon Beethoven the honour of actually freeing the Mass from its traditional confinement within the boundaries of a particular church. He even liberated it from the confines of ecclesiastical convention itself, and made it free of a region until then almost untrodden by composers—that land of true religion, wide as the human race, where the individual stands in immediate relation with the infinite life of which he is a spark.

Chapter XXXIX

MR. HYDE AND THE HELL-HOUNDS

Bad Faith with Publishers — Palliations — Did Beethoven Have a Higher Private Moral Code?—Weak Case for the Defense — Solicits Private Subscriptions for Missa *— Misrepresentations to Zelter — Letter to Goethe, February 8, 1823, Unanswered — Schindler Established as Factotum, 1822 — Liszt's Début, 1823 — Diabelli Variations, 1823*

Now comes a distressing matter. At the time when Beethoven's Dr. Jekyll had just finished such other-worldly music as the *Et vitam venturi,* the *Benedictus,* and the *Dona nobis pacem,* and was turning his thoughts to the sublimities of the Ninth symphony, Mr. Hyde flew into a bustle of pernicious activity along worldly lines.[1]

We have already heard how he said to the remonstrant "Falstaff" in the Rasoumowsky period, "Does he really suppose I think of his puling little fiddle when the spirit speaks to me and I compose something?" Now, in the above, Mr. Hyde could honestly have substituted for "his puling little fiddle" "my puling little publishers." For he was playing faster and looser with these so-called 'hell-hounds who licked and gnawed his brains' than he had just played with

---

[1] In *Dr. Jekyll and Mr. Hyde,* Thistle ed., 1901, p. 352, Stevenson's hero-villain wrote of the principles of evil and good within him: "It was the curse of mankind that these incongruous faggots were thus bound together—that in the agonized womb of consciousness, these polar twins should be continually struggling."

the sopranos by making them at one point enter the *vitam venturi* (or almost enter it) on four high B flats.

We shall not go into the details of these sordid business dealings. Are they not written in the books of the chronicles of Thayer? It will suffice here to give the summary in his third volume, for which Krehbiel, the American editor, accepted responsibility (p. 51 ff).

Careful readers of this biography can easily recall a number of lapses from high ideals of candour and justice in his treatment of his friends and of a nice sense of honour and honesty in his dealings with his publishers; but at no time have these blemishes been so numerous or so patent as they are in his negotiations for the publication of the *Missa Solemnis*—a circumstance which is thrown into a particularly strong light by the frequency and vehemence of his protestations of moral rectitude in the letters which have risen like ghosts to accuse him. . . . He was never louder in his protestations of business morality than when he was promising the mass to four or more publishers practically at the same time, and giving it to none of them; never more apparently frank than when he was making ignoble use of a gentleman, whom he himself described as one of the best friends on earth, as an intermediary between himself and another friend to whom he was bound by business ties and childhood associations which challenged confidence; never more obsequious (for even this word must now be used in describing his attitude towards Franz Brentano) than after he had secured a loan from that friend in the nature of an advance on a contract which he never carried out; never more apparently sincere than when he told one publisher (after he had promised the mass to another) that he should be particularly sorry if he were unable to give the mass into his hands; never more forcefully and indignantly honest in appearance than when he informed still another publisher that the second had importuned him for the mass ("bombarded" was the word), but that he had never even

[391]

deigned to answer his letters. But even this is far from compassing the indictment; the counts are not even complete when it is added that in a letter he states that the publisher whom he had told it would have been a source of sorrow not to favour had never even been contemplated amongst those who might receive the mass; that he permitted the friend to whom he first promised the score to tie up some of his capital for a year and more so that "good Beethoven" should not have to wait a day for his money; that after promising the mass to the third publisher he sought to create the impression that it was not the *Missa Solemnis* that had been bargained for, but one of two masses which he had in hand.

With this should be compared Beethoven's statement in a letter to the publisher Peters, June 5, 1822:

I love straightness and uprightness and am of the opinion that one should not discredit the artist, for alas! it is unfortunately true that however brilliant the outer aspect of fame appears, it is not granted him to be the daily guest of Jupiter on Olympus; unfortunately, in spite of his resistance, common humanity drags him all too often from these pure ethereal heights.

In mitigation of sentence on Mr. Hyde it should be remembered that money was harder for Beethoven to come by at this time, that deafness, ill-health, and many cares and distractions made him peculiarly susceptible to dubious "practical" counsel; made him morbidly suspicious of those with whom he had business dealings; made him produce more slowly and laboriously just when he was engaged on his larger works, and that his desire to keep and lay by money for his beloved nephew had become an obstinate obsession.

An instance of how he rationalized this altruistic avarice occurs in a letter to Peters (July 26, 1822):

I must consider his [Karl's] future, as we are neither Indians nor Iroquois [*sic*] who, as is well known, leave everything to the *lieben Gott*.

Mr. Sullivan comes to the defense of Beethoven by arguing that, while the Master did not recognize the claims of "business morality," he had a higher code of his own.[2] It was the sort of "artistic morality" shown by his threatening to kick General Kyd downstairs for having offered him £100 if he would compose a symphony in his own earlier manner. No doubt such a case of æsthetic rectitude can cover a multitude of business sins; somewhat as the sportsmanship, sincerity, and freedom from cant that characterize the post-war generation more than compensate for its selfishness and bad manners. And in the main our hero's musical conscience was upright and exalted.

But Mr. Sullivan overlooks the fact that, most of the time, Beethoven honoured the claims of business morality to such an extent that he must have had at least a theoretical respect for them. And he must have blunted the teeth of remorse in a very human way. After his dishonest lapses towards the publishers he probably rationalized, as the rest of us do, by telling himself that all was fair in the struggle with these "hell-hounds." And he probably even persuaded himself that the London Philharmonic was legitimately to be treated like the publishers.

In lauding Beethoven's "artistic morality" Mr. Sullivan

[2]*Beethoven: His Spiritual Development*, p. 188 ff.

also forgets the sheer artistic immorality of such works as the *"Battle"* symphony, the *Polonaise* (Op. 89), and those shoddy overtures which he fobbed off upon the Philharmonic.

Mr. Sullivan roundly declares: "Whatever moral canons Beethoven violated he did not violate his own." But how then may we account for his continual reactions of sincere remorse, when, as so often happened, he realized that he had treated his friends shabbily?

No, such a whitewashing cannot entirely convince us. But the author, for one, is glad that Beethoven was no alabaster saint who scrupulously observed all his own moral canons. We should never have had such gloriously human music from a saint as we had from this Dr. Jekyll. And on hearing his greater pages the importance of Mr. Hyde dwindles almost to insignificance.

When all is said, no very strong case can be made out for the defense. Even the sympathetic Dr. Deiters, Thayer's German editor, after putting all the extenuating circumstances before the jury of posterity, felt himself bound to add:

We pay the tribute of our profoundest sympathy for Beethoven in these circumstances; we know sufficiently well the noble impulses of his soul in all other fields; we are aware of the reasons which compelled him to try anything which promised to better his conditions; but the conscientious reporter cannot ignore facts which lie notoriously before him, and, hard as it may be, cannot acquit Beethoven of the reproach that his conduct was not in harmony with the principles of strict justice and uprightness.

Perhaps none but those who have suffered the plight of total deafness can feel more sympathy than repugnance in following the business history of the *Missa*. There is nothing like ear trouble for curdling the milk of human kindness. It can easily persuade a victim that the universe is in league to deride and defraud him, and that almost anything the minority may do is justifiable in such a lopsided war.

In his keenness for money the man who had freed the composer from the patronage system—even while he himself was profiting therefrom—and established him on a professional basis went back on his excellent principles. He postponed publication of the *Missa* and obsequiously solicited private subscriptions for it, at 50 ducats each, from those potentates whom he was fond of describing as "the princely rabble" and worse.

Keats may have been right in saying that beauty is truth; but it does not follow that the creator of beauty is always truthful. The Master's letters to Zelter offering the *Missa* to the Berlin Singakademie show rather crude prevarications. They intimate that the Mass would never be published in the ordinary way; also that this whole composition, unthinkable without the orchestra, "could be almost performed entirely *a la capella* . . . and there is already a movement in it which is entirely *a la capella*."

February 8, 1823, the same day as his first letter on this subject to Zelter, Beethoven wrote Goethe bespeaking his influence towards having the court of Weimar subscribe, and stating that the Mass would not be published in the ordinary way "for the present." Now Goethe was a close friend of Zelter's and may have discovered the discrepancy between these two statements about publication. At any rate, he had never forgiven Beethoven for the trick played on him at Teplitz. We know that Goethe fell suddenly and seriously ill on February 17, 1823. But even after his recovery a month later he treated Beethoven's letter to the same silence which he had meted out six years before to an unknown lad of twenty. This lad was named Franz Schubert. He had sent the *Erlkönig,* in a book of other manuscript settings of Goethe's lyrics, with a bashful request to dedicate them to His Excellency.

By 1822 Anton Felix Schindler, who had first met Beethoven eight years before, had become firmly established as his private-secretary-without-salary. He was tall and lean, a figure of comedy when he laid down the law in his nasal voice and with the angular gestures of a semaphore.

Naturally he never laid down the law to Beethoven, but used to annoy him with all manner of inept questions such as: "Will you tell me, in a few words, how to become an orchestral conductor?"

"Do you imagine," was the exasperated reply, "that a conductor can be improvised?"[3]

No wonder he called his famulus an irksome "appendix."

In April, 1823, Czerny's pupil, Franz Liszt, a twelve-year-old boy, gave his first public concert. On Liszt's own authority the world has long believed that Beethoven came, heard, wept, rushed upon the stage, and publicly kissed

---

[3]*Kölnische Zeitung,* June 28, 1845.

him, uttering complimentary prophesies. But the records of the Conversation Books and of contemporaries strongly suggest that this story was fabricated. It is doubtful whether Beethoven attended the concert. Even if he had, he could not have heard one note. And mere dumb show would scarcely have stirred him to the point of making such an emotional scene in public.

That same year Beethoven furnished a vivid illustration of the poet's chief function, which is to reveal the significance of the seemingly insignificant—to show forth the beauty, not of holiness, but of the apparently ugly. He performed a conjuring feat which recalls how he founded an important figure in the *Credo* of his Mass in C upon the absurd fumblings of a village violoncellist.[4]

A Viennese publisher called Diabelli, having written a waltz of the most perfect insipidity, invited a large number of composers, among them Schubert and Beethoven, to collaborate by contributing one variation each for his volume. Schubert accepted. Beethoven growled that he never collaborated; besides, he didn't want to write a variation on a cobbler's patch (*Schusterfleck*). Then he looked at the foolish thing again, burst out into a great laugh, and straightway fell to composing. It may have tickled his sense of humour that the tune was so much like the *scherzo* of a trio in E flat which he had written at the age of fifteen and never published.[5]

---

[4] See p. 266, note 9.

[5] It is worth noting that when this work was published in 1830, Diabelli was one of three old friends of Beethoven's to sign a guarantee of its authenticity. Perhaps he had based his own tune upon its *scherzo*.

Enthusiasm waxed, and he sent word to the publisher offering to write a whole set himself. Diabelli was delighted and offered him 80 ducats for six or eight variations.

"All right," said Beethoven, in high good humour. "He shall have variations on his cobbler's patch!" He had them—thirty-three in all.

This astonishing piece is a monument to Beethoven's learning, his resourcefulness, his humour, his rhythmical genius, his cosmic breadth,[6] but not throughout to his inspiration. Herr Ernest says a true word.[7] We miss here the evidence of that *"schaffenstarke Passivität,"* that "might of creative passivity," which underlies his supreme work. One feels too that in writing these variations the deaf Master was Utopian and intended them for a theoretical virtuoso playing a theoretical piano. But he was only recoiling *pour mieux sauter.*

---

[6] "Those incredible Diabelli variations . . . the whole range of thought and feeling, yet all in organic relation to a ridiculous little waltz tune." (Huxley, *Point Counter Point*, 1928, p. 294.)

[7] *Beethoven*, p. 395.

Chapter XL

THE CHORAL SYMPHONY

Choral Symphony, Begun before 1817, Finished 1823 —
Long Incubation Period — 1818, Memorandum for Ninth
and Tenth Symphonies — Fusion of the Two Schemes —
Echoes — Initial Difficulty in Composing — The Program
Question — Beethoven's Three Most Original Contribu-
tions — First Movement — Scherzo — The Kettledrum
Joke — Origin of First Subject — Adagio-Andante —
Choral Finale — Skill in Selecting Words — Merits and
Defects of Hymn to Joy

FOR three decades Beethoven carried about in his head part
of the Ninth symphony. Such long preoccupation recalls
the half century during which Goethe brooded and toiled
over *Faust*.

As has been already noted, it was the Master's custom to
write his symphonies in pairs. In an 1818 Sketch Book he
scribbled, among studies for the *Hammerklavier* sonata,
the following memorandum:

Adagio cantique; sacred song in a symphony in an old mode
(We Praise Thee, O God—alleluia), either to stand alone, or
as introduction to a fugue. The whole second symphony to be
based, perhaps, on its melody. The singing voices to enter in
the last piece, or as early as the *Adagio*. Orchestra, violins, etc.,
to be increased tenfold in the last piece. Or the *Adagio* repeated
in a certain manner in the last piece, the singing voices being
then first introduced little by little. In the *Adagio* the text of

[399]

a Greek myth—*Cantique-Ecclesiastique*—in the *Allegro,* festival of Bacchus.

It appears that these two symphonies were to be called "The English" and "The German." They were to contrast the worship of the pagan gods with that of Jehovah. The second was to have a vocal termination in an old mode. The first was to have a *finale* commencing with a glorious sweeping tune which, as we shall see, met a different fate. And there was to be an anagram movement based on Bach's name—perhaps as a contrast to the "festival of Bacchus."

When these paired ideas fell into the active volcano of Beethoven's unconsciousness tremendous seethings, fusions, and eruptions took place. The two dream symphonies melted and ran into one. But the pagan gods and the Bach anagram were violently rejected. The old mode and the sweeping *finale* tune were shot forth for later use in the A minor quartet (Op. 132). Various reminiscences of early work flowed in to replace them. And the Ninth symphony began to take definite form.

There are more memories in this symphony than in even the "memory" sonata in A flat.[1] The Trio of the *scherzo*

Ex. 155

---

[1]See pp. 369–372.

BEETHOVEN'S FACTOTUM
ANTON SCHINDLER

opens with a third-period version of the corresponding part
of the Second symphony.² This was taken from the venerable church tune on which *Non nobis* was founded.

Ex. 156   WM. BYRD, c. 1590

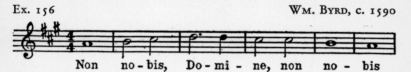

Non   no - bis,   Do - mi - ne,   non   no - bis

In the last eleven notes of its final theme, moreover,

Ex. 157

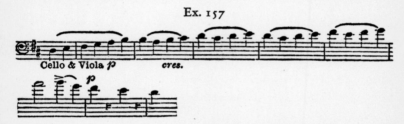

Cello & Viola *p*   *cres.*

the writer has chanced upon a smiling echo of the countryside atmosphere of an old English ballad, "My Man John,"³

Ex. 159

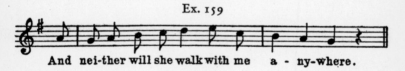

And nei-ther will she walk with me   a - ny-where.

---

²See the transposed Ex. 298, p. 584.

³The writer's friend Mr. Carl Engel contributes the suggestion that this echo may
have been a by-product of Beethoven's recent study of British folk-songs, many of
which he arranged. While Miss Marion Bauer points out that Humperdinck made
charming use of the same tune in the Forest Scene of *Hänsel und Gretel*:

Ex. 158

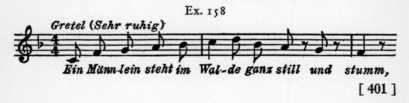

Gretel (Sehr ruhig)

Ein Männ-lein steht im Wal-de ganz still und stumm,

which may conceivably have been inserted as a gracious gesture to the land Beethoven had long admired from afar and for whose leading orchestra he was about to write the following inscription on the manuscript copy of the symphony:

> GRAND SYMPHONY WRITTEN
> FOR THE PHILHARMONIC SOCIETY
> IN LONDON
> BY LUDWIG VAN BEETHOVEN

Here we are pleasantly reminded of that youthful Anglomania which he probably acquired by contagion from his early patron Prince Lichnowsky.

The august opening theme

Ex. 160

of the *Allegro ma non troppo* is the *Storm* theme from the *Pastoral* symphony (at bar 23), raised to the *n*th power.

Certain other memories appear to have been overlooked. The opening of the second subject of the *Allegro ma non troppo*

Ex. 161

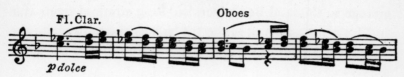

is taken almost literally from bar 100 of the *Allegro ma non troppo* in this same *Pastoral*. (See Ex. 308, p. 587.)

Another reminiscence is more subtle and interesting than a direct quotation. The writer stumbled upon it through Sir George Grove's footnote statement:[3]

> Dr. Charles Wood has pointed out to me that the bass of the first two bars [of the *Adagio's* first subject] is identical with that of the beginning of the slow movement in the *Sonate Pathétique* (Op. 13).

In studying Beethoven's sketches[4] for the movement with this hint in mind, it was noticeable that one of these sketches actually began in the treble with the first five notes of the *Adagio* of the *Pathétique*.

Ex. 162

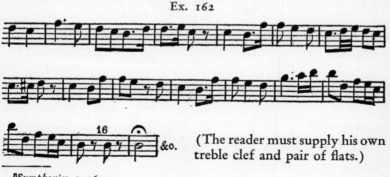

(The reader must supply his own treble clef and pair of flats.)

---

[3] *Symphonies*, p. 362 n.
[4] Nottebohm, *Zweite Beethoveniana*, p. 177, 2d example.

[403]

Comparing the final version of the two tunes, one saw that not only was the bass identical for three bars, but even the treble coincided in the third. It became apparent that the *Pathétique* might contain one of those hidden melodies which Beethoven had so often mined out of the interior of existing ones. We have already seen how he performed this feat in the *Allegretto* of the Seventh symphony,[5] the recapitulation of the first movement of the Eighth symphony,[6] and elsewhere. When the key and time signature of the *Pathétique* phrase had been transposed to conform to those of the *Choral* phrase, the surmise was found correct. The two go together even more smoothly than Dvořak's *Humoresque* goes with *The Suwanee River.*

Ex. 163

Ex. 164

[5]See p. 308.
[6]See pp. 323–324.

Skeptics are urged to try the pair as a duet for two pianos.[7]

In composing the *Choral* symphony Beethoven left its slow movement until the last. It was as though he despaired of finding any *Adagio* subject worthy to follow that puissant *Allegro* and that incomparable *scherzo*. Illness and trouble were making his ideas come more deliberately.

"You see," he confessed to Rochlitz in 1822, "for some while past I have not been able to write easily. I sit and think, and think, and get it all settled; but it won't come on the paper, and a great work troubles me immensely at the outset; once get into it and it's all right." This strange new handicap of initial inertia may explain why opus 125 ventured to climb upon the back of opus 13 to get up a few measures' momentum.

Less concretely than in the examples just cited, the opening movement of the Ninth recalls two earlier symphonies. The brooding chaos of the first measures is a third-period version of that prettier, smaller Haydn-oratorio chaos of the introduction to the Fourth symphony; while the main part of the movement is a mature, almost superhuman re-creation of the emotion surging in the terrific conflict that starts the Fifth. Only we feel that the latter conflict is raging in the soul of one who has now risen to the stature of a supreme conqueror.

---

[7]After this had been written the following footnote came to light, on p. 148 of the Bülow and Lebert edition of the sonatas (Schirmer):

"To the best of our knowledge no one has yet remarked the striking affinity of the theme of this movement, even with reference to its external melodic structure, to that of the loftiest *Adagios* of grandest scope from the Master's last period;—we mean the *Adagio* of the Ninth symphony, written almost a quarter of a century later."

It is distressing to find such learned musicologists as Herr Bekker solemnly and elaborately deliberating on questions like: "Where did he [Beethoven] find subject matter for his new work [the Ninth]?"[8] All of the numerous poetic programs which have been written for the *Choral* symphony, including Richard Wagner's impassioned rhapsody, can have—thanks be!—no more than a subjective validity for those who conceived them. Otherwise music would be something pathetically less than the infinite art.

Strip the Ninth of arbitrary interpretations. Remember that using the old idea of the Schiller Joy tune as a *finale* was a questionable afterthought which Beethoven later disavowed. And all that is left as a common programmatic denominator is much the same emotional scheme which Beethoven had often before used—notably in such masterpieces as the *Egmont* and *Leonore* overtures, the E minor quartet, and the Fifth symphony. It is *per aspera ad astra*, through struggle to triumph, passing by way of mystery, naïve trust, humour, abandon, reassurance, consolation, religious ecstasy, love, etc.

Three parts of this symphony are first-magnitude examples of what we shall find[9] to have been Beethoven's three most original contributions to music: the opening movement of titanic struggle, the Dionysiac *scherzo*, "that great spout of life,"[10] whirling the listener to undreamt regions of humour, abandon, and fantasy; and the visionary slow movement of mystic delight.

[8]*Beethoven*, p. 188.
[9]See pp. 499–500.
[10]In Mr. Lawrence Gilman's vivid phrase.

In the Ninth symphony these three are superbly represented and balanced. The opening subject of the first movement, founded on the D minor triad,

Ex. 160

is colossal, although it by no means bestrides the whole mighty symphony, as some writers insist.[11]

This herculean main subject with the eerie twilight of the starkly elemental introduction, the extraordinary richness of subsidiary matter, the sudden surprising gleams of tenderness, the terrific passage with the long *tympani* roll at the start of the recapitulation where "the Dark Tower of Childe Roland's encounter looms before us out of the swirling spiritual mists,"[12] the coda's dirge over a chromatic *basso ostinato* that seems crushed beneath the weight of universal woe—all this would clearly constitute the strongest, noblest page of Beethoven if it were not for the opening of the C sharp minor quartet, the *Et vitam venturi* fugue in the *Missa,* and the first half of the *Eroica.* Perhaps it is, in any case.

Though the first movement is rivalled by that of the *Eroica,* the *scherzo*

---

[11]See Paul Bekker, *Beethoven*, p. 193.
[12]To quote Mr. Gilman's interpretation again.

Ex. 165

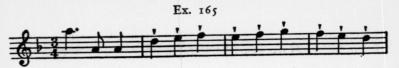

stands absolutely unrivalled among *scherzos,* and but little below any other movement whatever. There is one curious matter-of-fact reason for the power the *Molto vivace* has over us. At the right tempo, each four-measure group of twelve notes constitutes, according to the psychologists, approximately the largest musical unit which the human mind can absorb as a single impression.

This masterpiece of variety in unity, this "miracle of repetition without monotony," as someone has called it, is made up to a large extent of the dotted three-note phrase with which it opens.

Ex. 166

Such economy of material is very unusual even for an arch-economist like Beethoven.

After the first repeat, where the rhythm changes from groups of four to groups of three bars, there is a piece of deliciously subtle humour: *Ritmo di tre battute* (Rhythm of three beats) is the elegant Italian stage direction. The rank bassoons waggishly lead off. Then the kettledrums, no longer able to contain themselves, start the three-bar group four times with a loud, self-important

Ex. 167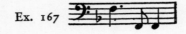

BEETHOVEN IN 1823
After the painting by Waldmüller

Mr. Grace writes charmingly about this passage:[13]

The drums, hollow of tone and slightly lacking in definition of pitch, change the humour from the polite to the broad. It is as if, impatient of their traditional rôle of mere rhythm-makers, and jealous of the busy bandying of the theme between other parts, the drums said, "Let us take a hand," promptly take it, and find themselves after all unable to improve on the feat with which they started in at the opening of the movement—i. e., the delivery of the first three notes of the theme.

The fifth time, however, they come in with total unexpectedness after *four* measures, but *diminuendo,* as though shaky in their minds.[14]

At the *première* of the Ninth symphony, the quick and creative Viennese listeners were so thrilled and excited by the humour of this passage that their applause quite interrupted the performance.

The three-note phrase underlying this movement is said to have come to Beethoven in a flash, as he went out of the dark into a dazzling light. And upon many a hearer it has a similar effect of abrupt nocturnal illumination. Then suddenly, with the Trio, he finds himself in the sweet and common daylight of an English countryside.

We have it on Czerny's authority, however, that the first subject of this *scherzo*—please look again at Example 165—occurred to the composer not in coming out of the dark but on hearing sparrows twittering in a garden. Assuming that

[13]*Beethoven,* p. 276.

[14]This proceeding, as Professor Donald Tovey points out, in his analysis of the Ninth, apparently reëstablishes the original four-bar grouping, though it really does nothing of the sort, because the fifth drum entry simply comes on the second bar of the three instead of on the first.

[409]

the deaf composer could have heard them, the sparrows may have had a voice in the nervousness of the hide-and-seek fugato part, and the garden itself in the rustic simplicities of the Trio.

The *Adagio-Andante* is one of the holiest, purest out-pourings of exaltation in the whole domain of mystical music. It is far more akin to the *Benedictus* of the *Missa* than to the *Adagio* of the *Pathétique,* where, as we have seen,[15] the first subject was found like a statue embedded in a block of translucent marble.

After two dozen measures we bring up against a double bar. Most unexpectedly the time signature changes to 3/4 *Andante moderato.* The key signature turns from B flat into D, and the second fiddles fervently intone a tune which Beethoven originally sketched to start this movement as an *Alla Menuetto,* then discarded, and finally brought back for a second subject, to the delight of nephew Karl, who scribbled in one of the Conversation Books, "I'm only glad that you've put in the beautiful *Andante.*"

Herr Bekker cleverly suggests that "the two themes of the *Adagio* are comparable to the two female figures in Titian's well-known picture, 'Sacred and Profane Love.' "[16] This may have resulted from Beethoven's original idea of contrasting symphonies, one Christian, one pagan. For the Ninth, as we have seen, came from a fusion of both plans.

In this *Andante* subject Beethoven's sympathy for the downtrodden, and the democracy of the feelings he was

[15]See pp. 403–405.
[16]*Beethoven,* p. 185.

about to express concerning Joy, caused him to take compassion on those peons of the orchestra, the second violins,
and assign them one of the most luscious tidbits in the work.
It is touching to hear with what a fevour of gratitude and
enthusiasm these poor fellows fall upon the tune—an enthusiasm which even the most magnetic or savage conductor
can scarcely restrain within the bounds of anything like the
piano enjoined by Beethoven.

This movement is kind to another sort of player as well.
The short, poignant dirge in D flat (bars 133–136)

Ex. 168

has for a century served as a fountainhead of inspiration to improvising church organists.

Beethoven's own description of opus 125 as "Symphony with Final Chorus on Schiller's ode 'To Joy,'" shows that he himself regarded the last movement as an addendum to the first three. Let us say at once all we can in its favour.

Less than half of Schiller's elaborate drinking song was used here. For Beethoven realized that some of the rejected stanzas lapsed into a sophomoric audacity which came rather close to the sacrilegious. For example

> *Lasst den Schaum zum Himmel spritzen!*
> *Dieses Glas dem guten Geist!*
>
> (Let the foam to Heaven go spurting!
> Lift this glass to the Good Spirit!)

which is as who should say: "*Prosit,* God!"

The composer's skill in selecting the right words to form a whole of far greater dignity than the original poem would have done credit to a poet of no mean power. Feats like this, and scores of remarkable passages in his letters, suggest that his literary ability has been underestimated. In one sense Debussy was mistaken when he wrote "Beethoven was not literary for two sous."[17]

There are two superlatively great things about the choral *finale:* the Joy theme itself,

---

[17]Quoted in J. de Marliave, *Les Quatuors de Beethoven,* 1925, xv.

[412]

Ex. 169

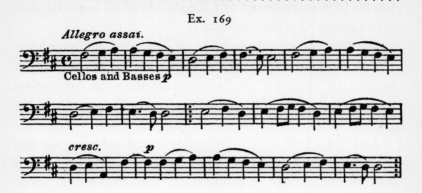

and the second intermediate theme of this huge cantata-rondo, beginning at the 595th bar, *Andante Maestoso,* through the *Adagio ma non troppo, ma divoto.*

Here Beethoven's studies in the Gregorian chant[18] bore more fruit than in all of the *Missa* to prepare for which he looked through the "church-chorals of the monks."

Those who have followed the long and painful evolution of the Joy theme through the Sketch Books, may more fully appreciate the force of Richard Wagner's remark:

Beethoven has emancipated this melody from all influences of fashion and variations of taste, and has raised it into a type of pure and lasting humanity.

It has the simple force, the limpid beauty, the generic quality of the greatest folk music. The tune haunted the

[18]See p. 381.

imaginations of those on whom Beethoven's mantle fell.[19]

The *Andante Maestoso—Adagio* section of the *finale,* just mentioned, has need of all the noble qualities it can muster. For it follows a sort of fife and drum corps march of an offensive triviality somewhat reminiscent of the *"Battle"* symphony. By the time this is reached Beethoven has been such a ruthless "tyrant over all the vocal organs" that the wretched sopranos have most of them stopped singing to begin screeching. And not long after this the work expires in a *prestissimo* amid the lamentable howls of these now agonized females, and what Mr. Ernest Walker has computed to be "one hundred and twenty-seven rapid bangs on the big drum and cymbals."[20]

The reliable Czerny told Jahn that, after the first per-

---

[19]Schubert put something very like it into his last symphony (C major),

Ex. 170

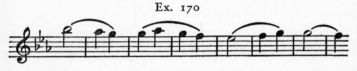

and Brahms let its accents be heard in the *finale* of that C minor symphony, which Von Bülow honoured by naming "The Tenth."

Ex. 171

At one of the early rehearsals of this symphony a certain nobleman ventured to call Brahms's attention to the resemblance. The exasperated composer ran true to his notoriously ungracious form. *"Das hört jeder Esel!"* ("Every donkey can hear that!") he growled.

[20]*Beethoven*, p. 56.

formance, Beethoven emphatically declared he was dissatisfied with the *Hymn to Joy* and wished to write another movement without vocal parts, to take the place of this failure. In the present writer's experience only two conductors have given the *Choral finale* so supremely as to make him cease for the moment to agree with its composer's severe verdict. But Signor Toscanini and Mr. Stokowski are men so creative that they can ennoble the tinsel tawdriness of *Ein Heldenleben.* They are such invincible bull operators that they can even send the watered stock of *Pini di Roma* soaring.

Such artists are unsettling to the equipoise of the critic But on both occasions, when the excitement of their magic had subsided, the writer reverted to his former conviction. Theoretically it was an inspired idea to reinforce the orchestra with the most natural, popular, and directly human of all instruments, the voice. And the experiment might have worked out with brilliant success if the hearers of that time had been prepared to accept what is gaining ground to-day —the voice as an orchestral instrument, used without dragging in the irrelevant and maltreated art of poetry whenever a singer opens his mouth.

The fatal mistake of the *Choral finale* was the mixture of poetry, the concrete and finite, with music, the abstract and infinite. Schiller's drinking song *de luxe* pulled the music down from the cloud-capped eminence of the first three movements to a humiliating materialistic basis. It imposed upon an art that should be all things to all men a belittling concreteness.

[415]

Chapter XLI

HE EMBRACES THE AMATEURS

February, 1824, an Address to Beethoven — His Indecision — Conspiracy of Friends — Announcement of Concert — Rehearsal — Concert May 7, 1824 — Deaf to Applause — A Financial Failure — Accuses Supper Guests of Dishonesty — Breaks Faith with London Philharmonic — Word Portrait by Rochlitz

FOR some years now the wild popularity of Rossini had elbowed Beethoven somewhat into the background— though not so far as the vociferous complaints, fed by his mania of persecution, would have led people to suppose. The great public had begun to cool a little. His old friends, however, were still faithful. When they heard that the Ninth symphony was finished the Lichnowskys, Graf von Fries, Zmeskall, and more than two dozen others sent him a charming round robin, begging him reverentially to let the *Missa* and the Ninth symphony be heard. Here are a few of the less flowery lines.

Shall we tell you with what deep regret we have felt your retirement? Do you need our assurance that, as all eyes turned hopefully towards you, all noticed with sorrow that the man whom we must name as the living mortal most eminent in his own sphere, silently looked on while foreign art pitched its camp on German soil, in the German muse's place of honour? . . . You alone can assure to the efforts of the best among us, a decisive victory. From you the art-union of the Fatherland and

[416]

PRINCE VON LICHNOWSKY
One of Beethoven's earliest and most generous patrons.
Painter unknown

the German opera await a fresh blooming, restored youth, and a new mastery of the true and the beautiful over the force which would subordinate to the fashion-spirit of the day even the eternal laws of art. Give us the hope of soon seeing fulfilled the wishes of all those who have ever been reached by the strains of your harmonies.

The composer was pleased. "That is really very beautiful!" he cried in a loud voice. "That gives me pleasure!"

He resolved to give an "Academy." But of late indecision had grown on him. It seemed that he simply could not fix on what he wanted and stick to it. So three of his friends formed a benign conspiracy. As if by accident they met at Beethoven's house and tried to wheedle him into signing a definite plan for the concert.

The suspicious genius saw through them, however, as swiftly as he had discovered the hidden tune in Mozart's theme. Before sunset he dispatched three summary notes:

To the COUNT LICHNOWSKY: I loathe treachery. Visit me no more. Academy is off. BEETHOVEN.

To MR. SCHUPPANZIGH: Let him visit me no more. I give no Academy. BEETHOVEN.

To SCHINDLER: I request you to come no more until I send for you. Academy is off. B———N.

But this was only a passing squall. Successful negotiations were soon resumed. The formal announcement of the concert read as follows:

GRAND
MUSICAL CONCERT

by

MR. L. VAN BEETHOVEN

which will take place
To-morrow, May 7, 1824

in the R. I. Court Theatre beside the Kärnthnerthor.

The musical pieces to be performed are the latest works of
Mr. Ludwig van Beethoven.

First: A Grand Overture.

Second: Three Grand Hymns with Solo and Chorus
Voices.

Third: A Grand Symphony with Solo and Chorus
Voices entering in the finale on Schiller's Ode
to Joy.

The solos will be performed by the Demoiselles Sonntag
and Unger and the Messrs. Haizinger and Seipelt.
Mr. Schuppanzigh has undertaken the direction of
the orchestra, Mr. Chapelmaster Umlauf the direction of the whole and the Music Society the augmentation of the chorus and orchestra as a favour.

Mr. Ludwig van Beethoven will himself participate in the
general direction.

Prices of Admission as usual.

Beginning at 7 o'clock in the evening.

[418]

The Overture was *The Consecration of the House*
(Op. 124). The three "hymns" were the *Kyrie, Credo,* and
Agnus Dei of the *Missa Solemnis.*

On May 6th the last rehearsal took place in the Kärnthnerthor Theatre. The orchestra was filled with famous players like Böhm and Mayseder. At the *Kyrie,* as an eyewitness
reports, Beethoven was "quite dissolved in devotion and
emotion." After the symphony he "stationed himself at the
door and embraced all the amateurs who had taken part"—
a proceeding more in the spirit of Schiller's

> *Seid umschlungen Millionen!*
> *Diesen Kuss der ganzen Welt!*
> (O you millions, I embrace you!
> Here's a kiss for all the world!)

than was the lamentable private scene which was to occur
late the following evening.

The house was packed for the concert. The public bestowed upon Beethoven so much more applause than was
usually given even the Imperial family that the commissioner of police angrily yelled: "Silence!"

Let us hope [Mr. Lawrence Gilman pithily remarks] that the
memory of this incident brought some consolation to Beethoven
two and a half years later, when the King of Prussia palmed off
on him a near-diamond ring in return for the Ninth symphony.

There had been but two rehearsals, the third having been
omitted in favour of a ballet! Naturally the performance
left much to be desired. But Beethoven heard neither its

[419]

defects nor its beauties. He stood in the centre of the orchestra with his back to the audience, following the proceedings in the score. The word "following" must be taken literally. For a lady named Grebner who, at the age of seventeen, sang in that historic chorus told Herr Felix Weingartner three quarters of a century later, that although Beethoven "appeared to follow the score with his eyes, at the end of each movement he turned several pages together."

The pianist Thalberg, another eyewitness, informed Thayer that the choir and orchestra were directed to watch Beethoven but to pay not the slightest attention to his beating of the time.

Tumultuous applause broke out after the *scherzo*. But Beethoven stood utterly deaf to it, fumbling with his score. Then one of the singers, Fräulein Unger, pulled his sleeve and pointed to the rapturous audience. When he turned and bowed there were few dry eyes in the house.

After the expansion and exaltation of this concert there was an equal and opposite reaction. The box office had taken in 2,200 florins. But after deducting the cost of copying and administration less than 420 florins were left. Beethoven boiled over. He had invited Schuppanzigh, Schindler, and Umlauf, the conductor of the concert, to supper with him at a restaurant with the ominously prophetic name At the Sign of the Wild Man. He had ordered what Schindler called an "opulent" meal. But the company had no sooner sat down at table than Mr. Hyde, harpy that he was, spoiled it all. He poured out a flood of what he had once described as "hearty, free words." In downright terms he accused Schindler and the management of having swindled him.

In vain Umlauf and "Milord Falstaff" sought to point out that all the receipts and expenditures had been checked by the two theatre cashiers and by nephew Karl; that, contrary to custom, the latter had been allowed to act as comptroller. But far from listening to them, the composer of

Seid umschlungen Millionen!

only grew more and more hearty and free.

Finally even the meekness of Schindler could stand no more. Gathering his few poor shreds of dignity about him, and seizing Umlauf's arm, he rushed from the room.

Schuppanzigh [remarks Thayer] remained behind just long enough to get a few stripes on his broad back and then joined his companions in misery. Together they finished their meal at a restaurant in the Leopoldstadt.

Before we turn to the last and most exalted chapter of Beethoven's career we must record one more shabby Hydean trick. For the sum of £50, Beethoven had contracted to write the Ninth symphony for the London Philharmonic Society. He had agreed to give that body exclusive possession of it during eighteen months. At the end of this period the property rights in it would revert to the composer.

The money was paid in December, 1822, soon after the offer had been accepted. Beethoven delivered the manuscript late in April, 1824. On the 7th of the following month he broke faith by having the symphony performed in Vienna.

And adding insult to injury he dedicated the work—to the King of Prussia.

This unpleasant chapter cannot close, however, without a word about Dr. Jekyll. Not long before these events Friedrich Rochlitz wrote:

He will give his last thaler to a man who has grievously injured him an hour before, and whom he has most violently declaimed against. . . . Once he gets up momentum, witticisms of rough power, droll inspirations, surprising, exciting combinations and paradoxes constantly occur to him. Therefore I say, in dead earnest: he gives you a lovable impression. . . . The dusky unlicked bear has such a trustful and true-spirited way with him, he growls too and shakes his tuftlets of hair so harmlessly and curiously, that even if he were indeed nothing but such a bear and had accomplished none of the things he has, one must needs rejoice in him and take to him.

Chapter XLII

THE CREATIVE LISTENER AND THE LAST QUARTETS

Project of English Trip Revived, 1824 — And Wrecked — Prince Galitzin Orders String Quartets — Preparation Necessary for Hearing Last Quartets — Alpine Blossoms of Experience — Anticipations of Man's Evolution — The Ineffable Residue of Reality — Our Debt to His Deafness — "Ditties of No Tone" — The String Quartet a Fit Vehicle — Invents New Forms — Aids for the Listener — How to Approach This Music

LATE in 1824, the project of the trip to England again came up. The London Philharmonic Society made Beethoven another generous offer. But after haggling with them for £100 more, which they refused, he raised so many difficulties as to wreck this project. This was bad for Beethoven's purse. But we are probably the gainers. If he had gone to London the last five quartets might never have been written.

A century ago wealthy Russian amateurs of music were doing as much for their art as M. Koussevitzky is doing to-day. When, in 1806, Beethoven had begun longing to write again in this form, Count Rasoumowsky had earned the enduring gratitude of all quartet lovers by ordering opus 59. Toward the end of 1822 Prince Galitzin, another Russian enthusiast, chose an equally happy moment. He ordered "two or three string quartets." This commission was heartily welcomed. Beethoven was weary of his long struggle with the text of the *Missa* and desirous of returning to his own field of absolute music—that art which escapes the profanation of concrete programs.

For the experience of hearing the last five quartets the listener should be prepared at least as carefully and seriously as a schoolboy for the university, or a freemason for initiation into the higher degrees, or a child for confirmation. Indeed, more carefully and seriously. For these quartets give a glimpse of an evolutionary stage not yet attained by many human spirits. They reveal the Alpine blossom of experience growing farther above the workaday levels of normal Twentieth Century humanity than most visions of the average scholar or freemason or churchman.

"Behold, I show unto you a mystery!" says the Master. He does not proceed to enunciate an enigmatic intellectual proposition such as "We shall not all die." Rather he sets beating within us the heart of the mystery itself. He actually exhibits to us the incorruptibility of this corruption. He shows forth the mortal in the very act of putting on immortality, and the will of the superman, by a supreme rite of renunciation and resignation, drawing the very sting of death itself.

In treating of the experiences communicated by these quartets, Mr. Sullivan writes:

The great artist achieves a relative immortality because the experiences he deals with are as fundamental for humanity as are hunger, sex, and the succession of day and night. It does not

[424]

I   II

Ferdinand Fürst Kinsky

III   IV

BEETHOVEN'S CHIEF PATRONS

I County Andreas Rasoumowsky   II Prince Josef Lobkowitz
III Prince Ferdinand Kinsky   IV Archduke Rudolph

follow that the experiences he communicates are elementary. They may belong to an order of consciousness that very few men have attained but, in that case, they must be in the line of human development; we must feel them as prophetic. Beethoven's late music communicates experiences that very few people can normally possess. But we value these experiences because we feel they are not freakish. They correspond to a spiritual synthesis which the race has not achieved but which, we may suppose, it is on the way to achieving. It is only the very greatest kind of artist who presents us with experiences that we recognize both as fundamental and as in advance of anything we have hitherto known.[1]

It is of Beethoven in this last rarefied phase that the writer always thinks in reading a superb page of Marcel Proust:[2]

There is a unique accent to which those great singers who are the original musicians elevate themselves, to which they return despite themselves, and which is a proof of the irreducibly individual existence of the soul. . . . Every artist seems thus the citizen of an unknown fatherland, forgotten by himself, different from that land whence comes, equipped for earth, another great artist. . . . This lost fatherland the musicians do not recall. But each of them remains forever unconsciously tuned in a certain unison with it; he is delirious with joy when he sings in accordance with his fatherland.

Proust goes on to say that this song is composed of all that

residue of reality which we are obliged to keep to ourselves, which words may not even transmit from friend to friend, from master to disciple, from lover to mistress, this ineffable something which qualitatively differentiates that which each has felt

---

[1] "Beethoven: His Spiritual Development," p. 250.
[2] "La Prisonnière, Vol. II, p. 73, in that great modern epic, A la Recherche du Temps Perdu.

and which he is obliged to leave on the threshold of phrases in which he may not communicate with another, except in limiting himself to exterior points common to all and without interest.

Then the great artist appears,

exteriorizing in the colours of the spectrum the intimate composition of these worlds which we call individuals and which, without the aid of art, we never would come to know. Wings, another respiratory apparatus which would allow us to traverse immensity, would be of no service to us. For if we went to Mars and to Venus still keeping the same senses, they would invest themselves for us with the same aspect as all this which we are able to perceive of Earth. The only veritable voyage, the sole true fountain of youth, would be not to seek new landscapes, but to have other eyes, to look upon the universe with the eyes of another, of an hundred others, to see the hundred universes which each of them sees, which each of them is; and this we may do with [great artists]; with beings like them we truly fly from star to star.

Some such experience of extra-terrestial grandeur awaits the music lover who can acquire ears and brains attuned to appreciate the last quartets of Beethoven. In them the Master attained such other-worldly altitudes that, in connection with this *finale* of his career, one might appropriately reverse the title of Strauss's famous tone-poem, and speak of Beethoven's *"Verklärung und Tod"*—his transfiguration and death. No pin-prick thoughts of his irritability, his avarice, his dishonesty can count for a moment in the atmosphere of the *adagios* of the E flat, the A minor, and the B flat quartets and the fugue which opens the C sharp minor.

[426]

We are eternal debtors to his deafness. It is doubtful if such lofty music could have been created except as self-compensation for some such affliction, and in the utter isolation which that affliction brought about. Perhaps that very deafness acted as a sort of protection against the too dazzling intensities of the mystic revelation. It may be that his shrouded hearing was like the veiled vision of him who was warned that he might not "see God and live." At times these quartets seem to have the celestial quality of

> The light that never was, on sea or land.

Only three years before they were begun, another great artist, in a distant land, sickening like Beethoven for his deathbed, wrote some lines[3] strangely applicable to this last and supreme work of his loftiest contemporary:

> Heard melodies are sweet, but those unheard
>   Are sweeter; therefore, ye soft pipes, play on:
> Not to the sensual ear, but, more endear'd
>   Pipe to the spirit ditties of no tone.

When one has entered into intimacy with them, these last "ditties"—the quartets that were of "no tone" to the Master's poor outer ear, gradually become "more endear'd" than any other mortal music.

Nothing could have been a fitter vehicle for Beethoven's swan song than the string quartet—the most perfect means for conveying absolute music yet discovered. It is made up of instruments strongly individual yet capable of merging

---

[3] John Keats, "Ode on a Grecian Urn."

their personalities into one. These instruments are almost uniquely equipped for pure intonation. They interpose less mechanism between hand and ear than the piano. They form an organism far more intimate and pliable than the orchestra—a perfect medium for the high subjectivity and the rich and independent polyphony of these last utterances.

The old quartet form did not suffice for the intense personalism of this music. So Beethoven invented new forms. In these the tempo changed more often and more capriciously than ever.[4] The usual four movements grew to five—six—and even seven, as if in memory of the rococo *divertimento* and Suite. There was less strictness in the sonata-form movements. Their modelling was not so formally pronounced. The second subject sometimes burst in unprepared. The development grew shorter and more polyphonically intensive (e. g., in the first movement of the B flat quartet). The most astonishing contrasts of naïve folk tunes with the music of philosophical reverie were forged into a whole by sheer sorcery. The voice-leading became wonderfully free and daring. In these quartets there are no neutral passages where the hearer may nod and recover. Every moment he must give all he has; for each note is packed with significance.

The only way to make these quartets one's own is by repeated hearings and much detailed study with score in hand. The excellent phonograph records of them now

---

[4]Not counting *ritardandos*, the quartets of the first and second periods usually change tempo about four times, reaching ten times in the Sixth Lobkowitz and the "*Harp*." But of the three greatest quartets of the last period the A minor (Op. 132) changes tempo twenty times; the B flat (Op. 130) twenty-one times; and the C sharp minor (Op. 131) no less than thirty-one times.

available[5] are godsends. They are powerful aids in speeding up the processes of comprehension.[6]

But a still more powerful aid is a knowledge of how to draw near them. They should be approached in the humble spirit which Mr. Havelock Ellis advocates as necessary for the comprehension of graphic art.

Schopenhauer long ago pointed out that a picture should be looked at as a royal person is approached, in silence, until the moment it pleases to speak to you. For if you speak first (and how many critics one knows who "speak first"!) you expose yourself to hear nothing but the sound of your own voice. In other words, it is a spontaneous and mystical experience.[7]

---

[5]See Appendix, p. 623.

[6]Readers will find much of help and interest in certain books of detailed analysis: Theodor Helm, *Beethoven's Streichquartette*, 3d ed., 1921 (Leipzig: Siegel); Hugo Riemann, *Beethoven's Streichquartette*, *Meisterführer* No. 12 (Berlin: Schlesinger); Joseph de Marliave, *Les Quatuors de Beethoven*, 1925 (Paris: Felix Alcan) (English translation, 1928).

[7]*The Dance of Life*, 1923, p. 329.

Chapter XLIII

"LA GAIETE"

1824, First Galitzin Quartet, E Flat — Its Emotional Unity — Suggestion of the Pathétique — And of the Missa — Inspires Schumann and Brahms — An Impish Passage — First Performance, 1825 — Two Shabby Tricks — Failure of Schuppanzigh — Replaced by Boehm — Holz Supplants Schindler — Domestic Troubles — Furious Letter to Copyist Wolanek — Minerva and the Sow — Beethoven Not to Be Judged by Ordinary Standards

LIKE all the last five the E flat quartet (Op. 127) has a superb emotional unity. The words *"La gaieté,"* scribbled in the Master's hand, were found in a sketch of its slow movement. These words might be taken to indicate the mellow, serene happiness of a man who has come out on the other side of catastrophe to find that he has thereby secured the most precious of all gifts—a creativeness approaching the divine. Understood in this deeper sense, *"La gaieté"* may well be the motto of this ripe work.

This quartet often seems festooned with the gold and scarlet foliage, and pungently sweet with the bursting grapes, of autumn. The somewhat crabbed *scherzo* serves as a dun background to heighten the autumnal glow, like a premonition of arctic rigours in that

> Season of mists and mellow fruitfulness.

It is curious to see how Beethoven's thoughts recurred to the *Sonate Pathétique* (Op. 13), not only in the *Choral*

symphony[1] and the quartet before it,[2] but also in this sub-
sequent E flat quartet. Like the *Pathétique*, *La gaieté* has a
short slow beginning which is thematically an integral
portion of the first movement and comes back twice before
its close.

The *Adagio, ma non troppo e molto cantabile* is the
supreme part of the quartet and constitutes one of the most
lusciously satisfying sets of variations in music.[3] It is natural
that echoes of the *Missa Solemnis* should ring through this
Adagio. For Beethoven worked on both compositions together. Here is a bit of the *Benedictus:*

Ex. 172

which is closely akin to the end of the delicious eighteen-
measure theme of the variations.

Ex. 173

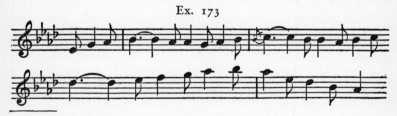

[1]See pp. 403–405.
[2]See pp. 567–569.
[3]Schumann was obviously inspired by it in the Variations of his string quartet in
F major.

To the author's mind there is a certain resemblance between part of the first subject of the first *Allegro*

Ex. 174

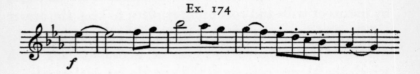

and the jolly second subject of the *finale*

Ex. 175

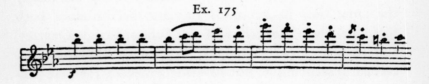

The opening subject of this *finale*[4] has five notes as the fecund germ of its first part:

Ex. 176

which makes, almost note for note, the same melodic outline as the first five notes (C–F–D–B flat–E flat) of the opening *Allegro*.[5]

The subject continues in dauntless fashion.[6] ➡➡→

Ex. 177

---

[4]See the transposed Ex. 344, p. 598.
[5]See the transposed Ex. 341, p. 597.

At the start of the *finale's* coda there is a passage through which Beethoven's impishness grimaces. He changed from *Alla Breve* to 6/8 time. But for three measures he managed, by means of trills and confusing triplets, to keep the hearer wildly guessing as to what on earth was happening rhythmically. One imagines the grin of *Schadenfreude* with which the Master conceived this strictly musical prank.

In bringing out the E flat quartet early in 1825 Beethoven was guilty of a pair of shabby tricks. At nearly the same time he promised the first performance both to Linke, the violoncellist of the Schuppanzigh Quartet, and to Schuppanzigh himself. At length "Milord" succeeded in securing it. But he made a mess of the first performance.

In a rage Beethoven showered reproaches upon his poor fat friend and replaced him with a better fiddler named Boehm. He himself attended the rehearsals; and though incapable of hearing a note he watched the bows and fingers so acutely as to be of great help to the players.

At the second performance *"La gaieté"* was given twice, and with such success that various publishers began a brisk

---

[6]Perhaps Brahms, when he began the slow movement of his G minor piano quartet (Op. 25) with the first four notes of Ex. 177, in the same key, and then used the first four notes of Ex. 176 to begin the second half of the great theme—

Ex. 178

—recognized this intrepid quality of his original, for he never penned a braver tune.

competition for it. Naturally "Milord's" nose was out of joint. The Conversation Books of those days show entries like:

Schuppanzigh is very angry at Boehm and the others.

. . . .

Schuppanzigh said he wouldn't have believed you would have done such a thing to him.

It was long before "Milord" forgave the affront.

About this time Carl Holz, the quartet's second violinist, began to supplant Schindler as Beethoven's factotum. He was young, intelligent, charming, had a lively sense of humour, and did the Master good by amusing him and taking him out a little into the world.

He had compassion for the composer's domestic troubles and was alert and clever in helping him out of them.

Beethoven [he wrote with characteristic wit] is an eagle who flies toward the zenith. Attached to his feet, not to his wings, is a cord that hangs to earth. It is firmly held by his housekeeper. Sometimes he abruptly tears himself loose and renews his flight toward the heavens. But if he thinks of earth and fain would stoop toward it, he lets the cord drop. Then she seizes and holds it fast.

Schindler hated Holz as only a bore can hate a wit who has elbowed him out of a privileged position. He called him Mephistopheles. And in the end he triumphed over him. For, shortly before the Master's death, Holz was preoccupied by his marriage and Schindler was again needed. But

[434]

not before Beethoven had appointed Holz his official biog-
rapher. Unfortunately Mephistopheles never took advantage of this authorization. He might have made the first
important Beethoven biography a more trustworthy and
readable affair than Schindler did.

"Milord" was not the only one in those days to be singed
by the blasts of Beethoven's temperament. Wolanek, his
Bohemian copyist, endured so many insults that he finally
ventured a politely ironic missive in defense of his remaining
rags of manhood. He was inclined to overlook Beethoven's
conduct with a smile. He wrote:

In the ideal world of tone there reign so many dissonances;
why not as well in the world of reality? One firm conviction
alone comforts me: that if you had been copyist to those cele-
brated artists Mozart and Haydn you would have shared a like
fate. I only beg you not to confuse me with those wretches of
copyists who are glad to be treated as slaves just for a bare existence.

In reply nothing would do but to make the worm who
dared to turn feel one hundred per cent. incompetent and
contemptible. On every available inch of this remonstrance
the Master gave vent to his "hearty, free" fancy in the
following endorsements, which may still be studied in the
museum at Bonn:

"Stupid fellow, conceited asinine fellow!" he scrawled across
the writing, in letters two inches high. Then on the lower
margin: "Pay compliments to such a ragamuffin who steals one's
money?—better to pull his donkey-ears!"

[435]

And on the blank reverse page:

BOTCHING–SCRIBBLER!

STUPID FELLOW!

Yesterday and even before then, it was decided *not to have you write any more for me.*

Correct the blunders your own ignorance, insolence, conceit and stupidity have perpetrated. This would be more fitting than wishing to teach me, for that is exactly as if a SOW should attempt giving lessons to MINERVA.

BEETHOVEN.

Do YOU do Mozart & Haidn *the honour* of not taking their names into your mouth.

One cannot help feeling that the poor copyist came out of this encounter first-best by a safe margin.

But let us cheerfully accept the bitter parts of Beethoven with the sweet, recognizing that they were all necessary ingredients of this particular genius. Let us be as large minded as Clara Schumann was about the bearishness of her friend Brahms.

She was always ready to pay the price which the creative artist has a right to ask of the world, as an inconsiderable token of thanks for his gifts, namely: consideration in his hours of creation.[7]

We do not expect a woman in travail to pay close attention to the precepts of the book of etiquette. And men like Brahms and Beethoven were constantly in travail.

When we are repelled by the Master's churlishness, his dishonesty, his priggishness, or any of his other disturbing

[7]Eugenie Schumann, *Errinnerungen*, 1925, p. 247.

traits, let us remember that, as Lord Macaulay remarked about Clive, exceptional men must not be judged by ordinary standards. And let us read again, as a possible antidote for ethical provinciality, these tender, wise, and comprehending words by Reichardt:

It often grieves me to the bottom of my heart when I see this thoroughly good, excellent man gloomy and suffering, although I am convinced, on the other hand, that his most original works can only be created in such peevish, bad-tempered moods. People who are able to enjoy his works should never lose sight of this, and refuse to take offence at any of his outer peculiarities. Otherwise they can never in reality be his true admirers.[8]

---

[8]Leitzmann, Vol. I, p. 103.

Chapter XLIV

THE A MINOR QUARTET

*Illness — 1825, Second Galitzin Quartet, A Minor —
Mottos of Slow Movement — Programs — Echo of Arioso
Dolente — Defect of First Movement — Economy in
Allegro ma non Tanto — Harmonic Syncopation — High
Lights*

IN APRIL and May, 1825, Beethoven was ill. Inflammation
of the bowels threatened. Nevertheless, he kept hard at the
A minor quartet. This was written second of the last five,
though by mistake it was numbered opus 132. Over the
Molto adagio beginning of the slow movement

Ex. 179

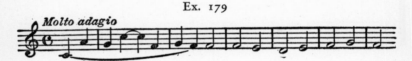

he wrote: *"Heiliger Dankgesang eines Genesenen an die
Gottheit, in der Lydischen Tonart"* (Holy song of thanksgiving to the Godhead, by one recovered from sickness, in
the Lydian mode) ;[1] and over the first *Andante* interlude:
"Neue Kraft fühlend" (Feeling new strength).

From this hint it has been easy for the tag makers to
turn the whole quartet into a circumstantial account of
Beethoven's sickness and recovery. According to them the

---

[1]His use here of the Lydian (consisting of the F major scale with B natural) foreshadowed that freer use of the old church modes which has more recently been
stimulated by the influence of Moussorgsky.

first movement shows the illness at its height; the *scherzo,* an exceptionally good day; the *Adagio,* recovery; the March, misgivings and a struggle to keep up appearances; the body of the *finale,* relapse; and its coda, complete rehabilitation.

Readers of *Point Counter Point* will recall that this *Dankgesang* movement was invoked by Spandrell, the murderer and suicide, in order to demonstrate to the tough-minded Rampion the existence of God. And Spandrell was as dogmatic about it as Lenz was about the thirty-two dagger thrusts in the *Eroica,* or Herr Emil Ludwig about the festivals and ceremonies in the Seventh.

Ex. 180

Ex. 181

etc.

Happily, the literalists cannot spoil such music for all people all the time. To the million who come to the A minor unprejudiced by programs it will convey a million different meanings. And each of these meanings, by the grace of music's infinitude, will be as authentic as Beethoven's fancy mottos for his slow movement were to him when he set them down.

It must be said, however, for the programmatists, that they have derived another hint about the pathological character of the *allegro* from the resemblance of its first tune (Ex. 180) to the *Arioso dolente* of the A flat sonata (Ex. 181)—that memory sonata which, like "the quality of mercy," is blest both in giving and taking. But it is hard to agree that the first movement's emotional tone is as despairing as most of the commentators feel it. The second subject has too much of the joy of creation for despair. But this movement has the same defect as the corresponding portion of the C minor quartet (Op. 18, No. 4)—insufficient contrast between the contours of the first and second subjects.[2] They are too consanguineous with one another and with the main tune of the *finale*.

The *Allegro ma non tanto* is a sort of *scherzo*, chastened by a strong strain of minuet blood on the mother's side. It might appropriately have been christened *Scherzo ma non tanto*. Even for this most thematically economical of all

---

[2]See Ex. 346, p. 599, Ex. 15, p. 68, and Ex. 12, p. 57.

musicians it represents a triumph of economy. Its main portion is built entirely out of a phrase of three notes:

Ex. 182

and another of six:

Ex. 183

In the Trio of this movement Beethoven invented a novelty which was destined to appeal to such lovers of contradiction as Brahms. We have already noticed the whimsical way in which the Master would sometimes displace a phrase out of its natural bar frame, as in the prophetically jazzian *scherzo* of the B flat quartet (Op. 18, No. 6) and the *scherzo-finale* of the G major piano sonata (Op. 14, No. 2). This invention he combined here with another precursor of jazz: harmonic syncopation. The harmony shifts on the unaccented part of the measure a beat before the ear expects the change.

Ex. 184

The most memorable parts of this quartet are the mystic ecstasy of the last *molto adagio* portion of the Song of

Thanksgiving, the forlorn gaiety of the little *Alla marcia*, and the glorious *presto* coda of the *finale*, where the tragic main tune turns minor to major in the spirit of Moody's poem—

> Of loss and doubt and dread
> And swift, oncoming doom
> I made a helmet for my head
> And a floating plume.

Chapter XLV

LESS LACK OF FANCY

*1825, Word Portrait by Rellstab — Beethoven Complains
of Neglect — Relations with Nephew — Loneliness —
Premonitions of Death — Karl Runs Away — 1825, Third
Galitzin Quartet, B flat — "Quartetto Scherzoso" — Bee-
thoven's "Leibquartett" — Cavatina Cost Him Tears —
Modesty — Contrapuntal Miracles in First Movement —
Influences Wagner — Fairy Music in Andante con moto —
The Great Fugue — Writes a New Finale*

As BEETHOVEN was preparing in 1825 for a plunge into the
B flat quartet (Op. 130)—the third of the Galitzin series—
he was visited by Ludwig Rellstab, the man who had first
called opus 27, No. 2 the "*Moonlight* sonata." This Berlin
author left an interesting vignette of the man, expressed in
the lush Biedermeyer manner of the period. After remark-
ing the kindly mouth, the jaundiced tone of the complexion,
and the small but eloquent eyes, he went on:

> I read on his countenance melancholy, suffering goodness; but
> not one hard trait, not one sign of the mighty boldness which
> characterizes the rhythms of his spirit could, even in passing, be
> noticed.
>
> In spite of all I have said, however, he lacked nothing of that
> mysterious magnetic force by which the outward appearance of
> great men enthralls us. For the suffering, the dumb burden of
> pain which showed forth there, were not due to a momentary
> illness. Weeks afterward I saw this same expression, when Bee-
> thoven felt in far better health. They were the results of his whole
> unique life—destiny.

Young Rellstab confessed that in saying good-bye Beethoven embraced him

in such a heartfelt German fashion [that] my whole heart, glowing with enthusiasm, was lifted up. . . . It was like a dream,—the great immortal Ludwig van Beethoven on my breast. I felt his lips on mine and he must have felt himself bathed by my warm happy tears that welled up unceasingly. And so I left him. I had no thought; only a glowing emotion that surged through my innermost breast—Beethoven has embraced me! And I will be proud of this good fortune to the last day of my life![1]

Towards the end of his career Beethoven complained bitterly that the Viennese were neglecting his works. But the records show that these complaints were as ill founded as his deathbed protestations of extreme poverty, with seven bank shares safely hidden in their secret cubbyhole.

He had a less imaginary grievance in the conduct of Nephew Karl. The lad had grown into a commonplace young man who had inherited his father's littleness and meanness with his mother's frivolity and inability to concentrate. There was no spark of the qualities for which we revere the Master.

The boredom, the exaggerated discipline, the fatuous spoiling, the loneliness, and the interminable harangues of a childhood alone with his uncle had turned out a young fellow who reacted naturally to all this. He had little appreciation of the great man's sacrifices or of his genius. In correspondence he referred to him as "the old fool" and wished only to be well rid of the eternal moralizing.

[1]Leitzmann, Vol. I, pp. 296–311.

In 1823 Karl had begun philosophical studies at the University of Vienna. But after a year and a half he tired of them and was allowed to enter a business course at the Polytechnic Institute.

During the summer of 1825, which Beethoven spent in the suburb of Baden, Karl would grasp any pretext for evading the weekly visit of duty to his uncle. Then Beethoven would seize his pen and pour forth alternate threats, admonitions, and pleadings.

Reading such lines as the following one does not know whether to sympathize more with the misguided genius or the misreared youth. On hearing that Karl had again been seeing something of his mother by stealth the uncle wrote:

If I suffer again the most loathsome ingratitude, nay if the bond between us is severed, so be it, but you will be hated by all unprejudiced people who hear of this ingratitude.

In pathetic contrast to such an ultimatum comes an inarticulate wail of loneliness:

As I live here, you know, with the cold weather besides, the perpetual being alone weakens me still more, for my weakness often actually borders on a swoon, O do not add to my illness, even so the man with the scythe will not grant me much further respite.

Again the mood changes:

God has never forsaken me, some one will yet be found to close my eyes . . . you need not come this Sunday, for true harmony and sympathy will never be between us while you act as you do.

[445]

But when Karl ran away, and there was no sign of him for days, the uncle's love burst out with such torrential force as his spirit had shown in the first movement of the *Eroica*:

MY DEAR SON:—

Only nothing further—just come to my arms, you shall hear no harsh words. O God, do not make way with yourself in your misery—you will be received with love as always—we will affectionately talk over what we must consider, what is to be done about the future, on my honour no reproaches, for they would be of no use anyway, from me you need expect only the most loving care and help. Only come—come to the faithful heart of your father.

BEETHOVEN.

[In French]

. . . *Si vous ne viendrez pas, vous me tuerez surement.* . . . (If you do not come you will certainly kill me. . . .)

Plagued as he was in body and mind, Beethoven fortunately could always flee to that "shadow of a mighty rock within a weary land"—his art. Sketches for the B flat quartet overlapped the finishing of the A minor. And so resilient were the resources of his vitality that several of the six movements rank with the most humorous, dainty, and light-hearted of his works.

These elements indeed are so prominent that the question arises whether the B flat does not deserve to be placed beside the Eighth symphony and called the "*Quartetto Scherzoso.*" It is the only quartet which has more than one *scherzo*-like movement. Indeed, it has several. For the *Alla Danza Tedesca* provides much the same sort of relief as a *scherzo*.

[446]

The *Andante* is labelled *poco scherzando*. And the *Presto,* or *scherzo* proper, is one of the most delicious bits of pure humour in the whole realm of absolute music.

Of course, when one considers the introduction, the serious portions of the witty first movement,[2] the *Cavatina* with its tender passion, and the ponderous, mystic solemnity read by most interpreters into the Great Fugue which originally served as *finale*, one feels that "*Quartetto Scherzoso*" might, after all, scarcely do. That is, until one hears such a light-hearted, almost sportive reading of the Great Fugue as Mr. Harold Bauer's[3] and remembers that the Master's last act was to write a new, jocund *finale* for this quartet, full of *scherzoso* quality, in which now and again the lower strings echo the drolly skipping octaves for bassoon from the *finale* of the Eighth symphony, as if to underline the quartet's kinship of wit with the "*Sinfonia Giocosa.*"

The creation of such high-spirited movements by a man in Beethoven's physical and mental extremity is one of the strangest and most affecting anomalies in the history of the arts. He had a special affection for this work. He called it his "*Leibquartett*," a term of familiar endearment which our language lacks, and needs. Indeed, not a few of its pages represent the most intimate emotional self-revelations which he has left us.

At the very end of his life the Master confessed that each time he recalled the melody of the *Cavatina* it stirred him

---

[2] Aldous Huxley labels this movement: "Majesty alternating with a joke." (*Point Counter Point*, 1928, p. 293.)

[3] When he takes a part in his own two-piano arrangement of this composition.

deeply and cost him tears. Surely, in the stammering accents of that portion of it marked *"Beklemmt"*

Ex. 185

one seems to catch the anguished, eloquently fragmentary style of such documents as the Heiligenstadt Testament, the letters to Amenda and Wegeler announcing his deafness, and that written to "The Immortal Beloved."[4]

"Mephistopheles" Holz once ventured the opinion that the B flat was the greatest of his quartets. But, with exceptional modesty, Beethoven answered:

Each in its way. Art demands of us not to stand still. You will find there a new way of voice-leading [part-writing] and, thank God! there is less lack of fancy than ever before.

Beethoven was right about the voice-leading. The art of contrapuntal part-writing for four instruments has never

---

[4]This was the movement which Joseph Joachim chose to play as his farewell to the *Beethovenhaus* at Bonn.

The writer remembers with what a thrill of pleasure he recognized, amid the puzzling confusion of a Sketch Book in the Prussian State Library, its ethereal opening melody, suddenly standing out from the page. In this instance, by exception, the first notation revealed it in virtually the form familiar to us to-day.

BEETHOVEN'S NEPHEW KARL
Photograph taken in later life

advanced in line or space since he conceived those highly compressed thirty-eight bars of development in the first movement. Into the three measures of the following example the Master succeeded in packing no less than five distinct motives:

Ex. 186

and he fused them with the utmost smoothness into a superb whole.

To the eye this example looks meagre enough. But here, none the less, may be found: both parts of the double first subject (a and b); two two-note motives from the second and fourth bars of the Introduction (c and d).

Ex. 187

And finally a new, hidden violoncello tune (e),[5] mined out of the conglomerate and owning allegiance, in its upward leap of an octave, to the second subject.

Ex. 188

How artless and innocent the little development passage, Ex. 186, appears; yet how artful and deep it is! It represents the height of the craft.

A close study of such *tours de force* helped and inspired Richard Wagner to pen pages like that in the prelude to *The Mastersingers,* where he kept all three of his main themes unostentatiously and smoothly going together. And about pregnant music like this the Bayreuth master wrote:

Here there is no longer anything added, there is no more framing of the melody, but all has become melody, every voice in the accompaniment, every rhythmical note—yes, even the pauses themselves!

So much for Beethoven's remark to Holz, quoted above, about "a new way of voice-leading." For light on that superb bit of understatement concerning "less lack of

---

[5]Remember Beethoven's other hidden tunes, which have often been mentioned.

fancy" the reader is referred to such a sympathetic performance of the *Andante con moto*

Ex. 189

as the London String Quartet gives on the stage or the Lener Quartet on the phonograph. Once he manages to know it well—and this is no light task!—he will find it an even more exquisite sort of fairy music than its prototype—the prototype of all its kind, the *Allegretto* of the Eighth symphony. This *Andante* marks, if people only knew, the most seven-leagued stride ahead in all the annals of fairy music. It may, however, be a long time before people do know; because it is hard for humanity, in the present stage of evolution, to sustain life at the rarefied heights where we now encounter Beethoven.

> For he on honey-dew hath fed,
> And drunk the milk of Paradise.

The B flat quartet is less copiously reminiscent than most of its immediate predecessors. In the subtlety and smoothness of its inter-movement thematic liaison work it shows an arresting gain.[6]

For the last hundred years most music lovers who could bear to listen at all to the Great Fugue which Beethoven wrote as the original *finale* of the B flat quartet have looked upon it as a thing of stern and almost unapproachable grandeur. When first played, what were taken to be its

---

[6]For the sake of the nontechnical reader both of these fascinating subjects are under sentence of banishment to Part II, pp. 527–528 and 560–563.

cryptic, sibylline utterances were sayings too hard for even the most sympathetic and devoted contemporaries of the Master. The work completely baffled even those talented Viennese listeners who, at the first performance of the *Choral* symphony, had been so feelingly responsive to the humour of that now famous kettledrum manœuvre in the *scherzo* and had burst forth into jubilant applause.

This sort of fugal ending to a quartet was a century ahead of the most enlightened performers and listeners in that audience.[7] They criticized, complained, and agitated until the publisher, in alarm, begged Beethoven to write a new *finale*.

The trouble with the Great Fugue has always been that its extraordinarily crabbed and cruel technical difficulties usually make it sound dry and dully ponderous in performance. Whereas Mr. Harold Bauer's half jest contained a large element of truth when he remarked to the late Oscar G. Sonneck: "The Great Fugue is more like a glorified polka-*scherzo*. People play it as if it were profoundly mystical, which it is not. They put philosophy into it instead of music."

Wonderful to relate, the man who had withstood the frenzied demands of embattled singers to revise the *Missa* and the *Choral*, gave way to the critics of the Great Fugue. He put his tongue into his cheek and, almost on his deathbed, as his last composition, wrote an *Ersatz-finale* that a child, though bouncing a ball, might understand.

---

[7]Even so intelligent a modern critic as Mr. Ernest Walker (in *Beethoven*, 1920), labelled it "practically unintelligible" and scored its "uncouth inconsequence."

But he did not connect it with the rest of the quartet, as he had connected the Great Fugue, by his customary thematic liaison work. He had been through that arduous labour once, and enough was enough. Its absence lends colour to the theory that he dashed down these pages in a somewhat cynical mood. Or perhaps he was too nearly spent to summon up pressure high enough for making this afterthought thematically an organic part of the quartet. The Great Fugue was published by itself as opus 133.

We are drawing near the last page of the story. But one supreme work is still before us.

> The best is yet to be,
> The last of life, for which the first was made.

Chapter XLVI

"SPANGY" IN THE BLACK
SPANIARD'S HOUSE

*1825, Moves to Black Spaniard's House — Renews Intimacy
with Von Breunings — "Trouser Button" — Relics — Frau
von Breuning — An Embarrassing Escort — Unconsciousness of Discord*

IN THE fall of 1825 Beethoven moved, for the last time,
to lodgings in the "Black Spaniard's" house. This structure
was so called because it had been built by Benedictine monks
from Spain. The Black Spaniard's House. How neatly it
fits young Ludwig's childish nickname of "Spangy"!

The man who had once been *"der Spangol,"* or the little
Black Spaniard of Bonn, chose his new house as if such a
name might have power to bring glimpses of those youthful clouds of glory which had been so prematurely obscured
by the vapours from Father Johann's bottle. Something,
at any rate, brought them back. For here he was soon to
write that swan song, the C sharp minor quartet, whose
second, fourth, and fifth movements look at us with young
eyes of limpid innocence, and whose other movements—we
may imagine—repeat: "Whosoever shall not receive the
Kingdom of God as a little child, shall in no wise enter
therein."

In the Black Spaniard's house he was to meet an untimely
end at the height of his powers, with his Tenth symphony

lying sketched in the desk—all done but the writing. As if exhilarated by the new home he spoke gaily of dwelling "on the heights of Black Spain," whence the vision roves across "barbaric Baden." Which is very much as if a cliff-dweller on Riverside Drive, New York City, should claim that his vision roves across barbaric Englewood.

Here Beethoven found himself the neighbour of his boyhood friend Stephan von Breuning and renewed the old intimacy. He became extremely fond of Gerhard, the twelve-year-old son of Stephan, nicknaming him "Hosen-knopf," or Trouser Button (because he stuck so close to father), and Ariel (because he was so light on his feet). When the lad took up the piano Beethoven prescribed the Clementi method as preferable to that of Czerny and made Gerhard a present of it. At the Von Breuning home in Vienna the writer handled this precious volume and the kindly letter that went with it. The grandson of "Hosen-knopf" showed him a magnificent nutwood desk which had been Beethoven's only fine piece of furniture. Also the funny little painted clock with iron weights, which always hung in the Master's kitchen, but which made such an eager and continuous racket that the Von Breunings had to stop it. Such a timepiece could be tolerated in action only by a very deaf person. If Herr von Breuning's forbears had as much charm as this young palæontologist-entomologist, one can well understand why Beethoven was attracted to them.

Frau von Breuning saw to the fitting up of Beethoven's kitchen and engaged his servants. In return the gallant

[455]

Master once accompanied her a long distance to a public bath. Emerging an hour later she saw with astonishment that he was waiting for her in the street.

This may have been an unwelcome attention. For his laugh was sudden, powerful, and piercing; his gestures, angular and eccentric. He was completely indifferent toward strangers. His speaking voice was loud. So that passers-by often stopped in their tracks, taking him for a madman, and the street boys followed him hooting. Of course Beethoven, deaf and absorbed, had no more idea that he was embarrassing the lady than why she hesitated to eat at his table. The truth was that she did not find the Master's neglected clothing and his eccentric behaviour appetizing.

Gerhard's sister Marie reported to Thayer:

Beethoven often told my mother that he longed greatly for domestic happiness and much regretted that he had never married.

The lady sometimes teased her husband to make Beethoven play. But Stephan always replied tenderly:

He doesn't like to do it, and I don't want to ask him, because it might pain him not to hear himself.

When he did, though, it sometimes gave exquisite pain to others. Rellstab tells how, by a trick, he induced the Master to press the keys of his Broadwood.

"I struck a chord lightly . . . in order to make Beethoven turn around. . . . 'That is a beautiful gift,' said Beethoven, . . . 'and it has such a beautiful tone,' he continued and moved his hands towards the keys without taking his eyes off me. He gently

GERHARD VON BREUNING

Nicknamed "Ariel" and "Hosenknopf"
("Trouser-button," the latter because
he stuck so close to father)

struck a chord. Never again will one enter my soul so poignant, so heart-breaking as that one. was! He struck the C major triad with the right hand and B as a bass in the left, and continuing to gaze uninterruptedly at me, repeated the false chord several times in order to let the sweet tone of the instrument reverberate; and the greatest musician on earth did not hear the dissonance!"[1]

It may be, however, that Rellstab's sorrow was supererogatory. Perhaps the composer of that up-to-date Twentieth Century piece, the Great Fugue, was deliberately trying the effect of polytonality on the critic. Perhaps the forward-looking mind which was already interested in steam and aviation agreed with the creator of *The Faërie Queene*,[2] that

Dischord ofte in music makes the sweeter lay.

---

[1] Translated from Leitzmann, Vol. I, pp. 307–308.
[2] III, II, 15.

Chapter XLVII

THE MASTER'S MASTERPIECE

Le génie de l'artiste est comme toutes les grandes choses du
monde: un acte de foi et d'amour.
—PAUL BOURGET, *Address on His Admission to the Académie.*

*C Sharp Minor Quartet Completed, 1826 — Its Pre-
eminence — Sketches — "Cribbed," yet "Spanking New"
— The Author's Own Reaction — "Twenty Minutes of
Reality" — From Heaven to Earth — The Opening Fugue
— "Consciousness Surpassing Our Own" — An Expression-
istic Allegretto — A Mighty Compensation*

EARLY in 1826 Beethoven finished that quartet which he
called his greatest, the C sharp minor (Op. 131). After
many flunctuations of taste, the author has come to feel
that Beethoven was right, and that this quartet is his greatest, with the A minor (Op. 132), the E flat (Op. 127), and
the F major (Op. 59, No. 1) pressing one another in close
competition for second place.

The Master took extraordinary pains with the C sharp
minor. The preliminary sketches for it bulk huge beside
the portly completed manuscript. Studying them in the
Prussian State Library in Berlin, one is filled with something
like awe at the infinite pains lavished by this dying man, and
the infallibility with which revision progressed from the
commonplace first thought to the inspired last thought.

In August, 1826, he sent the manuscript to Schott &

Sons, his publishers. On its title page he scribbled *"Zusam-mengestohlen aus Verschiedenem Diesem und Jenem"* (Cribbed together variously from this and that).[1] Schotts took fright and wrote, reminding Beethoven of their stipulation that the work must be an original one. To this the Master replied that the expression *"zusammengestohlen"* (cribbed together) had been only a joke, and the quartet was "spanking new" (*funkelnagelneu*).

"Spanking new" it unquestionably was. But was the *"zusammengestohlen"* inscription no more than a humorous lie?

Perhaps not quite. The more one studies this music the more miraculously "cribbed together" it appears. Many of its tunes were born and reared through childhood elsewhere.

The subject of the opening fugue

Ex. 190

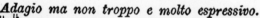

Adagio ma non troppo e molto espressivo.

is enough like that of the C sharp minor five-voiced fugue in Bach's *Welltempered Clavichord* to be its son. But, curiously enough, its component parts can be traced to Beethoven's own earlier works. As we shall see, Herr Bekker points out that the start of the introductions to the (earlier)

---

[1] The winning understatement of this inscription recalls Brahms's way of describing his MS. symphonies, when he first mailed them to friends, as "a bundle of little piano pieces."

A minor quartet and to the Great Fugue were perhaps echoed in notes 2 to 5 of the C sharp minor fugue.[2]

The germ of the first *Allegro*

Ex. 191

comes straight from the *Allegro ma non tanto* of the A minor quartet.

Ex. 183

The theme of the *Andante moderato* variation

Ex. 192

is drawn, with only slight alterations, from a pregnant phrase of the opening movement of this same A minor quartet:

Ex. 193

[2]See pp. 573-574.

The lone scrap of melody in the enigmatic *Allegretto* variation

Ex. 194

is borrowed from the *finale* of the A major sonata (Op. 101):

Ex. 195

In the *scherzo*, with its atmosphere of naïve and playful childhood, it is appropriate to find a quotation from the youthful quartet in G major (Op. 18, No. 2) whose first movement ends its main theme thus:

Ex. 196

Twenty-six years later this tune reappeared in the C sharp minor quartet at the place marked *piacevole*, but this time without its rococo trappings and wearing simple greatness as a child's light garment.

Ex. 197

The tune of the short sixth movement

Ex. 198

is not only related to that of the Bagatelle (Op. 26, No. 1)

Ex. 199

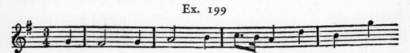

but also to the venerable Hebrew melody, *Kol Nidrei*, which antedates the Ninth Century.

Ex. 200

Last, the motto of the *finale*

Ex. 201

comes almost note for note from Mozart's *Fantasie* sonata in C minor.[3]

Ex. 202

This, in its turn, echoes the theme of J. S. Bach's *Ricercata* organ fugue in C minor from *Das musikalische Opfer*.

Here are nine "cribbings together" of thematic material from other compositions, not counting the inevitable source-motive[4] in fugue and *scherzo* which had already appeared more than a hundred times in his earlier works. Surely these are enough to lend a substratum of seriousness to the joke "*zusammengestohlen*," as well as to shed an additional lustre of the miraculous on the perfectly honest claim that the quartet was "spanking new." For, of course, the point of all this is not how he borrowed, but how magically he disguised, improved, and renewed his borrowings.

For a detailed study of the inter-movement thematic liaison work in the C sharp minor the reader is referred to Riemann,[5] who indeed carries his analogies to the length of declaring that the main themes of the second and seventh movements as well as the initial motto of the latter are rewritings of the subject of the opening fugue.

More than any other work of Beethoven, this quartet represents to the writer the gradual and painful acquisition of a taste long denied. For many years he had taken part in

[3]For this observation the writer is indebted to his friend Mr. Gustave Reese.
[4]See p. 601, (transposed) Exs. 352 and 353.
[5]*Beethoven's Streichquartette*, p. 147 ff.

playing and hearing it without much more response than annoyance at its length and obvious harshnesses. Not until after prolonged study, score in hand, of the phonograph record of the Lener Quartet, and hearing it repeatedly played in concert, did he begin to think it one of the supreme things in all art. It took him thirty years to realize that the C sharp minor uniquely blends the pure and unerring intuition of the child with the maturest experience of the supreme genius.

Without in the least offering a personal view of this quartet as the only valid one, he feels it may be of a certain interest to mention that, though the work affects him variously according to mood and tense, most often its first part offers him, in a language far more veridical than any words, the illumination of the mystic vision. Its "twenty minutes of reality" communicates directly, without recourse to such awkward conventions as the worn counters of speech, the secrets of the universe. He feels himself a completely balanced and integrated being. And he sees everything at a glance as an inevitable progress of clearly unified cause and effect. The past, present, and future are made to form one pure ring of burning light. There is "no more death, neither sorrow, nor crying, neither shall there be any more pain; for the former things are passed away."

Richard Wagner held the *scherzo* of this quartet to be the *chef d'œuvre* of all music. It stirs us with faint echoes from the Master's actual youth, now thirty years gone. It suggests that little *scherzo* which twice interrupted the second *Adagio* of the Serenade for string trio (Op. 8). But

[464]

it is strangely touching to notice that the opus 8 *Presto* sounds prosaically grown-up in comparison with that of opus 131, where one may overhear the mirth of such innocent and exuberant play as the "young-eyed cherubim" might enjoy on the shores of the jasper sea.

The last two movements bring a stirring change. Turning abruptly from the subliminal, they seem—to one listener at least—to intimate secrets even more important to the sons of Earth. They whisper that no man may gaze with impunity into the untempered brightness of the infinite. That we, whose ancestors so recently swung gibbering from branch to branch, are not yet intended to linger with the children of light on the plane of eternal bliss, neglecting our earthly home, like absentee landlords, to feast upon supernal glories. Those painful, resolute footsteps of the *finale's* heroic march fall on the ear like heartening exhortations to live out this phase of existence fully and courageously if we would develop the momentum of spirit necessary for the next.

When Richard Wagner declares that the opening fugue[6] is "perhaps the most heavy-hearted thing that has ever been said in tones," the writer fails to follow him. Its serenity, elevation, and fullness of life seem incompatible with melancholy. This fugue is beyond sorrow and joy, beyond good and evil, almost beyond ugliness and beauty.

Nowhere else in music [writes Mr. Sullivan] are we made so aware, as here, of a state of consciousness surpassing our own,

---

[6]See Ex. 190, p. 459.

where our problems do not exist, and to which even our highest aspirations, those that we can formulate, provide no key.

The experiences Beethoven here communicates

may belong to an order of consciousness that very few men have attained, but, in that case, they must be in the line of human development; . . . they correspond to a spiritual synthesis which the race has not achieved but which, we may suppose, it is on the way to achieving.[7]

This quartet was Wagner's chief inspiration in creating "the music of the future." And to-day, with *Tristan* and *The Ring* to its credit, it remains music of the future in a far deeper sense than any page left us by the seer of Bayreuth.

One is constantly surprised by new evidence of its forward-looking spirit. Study, for instance, the brief *Allegretto* which constitutes the fifth variation of the fourth movement. This cryptic page, which says little directly but suggests much by veiled indirection, is like some expressionistic story of to-day. Without apparent coherence or progression, without narrative or argument—almost without matter itself—it conveys a surprisingly significant and coherent account through shreds and patches of naïvely natural suggestion. This was a new style in the music of 1826. And, though the Marcel Prousts and the Virginia Woolfs have made an accepted and honoured place for the new style in literature, these notes of music are almost as fresh and novel and mysterious to-day as when they were first set down on paper.

[7]*Beethoven: His Spiritual Development*, p. 239.

For people of charm and endowment the world always baits snares. It was rare good fortune for us that Beethoven should have evaded these snares and come safe through to the time when deafness shut him more and more away from distractions and temptations and provided him with a terrible affliction which he had to redress by such mighty compensations as the C sharp minor quartet. A stroke of miraculous luck[8] for this none too lucky planet! In all probability we shall not look upon its like again.

Soon after presenting this gift to the world the Master received a shock that, in a few days, made him look like a man of seventy.

---

[8]In view of the striking superiority of the music which Beethoven wrote after 1818, one is inclined to endorse the proposal of Mr. Harvey Grace that all composers should be made deaf!

Chapter XLVIII

THE "MADMAN" AT GNEIXENDORF

Karl Goes from Bad to Worse — Lays Hands on His Uncle — Attempts Suicide — Decides to Be a Soldier — Beethoven Takes Him to Gneixendorf, September, 1826 — A Trying Guest — Homely Brother Johann — Beethoven's Habits of Composition Too Much for Cook — The Vine-Dresser Valet's Account — What the Natives Thought of Him — "A Bissel Stada!" — Friction

BEETHOVEN's desperate and pitiful attempts to make some sort of contact with humanity by rearing a worthy heir concentrated all the terrific power of his passionate affection upon one quite ordinary young man. Karl nearly died of it. He could not stand the perpetual change from suspicion and angry upbraiding to sentimental coddling. Holz came in one day and found the young fellow actually laying forceful hands on Beethoven.

Karl made debts. He neglected his studies and his uncle. Then he took to stealing. Finally he tried suicide *à la Werther*, among the picturesque ruins of Castle Rauhenstein. At the last moment his nerve partially failed, and two shots resulted in only one scalp wound.

This deed produced in Beethoven the old alternations of emotion: first fury at Karl's ingratitude; then a fervour of thankfulness for his escape, followed by the unconditional but temporary surrender of a loving heart.

[468]

Karl told the examining magistrate that he had tried to kill himself because his uncle tormented him too much. "I grew worse because he wanted me to grow better"; which is a reaction perfectly natural in an unwisely handled youngster.

He decided now to be a soldier. Baron von Stutterheim offered to take the boy into his regiment. In return he received from the grateful uncle the dedication of the C sharp minor quartet.

But before Karl put on the uniform his telltale scar must heal. So, on September 28, 1826, uncle and nephew went for a visit to brother Johann's four-hundred-acre estate at Gneixendorf. The name of this village reminded Beethoven's occasionally sensitive literary ear "somewhat of the breaking of an axletree."

His hatred of his sister-in-law, his deep distaste for Karl's growing friendliness with this same Aunt Therese, his suspicion, his irritability, his invalid's diet, and his eccentricities must have made him a difficult guest.

But Johann, too, must have been a trying house companion. He was an ignorant and unmusical but pretentious person who felt that, as the brother of the great composer, he must act the part of a musical Brahmin. After forcing himself to look knowing during several performances of the great E flat quartet, it developed that he had no idea he had ever before heard it. His near presence must have been trying to such a sensitive man as the Master. In one of the Conversation Books of this period we read a jotting in young Karl's hand, discreetly meant for Ludwig's eyes

[469]

alone, which may be euphemistically translated: "The brother is odoriferous!"

The Conversation Books also give us many a quaint touch of Johann's homely quality; as when he calls the violoncello by its long outlawed name, *Bassettl,* and by even the corruption of this old word, *Passedel.*

Johann was hard put to it to provide Ludwig proper attendance. The latter composed at a table, waving and stamping the tempo with hands and feet while he hummed and shouted what to himself, at least, represented tunes. This was too much for the cook, who made his bed. She was overcome with mirth. And Beethoven drove her out with "hearty, free words."

Then Johann tried one of his vine dressers as valet. Michael Krenn was more discreet. When he could no longer contain himself he rushed away and exploded with laughter at a safe distance. This peasant has left us a vignette of the composer in labour.

At half-past five he was up and at his table, beating time with hands and feet, singing, humming, writing. At half-past seven was the family breakfast and directly after it he hurried out of doors, and would saunter about the fields, calling out, waving his hands, going now very slowly, then very fast, and then suddenly standing still and writing in a kind of pocketbook. At half-past twelve he came into the house to dinner, and after dinner he went to his own room till three or so, then again in the fields till about sunset. At half-past seven he came to supper, and then went to his room, wrote till ten, and so to bed.

The neighbours as well as the servants felt that the strange stranger was not quite right in his head. He shouted and gesticulated so wildly as to stampede the same yoke of oxen twice in one day. Their driver asked Johann the name of the fool who had done this. "My brother." "A pretty brother, that he is!" exclaimed the peasant.

The picture of Beethoven at Gneixendorf following the inner gleam as he stormed across the fields, waving his arms like a windmill and roaring out unintelligible fragments of the last quartet to the consternation of the yokels, reminds us of Old Peter in that gem of Gilbert's *Bab Ballads*, "The Perils of Invisibility":

> At night, when all around is still,
> You'll find him pounding up a hill;
> And shrieking peasants whom he meets
> Fall down in terror on the peats.

It is recorded that one countryman, when the terrifying stranger appeared and made his yoke of oxen plunge, yelled, "*A bissel stada!*" which means in the local dialect, "Go a bit easy there!" This injunction neatly represents the typical reaction of average humanity to the waywardness of genius. If the Master had indeed gone through life "*a bissel stada*" he might never have quickened the heartbeats of either oxen or men.

Ludwig accompanied Johann on two different visits. The first was to the house of his surgeon, whose wife took the composer for a servant, spoke patronizingly to him, and gave him a jug of wine. The second was to a syndic who had as clerk an ardent Beethoven enthusiast.

SYNDIC: Who do you suppose that man was who stood so long by the door?

[471]

CLERK: He may be an exceptional case. But if you had not treated him so politely I should take him for an idiot.

Explanation and consternation. How were these simple folk to realize that he whom they held to be a fool or a madman was a great genius in parturition over a beauty full of the peace that passes understanding?

To Karl, life with this wild man, for whom he had now lost every spark of gratitude and affection, was rapidly growing unendurable. Witness his outbreak in one of the Conversation Books. Beethoven had evidently been scolding him for his reluctance to return to Vienna. The nephew replied:

If you want to go, good; if not, good again. But I entreat you once more not to torment me as you are doing; you might regret it, for I can endure much, but not too much. You treated your brother in the same way to-day without cause. You must remember that other people also are human beings. . . . I only want to be alone for a little while.—Will you not let me go to my room?

How the two unfortunate men grated upon each other's nerves can be read between the lines.

Chapter XLIX

RETROSPECT IN F MAJOR

Die Wirklichkeit wird zum Traum. Die Träume werden Wirklichkeit.[1]

October 30, 1826, Last Quartet Finished — Reason for Its Brevity — The Merchant of Venice — Op. 135, a Retrospect — "The Midway" Forecast — Origin of "Muss es sein?" — The Housekeeper Theory — Dembscher and the Canon

AT GNEIXENDORF, on October 30, 1826, Beethoven's last complete work, the quartet in F major (Op. 135), was finished. It consisted of four short movements. Only one other quartet of his, the G major (Op. 18, No. 2), can be performed in as brief a time. According to Holz the Master purposely kept down its length. He had bargained with Schlesinger for 80 ducats, but felt that the publisher had overreached him by sending 360 florins instead. "If a Jew," he exclaimed, "sends amputated ducats he shall have an amputated quartet. That's why it is so short."

All this about the Jew and the ducats; this insistence on the letter of what was nominated in the bond, reminds one of *The Merchant of Venice*. And when we hear the music, its easy mastery, its part-writing as lightly poised and balanced and transparent as the arcades of the Doge's Palace,

---

[1](Reality turns to a dream. Dreams become reality.) (Gustav Frenssen, *Otto Babendieck*, 1926, p. 1289.)

its crisp autumnal colouring, the freakish quality of the Gobboesque *Vivace,* the folk-tune flavour here and there, and the golden sunset glow that suffuses the *Lento assai*

Ex. 203

Lento assai

with idyllic poetry, we sometimes may still think of Shakespeare's masterpiece.

The F major is in the nature of a retrospect. The Master has fought his fight. Now he looks back over the arduous road he has travelled. In the confident happiness of the first movement, the sparkling vivacity of the second, the deep, brooding peace of the third, the firm but smiling resolution of the last, we see the stranger of Gneixendorf leaning on his staff and looking back toward the distant Danube. It reminds him of that Rhine of his boyhood, beyond which beckoned those castles in Spain.

And fragments of music float up the deep vista to lend him resolution for the facing of whatever may be before him. In snatches he hears the *Adagios* of his first quartet and of the Rasoumowskys, the Episode in the first movement of the *Eroica,* the beginning and end of the Fifth, the slow movements of the "*Emperor*" and of the "*Archduke,*" the *Arietta,* the commencement of the *Choral,* the immortal C sharp minor fugue, the *Dankgesang,* the *Et vitam venturi.*

[474]

"It will stand," he murmurs. And on his face burns for a moment the transfigured look that no man ever surprised there. Then a surge of pain obliterates it and he hurries back to the Wasserhof to see what mischief Karl is up to.

The F major is less "cribbed together" than any of the other last quartets.[2]

It is appropriate that this last work of the Master's should have had an eye to the future as well as to the past. At the 104th bar of the *finale* there is a curiously plain prophecy of that dusky tune which was to become so popular at the World's Columbian Exposition sixty-seven years later, and was to be christened *"The Midway."*

The *Muss es sein?* motto of this same *finale*

Ex. 204

was destined to suggest, almost note for note, the opening of Liszt's *Les Préludes;* and, far more gloriously, the start of César Franck's symphony in D minor.

The idea is current that this motto and its answering companion,

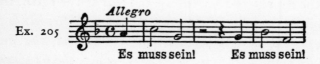

Ex. 205

was destined to suggest, almost note for note, the opening

---

[2] For Beethoven's use of his great source-motive in the *Lento* and *finale,* see pp. 602–603.

which are collectively entitled *Der schwer gefasste Ent-schluss* (The Difficult Resolve), arose from the Master's struggles with the demon of avarice (more serious than comic) during those painful moments every Saturday night when the old witch who kept house for him appeared to pull her eagle to earth by his cord—and demand the weekly house money.

Helm saw the conflict in the sick Master's revolt against the conventional necessity for ending the quartet with a fourth movement. But its true origin can be traced to an ardent amateur named Dembscher.[3] Dembscher wanted to have Boehm play the B flat quartet (Op. 130) at his own home. Unfortunately he had neglected to subscribe to Schuppanzigh's series in which this work had been first performed. He asked Beethoven for the loan of the manuscript. For once in his life the Master showed a little consideration for his bulky friend. He refused on account of Schuppanzigh's feelings.

Thayer[4] relates that

Dembscher stammered in confusion and begged Holz to find some means to restore him to Beethoven's good graces. Holz said that the first step should be to send Schuppanzigh 50 florins, the price of the subscription. Dembscher laughingly asked, "Must it be?" (*Muss es sein?*) When Holz related the incident to Beethoven he too laughed and instantly wrote down a canon:

---

[3]He was the violoncellist to whom Brother Johann referred as playing the *"Passedel."* See p. 470.

[4]Vol. III, p. 224.

Ex. 206

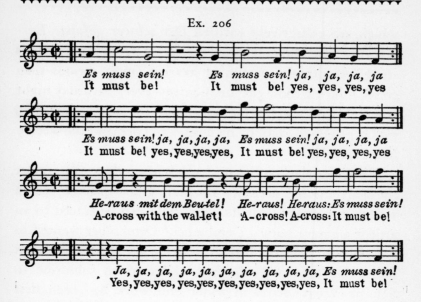

And out of this burlesque *jeu d'esprit*—just as the *Allegretto* of the Eighth symphony had grown out of the canon to Maelzel—grew the F major's serious, but not too serious, *finale*.

Chapter L

THE DIVINE COMEDY IS FINISHED

*Return to Vienna, December 2, 1826 — Last Illness —
Brave Wit During Operation — Sick-Room Conditions
— Enjoys Gift of Handel's Works — Confident of Pos-
terity's Verdict — Tries to Learn Arithmetic — Repre-
sentations of Poverty — Gift of £100 from Philharmonic,
February 28, 1827 — Was It Obtained Under False Pre-
tenses? — Rationalization — "A Stormy Flood" — Karl
Leaves Vienna — Mental Confusion — Schubert's Visit —
Last Handwriting, March 23 — "Applaud, Friends" — Last
Words, March 24 — Delirium — Death, March 26, 1827 —
Cause of Death — Finding the Secret Drawer — Philhar-
monic's Handsome Action — Burial, March 29 — Reburial,
1872 — Tomb*

ON DECEMBER 2, 1826, the weather was severely in-
clement. But Beethoven had determined to take Karl to
Vienna forthwith, and nothing could hold him back. Either
from riding in a crude open vehicle or sleeping in a cold and
wretched inn that night, he caught a chill and arrived
"indisposed."

In two days Holz sent for Dr. Wawruch,[1] who found
symptoms of inflammation of the lungs. These he soon
overcame, but on the eighth day a relapse was brought on
by a fit of rage. The cause was unknown, but it was prob-

---

[1] Thayer scotched the libelous tale of Schindler that Karl was too much interested
in billiards to call the doctor and sent the billiard marker instead, who at first forgot
the commission.

[478]

ably directed against either Karl or Johann. This paroxysm caused an attack of summer cholera, also jaundice, hard nodules in the liver, and dropsy.

The dropsy necessitated four tappings. But even during the operations Beethoven was his usual humorous and brilliant self. The first time the surgeon made the incision and applied the tube for the water to gush out, the patient observed whimsically: "Better from my belly than from my pen." Then, turning to Dr. Seibert: "Mr. Professor, you remind me of Moses smiting the rock with his staff."

With the rudimentary medical knowledge of a century ago, ignorance and carelessness combined to make that sickroom a cruel and disgusting place for a man to live or die in. Vermin came to complete the wretchedness.[2]

By the fourth operation Beethoven had lost hope. But still he had the wit to murmur: "My day's work is done. If there were a physician who could help me his name should be called Wonderful." This quotation from *The Messiah* alluded to the gift of Handel's complete works which his friend Stumpff had sent from London to cheer the Master's last days.

Young "Ariel" von Breuning used to bring the heavy folios and stand them on the bed against the wall. Beethoven was delighted. As he turned the pages words of admiration often burst from his lips. "I have long wanted these," he told the boy, "for Handel is the greatest, the ablest composer that ever lived. I can still learn from him."

In a Conversation Book some visitors scribbled: "Your

---

[2]Many of the nauseating details are given in Thayer, Vol. III.

quartet which Schuppanzigh played yesterday did not please." When they had gone the Master tersely remarked to "Ariel," who had found the entry: "Some day it will please them." He told the lad that he used his best judgment and would not permit himself to be carried away by the opinion of the moment.[3] "I know that I am an artist," he added simply.

Time hung so heavily on the patient's hands that, as the Conversation Books show, he even tried to learn elementary arithmetic from Karl, but soon gave it up. As usual, he devoted much anxious thought to that young man's financial future. This preoccupation and the anti-mathematical cast of his mind may help to condone the false representations of poverty and extreme need which he made at that time to the London Philharmonic Society through Stumpff, Sir George Smart, and Moscheles—against the friendly protests of Von Breuning and Schindler. They pointed out that Beethoven could not honestly plead poverty while he owned bank shares worth 7,441 florins. They declared that the fact, if known, would look ugly. But Beethoven insisted that he wished to leave this little fortune to Karl intact—and sent the letter. London took prompt action on February 28, 1827. The sick man was soon overjoyed at hearing from Moscheles:

The Philharmonic Society resolved to express their good will and lively sympathy by requesting your acceptance of £100

---

[3]One remembers how, deep in composing the Eighth symphony, he wrote to Amalie Sebald: "What people say means nothing, they are only people; usually they see in others only themselves, and that is just nothing; away with this, the good, the beautiful needs no people. Independent of external aid, here it is. . . ."

BEETHOVEN AT THE POINT OF DEATH

From drawings by Teltscher before he was driven from
the death chamber by Stephan von Breuning

sterling, to provide the necessary comforts and conveniences during your illness.

When the money was brought, Rau the banker suggested delivering it in two instalments.

I found poor Beethoven in a sad way [he wrote to Moscheles], more like a skeleton than a living being. . . . He acknowledged to me openly that he considered this money as a relief sent from heaven; and that 500 florins would not suffice for his present wants. I therefore gave him, according to his wish, the whole sum at once.

Beethoven left an estate which, allowing for the difference in purchasing power between 1827 and 1929, would to-day be worth about $8,800. Yet Sonneck attacked all adverse critics of the Philharmonic incident on the ground that they "naïvely overlook a determining psychological factor. In Beethoven's eyes his seven bank-shares did not exist for him; in his eyes . . . they belonged to nephew Karl, his sole heir. To have touched these for his own comfort would have been considered by Beethoven unpardonable thievery. One may disapprove of this excess of consideration for Karl's future welfare, but it was sincere. Hence, from his point of view Beethoven, logically enough, could not but look upon himself as a poor man."[4]

But Sonneck overlooked the fact that it is far from honest to proclaim one's self destitute while in possession of property, even though one may be filled with a burning desire to transmit this property posthumously. Suppose, for example, that some reader of these pages had accumulated a secret food supply, enough to sustain life for several years,

---

[4]*Beethoven Letters in America*, 1927, p. 37.

and that he nevertheless begged food from friends and strangers abroad on the ground that he was starving. Could he be cleared of a charge of obtaining food under false pretenses, even though he had set his heart on leaving the entire hoard to a relative? Sonneck wrote: "to have touched these would have been considered by Beethoven unpardonable thievery." But he forgot that Beethoven had already sold one of his accumulated shares on an occasion when he was particularly pressed for money;[5] and that, when on the point of selling another, he found he needed only to cash the coupon.[6] No, the sort of mental falsification of accounts which Sonneck attributed to Beethoven cannot fully relieve the dying Master of the charge of dishonesty; although his fault dwindles when we consider the ridiculous disparity between an estate of approximately $8,800 and the incalculable treasures he bequeathed to us.

As a rule, the greater the artist, the less he rationalizes about the quality of his own creations. He glosses over few misgivings on this subject. But he is human—often more so than most people—and has to strike a balance somewhere. So he usually compensates for his austere æsthetic probity by rationalizing his private life even more extravagantly than the average man.

The lofty artistic rectitude of the last sonatas and quartets, symbolized by the Kyd incident,[7] probably allowed

---

[5]According to records in the National Bank, Vienna, for July 13, 1819, Beethoven originally bought eight, not seven, bank shares. (Dr. Max Reinitz, "Beethoven als Bankationär," in Neue Freie Presse, May 28, 1916.)

[6]See p. 367.

[7]See p. 393.

Beethoven to make peace with his conscience for throwing a heavy stool at the servant's head and for obtaining money from the Philharmonic through false representations.

As Dr. Max Friedländer aptly says:[8]

The virtue of lofty natures is unminted gold which does not pass current in the business of daily life. Such men bless peoples more easily than individual people. It is more natural for them to bestow seed-corn than bread. Such a soul is no watering-can for the refreshment of someone's favourite gillyflower, but a stormy flood that quenches the thirst of wide fields and lofty oaks.

To everyone's relief, on January 2, 1827, after another quarrel with his uncle, Karl left Vienna and joined his regiment at Iglau. On the 3d Beethoven drew up a will making the young man "sole and universal heir" of all his property. A note to Schindler, probably written late in February, shows that the great mind had even then begun to grow confused. Schindler had evidently been laid up by some mischance.

About your accident, since it has happened, as soon as we see one another.—Without inconvenience I can send to you by somebody, accept this;—here is something Moscheles, Cramer; without your having received a letter, there will be a new occasion to write you Wednesday and lay my affairs to his heart, if you are not well by that time one of my . . . can take it to the post against a receipt.—*Vale et fave.*—There is no need of my assuring you of my sympathy in your accident—do take the food from me, all given from the heart—Heaven be with you.

Your true friend
BEETHOVEN.

---

[8]In an unpublished lecture.

It is not certain, but highly probable, that the shy and retiring Schubert visited Beethoven during these last days. Hüttenbrenner states that he took him to the house a week before the end and the sick man sent out word: "Let Schubert come first." At any rate, some copies of his songs were among the last things Beethoven enjoyed. And the Master is reported to have exclaimed: "Truly the divine spark dwells in Schubert." When eighteen months later the younger man finished the unfinished symphony of his own career the name of Beethoven was almost constantly on his lips.

The codicil to the Master's will, dated four days before the end, is the last thing we have in his handwriting.

Beethoven's Last Written Words.
Municipal Collections, Vienna.

Verbatim, it reads:

> Mein Nefffe Karle Soll alleini=[ger]
> Erbe sejn, das Kapital
> meines Nachlasses soll jedoch
> Seinen natülichen oder testamen=
> tarisch(isch?)en Erben zufallen.
> Wien am 23=März 1827
> luwig van Beethoen

[Translated:] My nep(p)hew Karle shall be so[le] heir, the capital of my estate shall however revert to his natu[r]al or testamentar(y?)y heirs.

> Vienna the 23 March 1827
> luwig van Beethoen

In signing it he was not fully conscious and had to be supported by Johann and Von Breuning. Notice the misspellings and duplications—mute testimonies to his condition.

The famous phrase *"Plaudite amici, comoedia finita est"* (Applaud, friends, the comedy is finished) was probably half-conscious half-quotation from several other famous deathbeds. There is some question as to whether Beethoven pronounced that lambent bit of sarcasm after receiving the Host or after a long consultation of physicians.[8a] A number of biographers, with more feeling for drama than for history, have assigned to the Latin phrase the rôle of the Master's last words. But one must believe Schindler's statement that his last authentic utterance, spoken at one o'clock on the afternoon of March 24th, was about nothing more

---

[8a]In the latter case, the author of *The Doctor's Dilemma* may well envy him this anticipatory specimen of Shavian irony. *"Plaudite"* was, of course, the conventional closing formula of Latin comedy.

momentous than a present of old Rhine wine from Schott, the publisher: "Pity, pity—too late!"[8b]

Towards evening began two days of almost uninterrupted delirium.

The strong man lay [wrote Gerhard von Breuning][9] completely unconscious . . . breathing so stertorously that the rattle could be heard at a distance. His powerful frame, his unweakened lungs, fought like giants with approaching death.

Late on the afternoon of March 26, 1827, there was a flash of lightning and a sharp peal of thunder. The then unconscious Master raised himself high in bed, as if answering the thunder. His eyes opened wide. He clenched and lifted his right hand, remained in this attitude for several seconds—and fell back dead.[9a] That clenched hand seemed to say:

> I was ever a fighter, so—one fight more,
> The best and the last!

Ironically enough, it happened that none whom Beethoven loved, neither Wegeler nor Holz nor the Von Breunings nor Karl, were there at the end to close his eyes; and that of the two present one was an acquaintance from out of town named Hüttenbrenner and the other his ancient enemy and sister-in-law Therese.

[8b]It is good to have this human touch in place of the *Plaudite,* etc., just as it is good to know that Goethe's last words were not the grandiose and apocryphal "More light!" but a tender phrase addressed to his son's wife: "Give me, then, your little paw!"

[9]*Aus dem Schwarzspanierhause,* p. 108.

[9a]Significantly, the last piece of tonal defiance—the last musical gesture of challenge on the part of this heroic fighter who had once cried out that he would seize fate by the throat—had been the opening movement of the *Choral* symphony, whose main subject was taken from the Thunderstorm in the *Pastoral.*

In the opinion of modern science, the immediate cause of Beethoven's death was cirrhosis of the liver. Long and vainly the friends searched for the dead man's fortune—not without some regrettable mutual suspicions and recriminations. Finally Holz pulled at a nail which stuck from an old cabinet. A secret drawer fell out. And there lay the seven bank shares, with the letter to the "Immortal Beloved" and a portrait of the Countess Therese von Brunswick.[10]

The friends also found the English £100, untouched. Like the wine, this gift had come too late. At first the Philharmonic asked for its return. But when Moscheles begged that it should go to Karl "in honour of the great deceased," the Londoners handsomely consented.[11]

The funeral on March 29th befitted the man who had set music free and had made a professional out of that lackey, the composer. For Beethoven's burial the schools of Vienna were closed, and the military were called out to hold in check a throng of twenty thousand.[12] The city was alert to do him honour.

Schubert, Hummel, Seyfried, Kreutzer, Czerny, and the faithful old quartettists Linke and Schuppanzigh were

---

[10]Nobody realized that Beethoven's papers would one day be worth fortunes. When the holograph score of the Fifth symphony was put up at auction it brought six florins.

[11]This whole action by the members of the Philharmonic, after the exasperating dishonesty shown them by Beethoven, is an admirable example of British sportsmanship. The wheel has recently come full circle through the graceful gesture of the Beethoven Association of New York in contributing £100 to the endowment fund of the London Philharmonic Society.

[12]To his pauper's grave only three people had followed Mozart—and those but a part of the way.

among the torch carriers and pallbearers in the procession
to the cemetery at Währing.

Forty-five years later the body was exhumed and re-
buried in Vienna's Central Friedhof. There in that greatest
of all musical pantheons, near the tombs of Mozart, Gluck,
Hugo Wolf, Schubert, and Brahms, he lies. Over him rises
an obelisk significantly marked in bronze by that ancient
emblem of divine creativeness, the serpent biting its own
tail. This encloses a butterfly—mute witness to the immortality of man's re-creative genius.

Chapter LI

HOW BEETHOVEN FREED MUSIC

A Versatile Emancipator — Established Composer on Professional Basis — Democratized and Universalized Music — No Disparagement of Bach Implied — Cultivated Nuance — Developed the Continental Concert — Matured the Art — Freed Form — Helped to Liberate Harmony — Created New Technic for Keyboard Instruments — Emancipated Modulation — Took Music Out-of-Doors — Freed It from Cloistered Outlook — The Luther of Church Music — And of the Dramatic Overture — Rid Music of Exhibitionism — Fought Venality — Developed Mechanism of Piano — And of Orchestra — Dissolved Time-Honoured Identity of Composer and Interpreter — Made Music More Self-Contained —Encouraged Rise of Creative Listening — Beethoven the Chief of Many Liberators

THROUGHOUT this book Beethoven has functioned as a versatile emancipator. We have seen him, by sheer personal magnetism, force of will, and intensity of genius, liberate the art of music from the long-standing indignity of being carried on by lackeys. We have seen him establish the composer's vocation upon a professional basis. No longer, thanks to Beethoven, would a musical genius sup, like Mozart, at the servants' table, or, like that unhappy lad, be kicked from the hall or discharged at a moment's notice. The poor

[489]

boy from Bonn was the first composer to attain the dignity of seeing his symphonies printed in score.[1]

We have seen Beethoven deliver the music of his day from the ignominious rôle of obsequious hanger-on of the fashionable world and make it a universal thing—a materialization of the utmost range of the human mind and spirit, omitting none of the peaks and abysses. We have followed this imperious figure as he emancipated personality in music, detonating in his scores such a profound charge of thought and passionate emotion that the world still vibrates with the shock.

Let it be noted that such claims as these imply no disparagement of the stupendous achievements of Johann Sebastian Bach. For, although, in our own day, Bach's works have had for the modern composer perhaps as potent a liberating influence as Beethoven's, some unhappy fate decreed that his influence was to remain merely potential during the lifetime of the Father of Music, and until long after Beethoven's death.

In this heroic campaign Beethoven did not scorn the most apparently trivial details. A factor in the triumphant emergence of personality in music was his minute and painstaking labour in developing nuance, through the extension and invention of dynamic symbols and other marks of expression.

He took Continental music from the salon to the concert hall; from the castle to the cottage, and made it the most democratic thing in the æsthetic world.

---

[1]Hermann Kretzschmar, *Gesammelte Aufsätze über Musik.*

> Through Beethoven melody has become emancipated from the influence of fashion and fluctuating taste, and elevated to an eternally valid type of pure humanity.
> —RICHARD WAGNER.
>
> To him we owe the absolute emancipation of instrumental music from the trammels of polite artistic society . . . his hand . . . gained for us the full measure of spiritual democracy which is our artistic heritage to-day.
> —ERNEST WALKER.
>
> The sum of his message was freedom, artistic freedom, political freedom, personal freedom of will, of art, of faith, freedom of the individual in all the aspects of life.
> —PAUL BEKKER.
>
> Freedom above all.
>
> —BEETHOVEN.

The Man Who Freed Music

He loosed this already grown-up art from the incongruous nursery and gave it a rightful place—for the first time on equal terms—among its adult brethren. For this act Richard Wagner paid him tribute:

Through these last, and to us still unknown works of our wondrous master [Beethoven's posthumous quartets], of all others, the power of musical expression has taken a direction from which the music of earlier periods was often bound to hold deliberately aloof; I will here call that direction *the tenderly and deliberately passionate*, through whose expression music has first raised herself to an equal height with the poetry and painting of the greatest periods of the past. While with this expression Dante, Shakespeare, Calderon, and Goethe, like the great masters

[491]

of painting in Italy and the Netherlands, took fee of every portrayable object in the world and man; and while it was this that first enabled them to paint the world and man: in music there had ruled an axiom which openly degraded her as a branch of Art, an axiom borrowed from the purely physical pleasure, the purely sensuous entertainment to be found in her.[2]

Beethoven liberated form, not from law, but from the specious compulsions of superficial and modish laws. He did much to free musical forms from slavery to the clogging conventions of formalism, and to give them that profound inner necessity through which they have ever since carried conviction. Nor was he wrecked on the reef of amorphism which has meant destruction to so many romanticists.

As a practical harmonist he broke ground for the skyscraper of Twentieth Century piano harmony. Philipp Emanuel Bach's innovation, the monodic style, had been used by Haydn and Mozart in their stand against the old polyphony. Beethoven's personal genius assimilated and hall-marked the contributions of these men and created a new harmonic, or chordal, technic for keyboard instruments. What was tentative, experimental in Haydn developed into Beethoven's characteristic idiom.[3]

He also freed modulation, brushing aside numerous hampering rules and enriching his harmonic scheme to match the liberty he had won in other departments.

This first great nature lover among composers took the

[2]In his report to King Ludwig II of Bavaria upon the establishment of a German music school in Munich.

[3]As early as the *finale* of the F minor sonata (Op. 2, No. 1) the *Largo et mesto* of the D major (Op. 10, No. 3) and the introduction of the *Pathétique* (Op. 13).

art out of the study, purged it of whatever smell of the lamp still clung to it, and gave it the run of meadow and forest.

He freed music from that cloistered outlook which ignored the march of events in the outside world of action, as Palestrina, Bach, and Haydn had ignored them.

By his choice of texts he presented vocal music with the freedom of the world of great literature—a pioneer accomplishment.

Through the accidental circumstance that the B minor Mass of Bach was not published until years after Beethoven's *Missa*, our hero became the Luther among composers, extricating the Mass from the bonds of convention and dogma.

He released the dramatic overture from subservience to that hybrid thing, opera; and the concerto orchestra from its abject servility as a mere accompanist to the solo part.

More than any previous composer, he rid music of the exhibitionistic taint of virtuosity for virtuosity's sake, and the reproach of composing to the order of outer compulsion rather than from inner necessity.

His ingenuity helped to throw open to the piano and the orchestra a new world of richness and sonority. The accident of his deafness freed the art in another way, by decreeing a divorce between composer and virtuoso and smashing the harmful old convention that the creative musician must necessarily fritter away his energies in interpretive work.

Perhaps his supreme achievement as emancipator was the exertion of a more potent influence than that of his greatest predecessors towards freeing music from the shackles of literature, whose servant it was in the beginning. By pouring into music a wealth of suggestive factors which made it so much more opulent and self-contained than ever before, he made it easier for the imagination of the ordinary listener at length to escape from the weakening incubus of cliché programs and, under the stimulus of this powerfully independent art, to fashion its own poetic interpretations.

Beethoven did more than any other composer has ever done toward realizing that utopian dream of the day when "all men shall be poets." It was scarcely his fault that mistaken inferences drawn from the *Pastoral* symphony, and from the regrettable *finale* of the *Choral* (which, too late, he himself regretted), should have led to a new enslavement of music by the poetic idea. Happily our own day is witnessing a fresh revolt from this degradation. The true lover of music must rejoice that, from the time when centenary thoughts of the Master commenced to hold the minds of all musicians, the world currents of thought and inclination seemed to begin setting away from the compromise relativities of opera and program music toward the pure absolutism of Bach, Brahms, Franck, and Beethoven.

Beethoven found the art of music narrowed to the pastime of a special class. He made it broadly human. He left it superhuman. Of course he was far from being the only man who ever freed music. In many ages and lands the art has been enslaved and has found its liberators. But the most potent of all these was Beethoven.

[494]

Chapter LII

WHAT BEETHOVEN MEANS TO US

A Supreme Master of Construction — Novel Architectonic Method — Made Forms "Internal" — Developed Them — Closely Knit Structures — Lengthened Sonata and Symphony — Multiplied Movements — The Germ-Motive — The Source-Motive — Modified the Rondo — And the Fugue — Three Greatest Contributions — The Titanic Allegro — The Scherzo — The Mystical Adagio — Treatment of Variation Form — Originality — Dramatic Power — Unexpectedness — Lavish Vitality — Economy — Concentration — Large Calibre — The Beethoven Religion — Beethoven as Physician — Conscientious Idealism — Trough and Crest — Fluctuations of Fashion — A Gift from Nature

A CENTURY after his death, why does Beethoven stand as the central—if not the chief—figure in music?

For one thing, because he was perhaps an even greater master of construction than the men who made the frieze of the Parthenon, Macbeth, the Sistine frescos, the B minor Mass, and Chartres Cathedral.

By forcing himself to sketch the plan of a movement before he had its subjects more than dimly in mind, he brought into music an architectonic idea hitherto foreign to it. This is the way masters of the other arts often work. The novelist and dramatist frequently start with the plot and build up their architectural plan before the characters take on life. or the setting emerges. The painter finds it natural to determine his colour scheme and emotional out-line before he knows exactly what figures are to appear in his fresco. The sculptor blocks out the important bony planes of his bust before focussing on details of features or drapery.

For a composer this way of working requires more con-centrated imagination than for any other artist. But it is capable of accomplishing inestimable results. When Bee-thoven adapted to music this commonplace method of the other arts he performed a creative exploit of the first im-portance.[1]

We have seen how he took the charming, graceful, pol-ished forms handed down to him by Haydn and Mozart, purified them of their superficial formalism, filled them instead with his own generous and fiery spirit, and made them "internal as well as external."[2] "His emotions," writes Mr. H. L. Mencken, "at their highest flight were almost godlike; he gave music a sort of Alpine grandeur."

In sonata-form movements we have watched him make a clean sweep of the star-play of "brilliant passages," the "dish-clatter" of bridge-work, and the cut-and-dried sort of development in which the hearer knew all too well what was coming next because it advanced and retreated like certain armies in the late war, "according to a prearranged plan." We have followed his iconoclastic progress as he remodelled the anticlimactic "cracker-box" type of re-

---

[1] For a most readable discussion of this subject see Newman, *The Unconscious Beethoven*, p. 115 ff.

[2] See Sir Hubert H. Parry's article: "Form," *Grove's Dictionary*, 3d ed.

BEETHOVEN'S FIRST GRAVE,
IN THE CEMETERY AT WÄHRING

capitulation which vainly tried to raise two laughs with the same story. And we have watched him replace it with a new and unpredictable version of the exposition. We have marvelled as he took the ancient coda, which brought the old-fashioned movement to a close as briefly and formally as the word "*finis*," and made of it a glorious and significant thing that sometimes rivalled all the rest of the structure in size, interest, and splendour. This coda exploit was much as though he had found a cathedral consisting of nothing but a large entrance portal, a nave, and a bricked-up transept, in the east side of which there was a tiny door for egress. It was as though he had converted this door into a tremendous breach and had then completed the cathedral with an apse generous and radiant as the choir of Beauvais.

We have seen Beethoven growing all his life progressively farther from the rococo procedure described by Sir Hubert H. Parry:

> Prior to Beethoven, the development of a long work was based upon antitheses of distinct tunes and concrete lumps of subject representing separate organisms, either merely in juxtaposition, or loosely connected by more or less empty passages.[3]

But the Master progressively changed all this. Until, in the last sonatas and quartets,

> the material is so continuous and unified that we are barely conscious of the passage from one theme to another. Sometimes the structure is so closely knit that even the searching eye of an analyst is defied.[4]

---

[3] Article: "Sonata," *Grove's Dictionary*, 3d ed.

[4] Grace, *Beethoven*, p. 214.

This, however, was by no means all that Beethoven did to form. He began with sonatas as long as the Mozart symphonies; went on to make symphonies twice as long as these; and finally, in the *Hammerklavier* and the C sharp minor, lengthened the sonata and the quartet to correspond. Taking a cue from the suite of Bach's day, he increased the prescribed number of quartet movements to six or seven. In a word, he regenerated the formalism of sonata-form and made it a thing of enhanced beauty, vitality, and expressiveness.

Meanwhile he carried his audience along with him; for by some fortunate chance this man appeared at just the moment when music lovers had begun to find their way about in the neatly demarcated sonata-form of rococo days and sighed for more difficulties to conquer.

Those readers who look into Part II, chapter LIV, may follow in detail the development of Beethoven's skill in the use of that interlocking thematic device we have called the germ-motive, by which he, first of composers, brought about complete inter-movement unity in long works.

This development of inter-movement liaison had important results. It led to such unified one-movement sonatas as Liszt's B minor, and to that suppression of pauses between different sections of symphonies which, combined with the influence of the *Pastoral,* ended in the one-movement symphonic poem.

In Part II, chapters LV and LVI, will be found studies of Beethoven's equally remarkable use of what we have called source-motives which lent thematic unity to his life work.

Beethoven changed for the better almost every form he touched. Even such a trivial and crystallized affair as the rondo he diversified, made more spacious, and endowed with elasticity, bringing it closer to sonata-form.

But he was not quite so successful with the strict fugue. He experimented at combining this with other forms. These experiments were seldom entirely happy, because the foreign matter introduced for relief tended to injure the fugue's essential one-ness and make it too diffuse. Yet, after all, this originality was sometimes justified by magnificently satisfying examples, such as the *finales* of the Third Rasoumowsky quartet and of the A flat sonata, the *Et vitam venturi* from the *Missa*, and supremely by the perfect opening of the C sharp minor quartet.

Of all Beethoven's concrete contributions to the art of music three were most original and powerful. There was (1) the first movement of titanic and elemental struggle (*Eroica, Serioso* quartet, Fifth, *Choral*).

There was (2) the *scherzo* of tumultuous humour and Dionysiac exultation or of elfin wit (*Eroica,* First Rasoumowsky, *Hammerklavier, Choral*). He did not invent the name *scherzo*. Haydn first quickened the minuet and called it by this attractive name. But Beethoven took what was handed him; broadened, deepened, elevated, and generally rebuilt it physically, intellectually, and emotionally into one of his most brilliantly original creations.

There was (3) the ethereal slow movement of mystic exaltation (*Choral*, B flat trio, Twelfth, Thirteenth, and Fifteenth quartets, *Benedictus* of *Missa*, and C minor sonata, Op. 111). His supreme *adagios* in variation form decidedly outnumber those in song form.

Beethoven's treatment of the variation-form is singularly interesting: it may be briefly described as a gradual advance back to the methods of Bach . . . in [his] colossal "Goldberg" variations (founded solely on the bass of the theme), which reaches its climax, in Beethoven's works, in the late pianoforte variations on a waltz of Diabelli. In this final aspect of the variation-form the merely melodic connection is secondary or indeed frequently non-existent: harmony and structure are the chief essential points, and though these may be altered to almost any extent, yet there is always, so to speak, the same intellectual thread running through the whole; and in place of the old rigid and merely decorative ideal, we have an ideal of unity in diversity, of the same subject presented in continually shifting and new lights.[5]

Beethoven was elementally original. Whenever the spirit moved him he could squeeze blood out of bricks. And he made rubies of the blood, and platinum of the residue of the bricks, and organized these products into miracles of design that would have put Benvenuto Cellini to shame. He could find laughter, beauty, and wonder in his own blaze of farcical fury over the loss of a groschen. (And he was capable of real fury, as well, on such an original provocation.) He could make an evolutionary epic—or the crack of doomsday—out of the peep of a small bird which was all but inaudible to his deaf ears.

---

[5]Ernest Walker, *Beethoven*, 1920, p. 159.

Mr. John Middleton Murry's statement about the simple originality of Jesus might apply, almost word for word, to Beethoven.

His qualities were all new: his quickness of apprehension, his profound simplicity of speech, his astonishing power of revealing an abysm of meaning through a transparent phrase—these appear before us in a combination so harmonious that we take them, as it were, for granted. They seem natural; and they are natural. Nothing is so new as a new naturalness, none so difficult to apprehend. A new simplicity is the most baffling of all human achievements, and the most perdurable.[6]

One reason why the musical embodiment of Beethoven's emotions was more original than that of his predecessors was this: He thought more deeply than they, and his music represented that deeper thought sublimated into feeling. This music was an unprecedented thing under the sun. In spite of its liberal use of borrowed thematic material, it differed astonishingly from other music. The contrast was almost as sharp as if a winged man had suddenly begun beating his majestic pinions and flashing his irised mail above the stupefied picnickers in the Viennese *Prater*.

It was not merely [writes Mr. W. J. Turner] that music had been more formal in shape, more restricted in content, but that nobody before Beethoven had lived in his music, had imaged his life so fully in music. Earlier composers, Monteverde, Palestrina, Bach, Handel and Mozart, no doubt lived to some extent in their music. But we do not get from it the same impression of personality.[7]

[6] *Jesus, Man of Genius*, 1926, pp. 162–163.
[7] *Beethoven*, 1927, p. 31.

A strong factor in Beethoven's originality was his dramatic power. This was best shown when unhandicapped by librettos, in overtures like *Egmont, Coriolanus,* and those named *Leonore.* The Master could condense more drama into four notes and a pause than Lord Tennyson could get into four acts, a prologue, and an epilogue. He could imply the momentousness of true dramatic suspense and conflict not only by the opposition of *mf* to *ff* and of *sf* to an abruptly following *mp,* but by the contrast with each other of phrases, subjects, sections, movements, and whole works within a group.

In these ways he was a tremendous innovator. And his dramatic sense even extended beyond nuance to a remarkable use of the symbols of literary expression. For example, in a letter to Schindler, 1823, he referred to his next of kin in these terms: "my brother?!"

The unexpectedness of Beethoven—even at the fiftieth repetition—is one of the major clues to his power over us. For he is so extremely unforeseeable, yet after all so inevitable, that we more easily forget how his music goes than in the case of other composers. He tricks us, artfully holds us in harrowing suspense. By implication he strews between the lines of his staves the impalpable largesse of wisdom, of delicate allusion and sheer loveliness, for us to ferret out as we may. He tickles our curiosity by offering two alternative solutions equally plausible, only to settle on a third, undreamt-of but utterly convincing. He mocks our tender emotion by drumming on the keys with the shaft of his ruthless quill and the flat of his great paw. When

[502]

we embark with him on some foaming tide of Gargantuan fun he leaves us abruptly in the lurch.

> And our sincerest laughter
> With some pain is fraught.

He is always surprising, perennially unpredictable. A chief reason why he charms us so completely is that almost every musical expedition on which he allows us to accompany him turns into a hidden treasure hunt—in the right spot.

He left [declares Dr. Dyson] thirty-two piano sonatas and nine symphonies, yet the more intimately they are known the less can one hazard even a guess as to what the thirty-third sonata or the tenth symphony would be like. They would be Beethoven, and that is but the statement of a formal enigma. How many movements they would have, and which would be which; what would be the psychological mood of any or all of them either in detail or as a whole; whether the theme would be slight and the handling sublime; whether there would be an orgy of rhythm or a feast of melody, or both; whether they would follow an old form or invent a new one; all these are matters on which nothing intelligible can be said. He would state, in some new and surprising way, ideas which so soon as they were grasped would seem to be as inevitable as they were unaccountable. We talk somewhat glibly of sonata-form and attach it to the name of Beethoven. There never was a greater deception. It is no doubt possible to extract from his movements two themes and a coda, and to say that here is, or might be, or should be, a double bar, and so forth. But it is often equally possible to extract three or four or five themes, though what will be their order of importance is beyond anyone to lay down. . . . The late sonatas and quartets are admitted to be beyond formal classification. He was descended in a measure from Haydn and Mozart, but it is none the less true that the moment we recognize his models we lose him. The things he himself said were just those that had no place in his inherited architecture. Beethoven is the creative iconoclast.[8]

He had that infectious intensity, that almost superhuman vitality characteristic of the great. His canvases suggest as profuse a lavishness of life as those of Rubens and Rembrandt, of Balzac and Dante and Shakespeare. Yet they are never centrifugal. They reveal instead the economy and concentration of a New Testament parable.

Whatever he may have sometimes been as a man, when it came to music Beethoven was nearly always big. It was not his way to let the notes hide the melody or the details conceal the essentials. What artist of smaller calibre could have stood like a colossus with one foot in classicism and one in romanticism, taking the best of each and fusing them into that higher thing which we have called "Beethovenism"?

Ever since he scrawled those memorable words beneath Moscheles's piano score of *Fidelio*,[9] Beethoven's "Man, help thyself!" spirit has been a growing inspiration to humanity. Since the Great War a strong movement has actually started in Germany and Austria towards a modern religion of strength and self-dependence, with Beethoven as its founder.

But even if he should fail as a prophet and the founder of a new religious order, he is already recognized as a potent

---

[8]*The New Music*, 1923, pp. 121–122.
[9]See p. 349.

physician. There is in his music something for everybody, everywhere, always. He is the healer, friend, and consoler[10] of humanity. If we are sad, tired, agitated, dull, wakeful, blue, bored, faint-hearted, oppressed by ugliness; if we suffer from a torpid imagination or from having the world too much with us, we may find in his music a richer variety of effective antidotes than in that of any other composer.[11] And, having found, we may echo that closing line of Miss Millay's sonnet: *On Hearing a Symphony of Beethoven:*

Music my rampart, and my only one.

After taking a Beethoven cure one understands why this man was the chief consoler and fortifier of the Central Powers in the Great War and of those Allies who were so large-minded as not to let national bitterness taint the world of beauty. One is not surprised to learn that the Bolshevists adopted Beethoven's as the official music of their movement. And one grasps more fully the truth in that remark of his to Bettina: "He who truly understands my music must thereby go free of all the misery which others bear about with them." Would that the poor physician had been able to heal himself!

As a healer he will be found 99 per cent. Jekyll and 1 per cent. Hyde. Like the ideal man of medicine, this man

---

[10]Readers of Proust's great novel will recall that, on the death of the hero's grandmother, her sisters telegraphed the single word "Beethoven." What piece did they have in mind? Was it the *Cavatina*, or the slow movement of the *Pathétique*, "*Apassionata*," Second Rasoumowsky, "*Archduke*," or *Choral*? (*Le Coté de Guermantes*, Vol. II, p. 34.)

[11]See chapter, "The Musical Pharmacy," in *The Musical Amateur*, 1911, and "Directions" and musical recipes in *The Poetry Cure with Music and Pictures*, 1927; both by the author.

almost never spared himself. With incredible faithfulness and courage he kept pouring out his force through his pen until the music was as good as it could be made. As Voltaire said of another artist, "He laboured at every new work as if he had his reputation still to make." The mass of sketches for the C sharp minor quartet alone is staggering to contemplate, especially when one notices the amount of splendid material he set down and then rejected as not good enough. His six false starts on the fourth movement alone make a thrilling object lesson on the conscientious idealism of genius and on the steadfastness and desperation of effort which often goes to the making of immortal things.

Naturally no man's work can be all best; otherwise there would be none of those contrasts on which the very nature of the superlative depends. His personal life was a succession of trough and crest, and his work more or less followed suit. One might graphically show the comparative quality of the nine symphonies by some such arrangement of type as this:

1 2 3 4 5 6 7 8 9

Viewing his whole life work in the large, one can roughly discern something of the same periodicity, though in *largo* time, which one sees in the *presto agitato* ups and downs of his relations with his much-enduring friends. Though his works were not written in the strict order of their opus numbers, these numbers nevertheless form a chronological sequence roughly correct enough for a bird's-eye view. Of Beethoven's first one hundred numbered works (with the single exception of the glorious opus 60's) the successive groups of ten, taken as wholes, oscillate from weaker to stronger and back to weaker. The groups beginning with Op. 10, 30, 50, 70, and 90 all contain better music than those beginning with Op. 1, 20, 40, and 80.

After the Napoleonic Wars a new generation arose which preferred to Beethoven the more easily comprehended music of Italy. The German Master was partially shelved as *vieux jeu*, only to regain his popularity after some years. A century later, in the United States, a similar thing happened to him. During the Great War the "Hun" Beethoven was taboo. And even after peace came the fashion-worshipping youngsters regarded him as a fossil. But before the centenary of his death he was again in high favour. The Beethovens can afford to disregard the fluctuations of fashion and to say, as the Master remarked when told that his work did not please: "It will please some day." Such a person is not for a day "but for all time." He is not for a nation but for all people. To him might better be applied the words of the Chevalier de Boufflers about Voltaire: "This man is too great to be contained in the bounds of his country; he is a gift from nature to the whole earth."

PART II

BEETHOVEN'S WORKSHOP

Chapter LIII

THE BORROWING ALCHEMIST

Prospecting Adventures in Beethoven — True Value of Such Researches — Beauty in the Making — Plagiarism vs. Genial Appropriation — Choice of Subject Matter for Part II — Beethoven Borrows from Haydn and Mozart — From Himself — Foreign Folk Tunes — From Himself — The Rust Imposture — Mozart Fathers the Joy Tune — Echoes in the Last Quartets

PART II is a study of Beethoven's creative processes. It has been written for the musical reader. All others are counselled to skip the next four chapters.

There are few more engrossing, thrilling, or rewarding forms of adventure than a prospecting expedition through the works of Beethoven, in search of indebtedness, loans, inter-movement, and inter-work relationships. Sometimes —though rarely—these are found on the surface. But the most exciting and rewarding discoveries are of those deeply and subtly hidden facts which call for stubborn exertion with spade, pick, and pan.

The writer would again disclaim any fatuous idea of "explaining" a piece of music in tracing the origin or other relationships of its themes. The interest and value of such studies lie in the light they shed on the richness, economy, and variety in unity of Beethoven's creative processes.

These pages show how successfully, how almost unrecognizably, this man could transmute his own earlier ideas and those of others, then use them not only in locking together the parts of a single movement or composition, but to compass scores of works as well into a larger unity.

The study of beauty in the making is valuable both in itself and for the fresh illumination it sheds on finished works of art. Writing of the creative processes of Coleridge, another great and unfortunate genius, one of the foremost scholars of our day declares:

It is because the worth of beauty is transcendent that the subtle ways of the power that achieves it are transcendently worth searching out. . . . For a work of pure imagination is not something fabricated by a *tour de force* from nothing, and suspended, without anchorage in fact, in the impalpable ether of an imaginary world. No conception could run more sharply counter to the truth.[1]

Beethoven was one of those rare men who could miraculously steal a tune and then invest it with dazzling novelty. The writer would no more dream of belittling the originality of such a feat than of attempting to "explain" a sonata or symphony. He agrees with Anatole France that the old distinction between plagiarism and genial appropriation for re-creation might well be revived and furnished with expressive designations, for our present vocabulary is inadequate to deal fairly with such matters.

It is absurd, this quibbling about plagiarisms which the vainglorious Nineteenth Century, with its notorious mania for

[1] John Livingston Lowes, *The Road to Xanadu*, 1927, p. 240.

originality, has invented. Formerly all subjects belonged to everybody and each took his property where he found it. Most certainly the idea of plagiarism existed, but it meant theft committed without talent or intelligence, the clumsy disfiguring of what was taken. In this sense,—the only true one, and which forbids a writer to do less well than his predecessors,—all of us are plagiarists if we amount to anything. . . . According to the merit of each one you can tell almost in advance if he is really a plagiarist. [France is now giving the word its usual derogatory sense.] Sardou is, fatally, because he borrows, and Shakespeare never was, although he stole infinitely more than the other. He struck the entire world for a loan, did Shakespeare! But he had a way with him! The whole thing lies there.[2]

That, as a borrowing alchemist, Beethoven had quite as much of "a way with him" as Shakespeare had, the reader of Part I may already have noted in connection with such works as the Fifth, Seventh, and Ninth symphonies, the *"Memory"* sonata (Op. 110), and the C sharp minor quartet.

The subject matter of Part II was chosen more with a view to freshness than comprehensiveness. Without wholly neglecting the discoveries of Grove, Nottebohm, Helm, Riemann, Marliave, Cassirer, Ernest, Frimmel,[3] and others, the available space has been chiefly given to those discoveries made by the writer and his liberal friends, which have not yet been announced in print.

Beethoven's predecessors wrought very much in the generous spirit of the old mastersinging cobbler of *Rothenburg*

---

[2]Nicolas Segur, *Conversations avec Anatole France,* 1925, p. 53.

[3]An able article on this subject will be found in Frimmel's *Beethoven Handbuch,* 1926, Vol. I, p. 11.

ob der Tauber. An inscription on the front of his house is still to be deciphered.

> *Im Hause meiner Väter*
> *Klopf ich allhier das Leder,*
> *Und Mache meinen Reim dazu,*
> *Ich sorge nicht wer's nach mir thu'.*

> . . . .

> (Here in the house of my *paters*
> I hammer and hammer on leather,
> And thread my rhymes together,
> Careless of imitators.)

If Bach, Handel, Haydn, and Mozart were "careless of imitators," who was Beethoven to refuse such bounty? Light-heartedly and light-fingeredly he took his tune where he found it.

This chapter will not attempt to exhaust the subject of Beethoven's thematic indebtedness to his predecessors and to himself. A full treatment of this interesting field might call for additional volumes.

The opening theme of the F minor piano sonata (Op. 2) can be traced back, as we have already seen on p. 222, to the *finale* of Mozart's G minor symphony. Because this arpeggio motive was a favourite with the Mannheim school of composition it was known as the "Mannheim rocket." But, as it can be traced still further back, to the first piano sonata in F minor of the Hamburg master Philipp Emanuel Bach, perhaps it should be known instead as the "Hamburg rocket." Note that these sonatas are in the same key.

The *finale* of the C minor string quartet (Op. 18, No. 4) owes an unpayable debt to Haydn's famous *Gipsy Rondo;* and, as we have seen,[4] one of "Papa's" best Sunday tunes, from his fifty-eighth sonata, is clearly recognizable in the Trio of the minuet of the A major quartet (Op. 18, No. 5).

Ex. 207

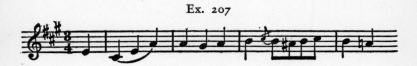

In the opening *Allegro* of the First symphony, the bridge-work between the first and second subjects evokes a vision of scissors, paste, and Mozart's *Don Juan* overture. While the beginning of the *Andante cantabile con moto* is a not wholly legitimate scion of the *Andante* in the same composer's G minor symphony.

It made small difference to Beethoven whether his tunes originated with one of the old masters or with a band of gipsies or his own earlier self. The *Eroica* Funeral March opens

Ex. 26

---

[4]See pp. 369–370.

with more than a suggestion of the most forceful *Allegro* he had, up to 1804, given to chamber music, the start of the C minor quartet (Op. 18, No. 4).

Ex. 208

The theme which opens the *Pastoral* symphony[5]

Ex. 209

appears to have been taken from an old Slavonic folk tune.[6] And strangely enough this same tune is to be found in one of the *Grands,* or wordless songs, of the cattle drovers of Auvergne. Stranger still, M. Canteloube has discovered[7] that the oboe solo at bar 91 of the *Pastoral scherzo* closely resembles an old Auvergne *bourrée;* while the Trio's rough

[5]See p. 262.
[6]See F. X. Kuhac's collection of folk songs, Agram, 1878–1881.
[7]J. Canteloube, *Beethoven et l'Auvergne, Le Courrier Musical*, Feb. 1, 1927.

country dance is curiously like a certain *Montagnarde* of that land.

Earlier in this book it has been asserted that the *"Geister"* trio (Op. 70, No. 1) "sounds like a sort of abridged edition *de luxe*" of the D major sonata (Op. 10, No. 3). Both present the contrast of a magnificent and gloomy D minor *Largo* set between more cheerful, fast movements in D major. The first movements of both begin with themes similar enough to be first cousins. Compare that of the *"Geister"*

Ex. 87

with the opening of the sonata.

Ex. 210

Both commence with resolute unison passages of four bars, the first notes of which run D–C sharp–B–A.

Notice that this theme in the sonata (see Ex. 210) ends with an upward scale like that in the first tune of the trio's *finale* (see Ex. 90). The earlier theme (Ex. 210) apparently held both of these later ones (Ex. 87 and 90) in solution. This sort of relationship also holds, though more distantly, between the first subject of the trio's *finale*

Ex. 90

and the *Menuetto* of the sonata.

Ex. 89

When he wrote the new work Beethoven must, for some reason, have been saturated with the old one. He even used a figure that had occurred once only, and then as if by

[518]

accident, in the recapitulation of the sonata's first movement.

Ex. 211

This recurs almost identically, and with increased importance, in the trio's *finale.*

Ex. 212

The inter-relation of the E flat trio (Op. 70, No. 2) and the E flat sonata (Op. 31, No. 3) has already been mentioned.[8] An additional reason for not making this trio a sonata, as the composer seems to have at first intended, may have been this: He felt that the fast 6/8 movement in each work piled up the resemblance. And he must have seen that the *Allegretto ma non troppo* of the trio

Ex. 213

Allegretto ma non troppo

Viol.

Pfte.

---

[8]See p. 229.

[519]

was too similar in contour and style to the already popular *Menuetto* of the sonata.

Ex. 214

This resemblance between opus 70 and opuses 10 and 31 is but a single rather marked example of Beethoven's growing habit of harking back to his pre-*Eroica* themes and remoulding them "nearer to the heart's desire." The older he grew, the more he seemed to enjoy working over his early ideas. In the *scherzo* of the C minor string trio (Op. 9), this tune—

Ex. 215

is surely a foretaste of the way in which the *finale* of the *Serioso* quartet (Op. 95) was to open.

Ex. 216
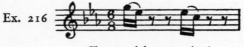

(Transposed for comparison)

But the Master also enjoyed echoing his own recent themes. Notice how in the *"Emperor"* concerto at bar 19 of the first movement the oboes and bassoons bring in a quasi-reminiscence of the second theme of the Violin concerto's first movement. And in the next bar (20) the piano has an echo of another theme in the same movement. At that time Beethoven must have been full of his beautiful, three-year-old violin piece.

It is curious to observe that the *"Archduke"* trio (B flat, Op. 97) begins

Ex. 217

with the Hero theme of the *Eroica* symphony, if one disregards in Ex. 217 the purely auxiliary third note. See also how the end of the second subject of the *"Archduke's"* first movement

Ex. 218

recalls the opening of the First Rasoumowsky quartet:

Ex. 219

In his *Beethoven*[9] and in his editions of T. W. Rust's music M. D'Indy stated that Beethoven had borrowed material from the older composer. Among other particu-

---

[9] Pp. 19, 21.

lars he specified that "the *Adagio* of the sonata for violin and lute [written in 1791], by Rust, bears an astounding resemblance to the melody of the superb *Andante* which forms the middle [*sic*] movement of the trio Op. 97."

Here is the beginning of the Rust movement:

Ex. 220

And Beethoven's *Andante* starts as follows.

Ex. 221

[522]

At first glance, this assuredly looks like borrowing. But if the distinguished French musician had studied the original sketches of the B flat trio and followed there the slow, painful evolution of the immortal theme from some such crude and alien inception as this:

Ex. 222

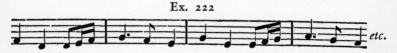

(the reader must supply the treble clef and two sharps, because the Master was far beyond such details), he would have seen that Beethoven had reached his goal independently. For him to have deliberately copied Rust's *Adagio* would have been a curious parallel to the aged Velasquez's act if he had deigned to crib the idea of Guido Reni's canvas[10] for that Venus and Cupid which is now one of the chief treasures of the National Gallery.

The Master's indebtedness to Rust, however, has been disproved much more definitely than the Sketch Books could disprove it. Since the publication of M. D'Indy's *Beethoven* and of his noteworthy prefaces to the modern editions of this so-called pioneer, the researches of Neufeldt have demonstrated that the blameless old T. W. Rust has been turned, in his grave, into an impostor. It now appears that his grandson Wilhelm (one of J. S. Bach's successors as cantor of the Thomas Kirche in Leipzig) deliberately doctored his grandfather's naïve music so that T. W. Rust should seem to have been thematically a most important

---

[10]Now in the Alte Pinakothek in Munich.

precursor of Beethoven and of Wagner; with the result that M. D'Indy was completely duped by the most impudent and amusing imposture in the history of music.[11]

In the first violin part of the *Vivace* of the Seventh symphony

Ex. 223

the writer stumbled upon a phrase which is the ghost of a snatch from the *Egmont* overture.

Ex. 224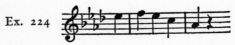

This suggests how, when composing the Seventh symphony in 1812, the Master's mind was still obsessed by his labour of love over *Egmont* two years before.

As this chapter was being revised, Miss Marion Bauer kindly contributed a discovery—the probable source of the D major Joy theme in the *Choral finale*.[12] It is the Trio of the *Menuetto* from Mozart's *"Haffner"* symphony (D major, Köchel No. 385)

Ex. 225

---

[11]The reader may find full information about the sensational episode in T. de Wyzewa, *Beethoven et Wagner*, 1914, p. 173.

[12]See Ex. 169, p. 413.

The *"Haffner"* was composed in 1782. Beethoven probably heard it in the most impressionable part of his youth;
and he was blessed with a tenacious memory.[13] He must have
had the tune in mind, consciously or unconsciously, when
he wrote those songs which were to be the forerunners of
the Joy tune. *To Hope*,[14] besides starting with the same
melodic progression as Ex. 225, is likewise written in 3/4
time. And *Mit einem gemalten Band*[15] even echoes the third
and fourth bars of the Mozart melody, which fall away
in the *finale* of the *Choral*. In its power and breadth and
almost epic "folk" quality the Joy tune contrasts so strongly
with its dainty aristocratic ancestor, the *"Haffner"* tune,
that one is reminded of Lenz's remark: "Between Mozart
and Beethoven came the French Revolution."

Notice the consanguinity between the exciting march
which takes the place of a *scherzo* in the A major sonata
(Op. 101), and the *finale* of the C sharp minor quartet
(Op. 131), and the *Alla marcia* of the A minor quartet
(Op. 132). All three of these movements were destined
to make an almost obsessionary impression upon the sensitive minds of Schubert and Schumann.

The second subject of the opening *Allegro* of the A minor
quartet

Ex. 226

---

[13]Mozart, for his part, had borrowed the melody from Sandrina's aria, *"Una voce
sento al core,"* in his own early opera *La Finta Giardiniera*. Even if Beethoven had never
heard it in the symphony he assuredly had in its embryonic form in the opera.

[14]See Ex. 281, p. 573.

[15]See Ex. 282, p. 573.

recalls the end of the *Allegro con brio's* first subject in the D major violoncello sonata (Op. 102):

Ex. 227

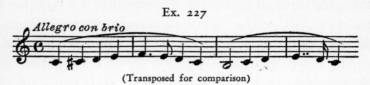

Allegro con brio

(Transposed for comparison)

The *scherzo* of the E flat quartet (Op. 127) starts with a recitative-like enunciation of the theme

Ex. 228

which apparently fathered the recitative passage for the lower strings at bar 92 of the A minor quartet's *Allegro*.

Ex. 229

The curious fact has been apparently overlooked that Ex. 228 is the same tune as the bracketed portions of Ex. 229, but with the accents and time-values shifted.

Another recitative is also reminiscent. When one remembers that Beethoven originally sketched the glorious main tune of the A minor's *finale* to end the Ninth symphony, one cannot wonder that it should be introduced by a recitative recalling those given out by the double basses when they usher in the *Hymn to Joy*.

The theme of the *Andante* interludes in the slow movement of the A minor quartet is actually an echo of "one

[526]

of the German dances written for the Ridotto balls fully thirty years before."[16] This dance is the eighth in A major. Probably through a misprint, Thayer finds it echoed not in the slow, but in the "first" movement. In the *Allegro* a memory of the great A flat sonata has already been noted.[17]

The B flat quartet (Op. 130) gives, in the transition between the first and second subjects of its opening *Allegro* (at the 41st measure),

Ex. 230

a reminder of the second subject of the "*Harp*" quartet's corresponding movement.

Ex. 231

There is also a parallel between the latter work and the C sharp minor quartet. The *Adagio* of the "*Harp*" quartet,

Ex. 232

---

[16]Thayer, Vol. III, p. 215.
[17]See p. 440.

at the second *espressivo*, gives a foretaste of the breathless, inarticulate anguish of the *Cavatina*'s "*Beklemmt*" portion.

Ex. 185

Starting at bar 38 of the first movement of the F major quartet (Op. 135), the accompaniment figure

Ex. 233

in triplets gives a quotation from the F major *Pastoral* symphony—an echo of the start of the *Peasants' Merry-making*.

And the *Es muss sein* theme

Ex. 205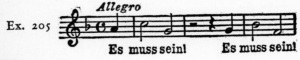

Es muss sein!   Es muss sein!

MOZART

Who said of young Beethoven, "Watch that chap!
Some day he will make the world talk about him"

of the *finale* of this last quartet reverses the beginning of the great A flat sonata fugue

Ex. 234

But let us turn from Beethoven's borrowings to the vastly more interesting subject of his constructive alchemy.

Chapter LIV

BEETHOVEN INVENTS THE
GERM–MOTIVE

Germ-Motive vs. *Source-Motive* — *New Meaning of the Word "Idea" — Beethoven Feels His Way — A Consciously Used Device — Treatment of Germ-Motive in Part I — Progenitor of Leitmotif — Early Experimentation — First Elaborate Use in* Pathétique — *C Minor Quartet — Violin Sonatas A Minor and F Major — Second Symphony — "Kreutzer" Sonata* — Eroica — *"Appassionata" — C Minor Symphony* — Serioso *Quartet — B Flat Trio — Eighth Symphony — A Masterpiece of Camouflage — Beethoven Describes His Own Creative Processes — Initial Germ-Motive in Last Sonatas —* Choral Symphony *— Last Quartets*

To INSURE full understanding of this and the following chapters it is well to recall the distinction between a "germ-motive" and a "source-motive." A germ-motive is a musical phrase which recurs, more or less disguised, in different movements of a composition to lend the whole thematic unity. A source-motive, on the other hand, is a phrase which recurs more or less identically in a number of distinct compositions.

To illustrate: A scrap of tune may—though rarely—confine itself to the retail business of being a germ-motive, like phrase (e) beginning the Eighth symphony.[1] Or it

[1]See p. 547 ff.

[530]

may—almost as rarely—specialize in the wholesale trade of being a source-motive, like the phrase from *Adelaide*.[2] Or, as usually happens, it may carry on both wholesale and retail activities simultaneously, like the rhythmical source-*cum*-germ-motive that opens the C minor symphony,[3] or the triad that begins the main movements of all the other symphonies except the Sixth and Seventh.

Though the writer has been obliged by the poverty of the existing technical vocabulary to coin the expressions germ-motive and source-motive, the nature of what they denote has long been understood. Sir Hubert H. Parry has written vividly upon the function performed by the germ-motive.

Before Beethoven, the development of a long work was based upon antitheses of distinct tunes and concrete lumps of subject representing separate organisms, either merely in juxtaposition, or loosely connected by more or less empty passages. There were ideas indeed, but ideas limited and confined by the supposed necessities of the structure of which they formed a part. But what Beethoven seems to have aimed at was the expansion of the term "idea" from the isolated subject to the complete whole; so that instead of the subjects being separate, though compatible items, the whole movement, or even the whole work, should be the complete and uniform organism which represented in its entirety a new meaning of the word "idea," of which the subjects, in their close connexion and inseparable affinities, were subordinate limbs. This principle is traceable in works before his time, but not on the scale to which he carried it, nor with his conclusive force. In fact, the condition of art had not been sufficiently

[2]See p. 575.
[3]See pp. 152–154 and 540.

mature to admit the terms of his procedure, and it was barely mature enough till he made it so.[4]

In learning to handle the germ-motive, Beethoven felt his way slowly and cautiously, very much as he did in acquiring the technic of any new means of expression, like the quartet, the symphony, or the Mass. He made small systematic use of subtly camouflaged versions of identical germ-tunes, in any type of composition, before he had gone a considerable way in the mastery of that particular vehicle. For example, he did scarcely any inter-movement liaison work before the eighth of the thirty-two piano sonatas, the last of the six trios, the fourth of the ten violin sonatas, the eleventh of the sixteen string quartets. In his symphonies he began earlier, with the Second. But it should be borne in mind that he deferred this composition until his thirty-second year. His vocal writing shows fewer traces of thematic interlocking. Perhaps he felt that the text gave it unity enough.

In reading the manuscript of this book the late Oscar G. Sonneck noted:

I believe that what you call the principle of the germ-motive, one of the fundamental characteristics of Beethoven's creative style, was consciously used by him for the sake of organic cohesion. Of course, Beethoven's having acquired it does not mean that he applied it pedantically to every composition. He probably applied it or not according to occasion, character of work and fitness of things. However, its absence in any work, does not argue against his having acquired such structural principles,

---

[4]Article: Sonata, *Grove's Dictionary*, 3d ed., pp. 828–829.

and against their *deliberate* application, when he considered that advisable.

Throughout Part I of this book the germ-motive has played an important rôle in connection with such highly integrated compositions as the *Sonate Pathétique,* the *Eroica,* the C minor and *Choral* symphonies, and the "*Quartetto Scherzoso*" (B flat, Op. 130). Even if this invention did not represent one of the most important artistic advances ever made in the direction of economy of material and variety in unity, its distinction as the father of the Wagnerian leitmotif would alone entitle it to the dignity of a separate chapter.

By long practice Beethoven learned to conceal his inter-movement liaison devices so deftly that he could join his materials into an organic whole without letting any mortar appear between the stones. The more subtly he performed these secret *coups de maître* the more thrill they impart to their discoverer. The germ-motives which the writer has been fortunate enough to find in the *Eroica* and Eighth symphonies, the *Serioso* and the "*Archduke*" have given him more pleasure than stumbling upon the prophecy of the A flat sonata fugue in the *Eroica,* or the B–A–C–H anagram in the Second Rasoumowsky quartet. For the latter discoveries were more in the class of curious facts, while the former proved to be aids in deepening the understanding, appreciation, and enjoyment of these works by turning new light on the marvellous economy and unity of their variety.

[533]

One of the Master's earliest experiments with the germ-motive took place in the First sonata (Op. 2, No. 1), where the middle section of the *finale* is a modification of the "Mannheim rocket" subject[5] which begins the opening movement. But his first elaborate use of this device was the somewhat obvious one which has already been noted in connection with the *Sonate Pathétique*.[6]

In the C minor quartet (Op. 18, No. 4) Beethoven used an even simpler unifying device than the patent and literal tune-repetitions of the *Pathétique*. This mechanism was to recur in important works like the "*Kreutzer*," the "*Appassionata*," the last sonatas, and the *Choral* symphony. It consisted merely in starting the several main divisions of a composition with the same interval. The first three movements of the C minor quartet begin with a rising fourth (G–C). In a sense both intermediate sections of its rondo-*finale* open similarly. Indeed, in the first and third movements the correspondence is carried even further. For both of these begin with the progression G–C–E flat. This sort of unifying device is so rudimentary that it might perhaps be more suitably called a sub-germ-motive.

As this book goes to press Miss Marion Bauer discovers[7] that the opening phrase of the A minor violin sonata (Op. 23), C–D–E–D–C–B–A is a germ-motive. It recurs in the first themes of the *Andante scherzoso* and of the *finale*.

---

[5] See the transposed Ex. 82, p. 222. Also p. 514.
[6] See pp. 53–55.
[7] Too late to admit of engraving the musical examples.

The same friend finds another germ-motive running through the first subjects of each movement in the "*Spring*" violin sonata (F major, Op. 24).

Although there are attempts in Mozart's G major trio (Köchel No. 496) and his D major quartet (Köchel No. 575) at a thematic interlocking of movements, and although we take into account the liaison work in Beethoven's C minor quartet[8] these violin sonatas occupy in their own sphere the same innovative position which the *Pathétique* holds in piano music and the Second symphony in orchestral. They mark the first mature, elaborate, and fully successful employment of the germ-motive in chamber music.

As we have already seen,[9] the Second symphony employed the triad source-motive extensively as a germ-motive. It also used two lesser germ-motives—and used them much less openly than the triad.

Melodically speaking, the first two measures of the *Larghetto*

Ex. 236

are closely imitated by the third and fourth measures of the *scherzo:*

---

[8]See p. 534.
[9]See pp. 110–111.

Ex. 21

for the upper D in the third bar of Ex. 21 is so orchestrated as to be the melodic note of that chord. The first four measures of Ex. 236 go on to provide material for the opening of the Trio of the *scherzo*.[10]

Ex. 237

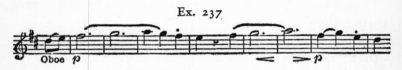

There is small finesse about the *"Kreutzer"* sonata's simple interlocking device. This whole work is built largely on a two-note phrase.[11] The second note falls or rises the interval of a second. This germ-motive first appears (marked by a bracket) in the fourth bar of the slow Introduction,

Ex. 238

---

[10]Ex. 237 was to sire the first half of the Trio of the *Choral* symphony's incomparable *scherzo*. (See pp. 400–401.)

[11]As Mr. Louis von Gaertner has kindly pointed out to the writer.

and soon after in inverted form. It leads off the opening
Presto, inverted in the treble

Ex. 239

but normal in the bass.

The second subject begins with the phrase first rising,
then falling.

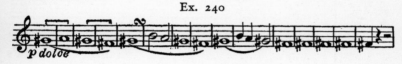

Ex. 240

A large part of the variation theme is made up of these
two notes, in both forms;

Ex. 241

while the same may be said for the opening subject of the
finale.

[537]

Ex. 242

Notice how, at its first occurrence, the motive simultaneously goes up in the violin and down in the piano, while the second subject, like that of the earlier *Presto*, starts with two successive announcements of the phrase, but both times falling.

Ex. 243

Not until the *Eroica* period did the Master learn how to fuse together the parts of a great work so subtly that the means disappeared and only the artistic end—a mysteriously convincing unity—remained apparent. In an earlier chapter[12] we have seen Beethoven arrive at the Hero theme by first telescoping the *Prometheus* theme, and then making the whole symphony revolve around this fundamental tune.

Notice how the *Eroica* is founded almost as completely as the Second upon that germ-source-motive, the triad. Turning back to chapter XVI one may see that this chord

---

[12]See pp. 126–131.

underlies examples 25, 26, 28, 30, 46, 51. While the *Prometheus* theme itself (Ex. 31) seems like an elaborate prelude and postlude to its own triad E flat–G–B flat.

The "*Appassionata*" shares with the "*Kreutzer*" its thematic countersign, the rising or falling interval of a second.[13] Throughout its opening *Allegro assai* much is made of the end of the first subject with its rhythmic premonition of the Fifth symphony in the bass.

Ex. 54

The beginning of the variation theme consists of little else but the "countersign"—the interval of a second.

Ex. 55

[13]For this fact the writer is indebted to his friend, the Dutch composer, Mynheer Julius Roentgen.

And the first subject of the finale—merely its beginning is quoted—

Ex. 244

rigorously follows suit.

The Fifth symphony, like the Second, uses a favourite source-motive as germ-motive. The Second keeps to the triad and the *Pathétique* motive. The C minor is loyal to the triad and the so-called *"Fate"* motive.

Ex. 77

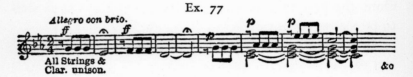

In the first movement this rhythmic formula is absent from but three of the thirty pages of score. It recurs like a faint promise of hope at the 23d bar of the variations. It is hurled in what might be a defiant personal assertion from the 19th measure of the *scherzo*. It raises its voice in something like a frenzy of victorious exuberance at bars 44 and 65 of the *finale;* and reappears in that miraculous echo of the *scherzo* (at bar 160) which seemed to Beethoven's envious contemporary, Spohr, the only part of the Fifth worthy of unreserved praise.

The *Serioso* quartet (F minor, Op. 95) is a masterpiece of secret interlocking. Compare with the first subject of the opening *Allegro con brio,*

Ex. 110

the eight-note motto which introduces the slow movement.

Ex. 245

Omit the first two notes of Ex. 110, and Ex. 245 is seen to be a slow variant of it.

Then consider that memorable fugato, the second subject of the *Allegretto ma non troppo*

Ex. 108

(which, by the way, reminds one of a passage in the slow movement of the C major Rasoumowsky). Prune away its passing notes and it becomes a chromatic variant, as Riemann pointed out,[14] of Ex. 245. And its beginning and end

---

[14]*Streichquartette,* p. 96.

are also seen to be developments of a characteristic little motive from the closing part of the first movement's exposition (bar 52).

Ex. 246
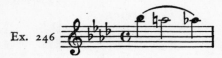

These three notes also furnish the stuff of the coda.

A tempestuous *Allegro assai vivace ma serioso*, does duty for a *scherzo* in this serious work. After the two spasmodic, baulky false starts, and the two long pauses which serve as introduction, the first bars

Ex. 247

might conceivably be taken as a scherzification of the descending portion of Exs. 110 and 245, while the last three notes of these examples are echoed at the notes D flat–E flat–F flat in the chorale-like tune of

Ex. 109

The little ascending motive just mentioned, now transposed and modified into B flat–C–D flat, reappears in Part II of the long tripartite first subject of the *finale.*

Ex. 248

Herr Ernest considers[15] that bars 5 to 8 of that short, happy ending, the final *Allegro,* are a mere jazzing up, so to speak, of the first two measures of Ex. 248 (Pt. I). And Riemann[16] traces a few subtle and minute resemblances between the first three movements. With these exceptions, curiously enough, the inter-movement relationships, which weld the *Serioso* into such a strongly unified personality, seem to have escaped the notice of the commentators. Since the *Pathétique* we have met with no composition but the

[15]*Beethoven,* p. 528.
[16]*Streichquartette,* p. 99 ff.

Eroica that observed such a rigid four-movement economy of material or was thematically so tied up into a single homogeneous parcel.

In the "*Archduke*" trio (B flat, Op. 97) the liaison work, though more varied than in the *Serioso*, is no less skilfully concealed.

The first and second subjects of the first movement run as follows:

Ex. 249

At the start of the *scherzo*

Ex. 250

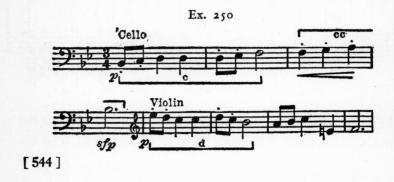

notice how (c) is derived from the last five notes of (a) in
Ex. 249 and (cc) from (a)'s last four notes. Each bar of
(c) also sounds very much like (ab) upside down, while
(d) imitates (ab) with lopsided approximateness.

The beginning of the *scherzo's* Trio

Ex. 112

is an elaboration of the last four notes of (a) in Ex. 249.
It is as if (a) were a snowy hill and Ex. 112 a climber who
slipped back a step for every other step up.

In the *Andante con moto*

Ex. 251

the progression (de) of Ex. 251 amounts to the tune (ab)
in Ex. 249, with a suitable change of rhythm. And the

whole melodic scheme of Ex. 251 may be found summarized in Ex. 250 by humming the second bar of (d) before the first bar of (d).

At the start of the *finale*

Ex. 252

disregard the passing notes of (e), Ex. 252, and notice that the phrase comes from the first three notes of (a) in Ex. 249. The phrase (f) bears a family resemblance to (b), Ex. 249, while the whole of Ex. 252 follows the general contour of Ex. 250.

This enumeration has far from exhausted the germ-motive work in the "*Archduke*." We can only hope the reader himself is as far from exhaustion.

The Eighth symphony is a surprising example of the skill which Beethoven had now developed in the use of his inter-locking invention. With self-effacing thrift he built the greater part of this work out of the seemingly careless and unsophisticated seven bars with which the symphony opens. In the case of the *Eroica*[17] and the "*Archduke*"[18] we have seen how he could group more than one germ-motive into a single subject. His easy mastery of complicated liaison

---

[17]See chap. XVI.
[18]Pp. 544–546.

work grew until he created the long, apparently naïve opening of the Eighth symphony

Ex. 253

as a sort of "host," if one may term it so, for a swarm of little germ-motives. Or perhaps one might better call the start of the *Allegro vivace* the Alma Mater of a blithe crowd of whistling students. Notice how the four-note phrase marked (a) in the melody just quoted reappears all through the opening portion of the second subject.

Ex. 124

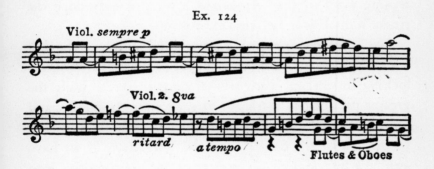

Look again at Ex. 253 and observe that out of the equally short phrase marked (b) is evolved the closing part of the second subject (after the first bar of Ex. 254).

Ex. 254

See the growingly intensive economy of material in the dotted rhythm of bar 1, Ex. 254, which is conjured out of (d), the two middle notes of (b) (Ex. 253).

Consider the hidden spun-sugar-and-white-mice tune,[19]

Ex. 125

which Beethoven, that genial conjuror, produced by sleight of hand from the mouth of the recapitulation. And see how the four-note phrase ending bar 4 is simply (a) standing on its head; a statement which holds just as true of the notes

---

[19]See pp. 323–324.

marked (aa) in the second subject of the *Allegretto scher-zando.*

Ex. 255

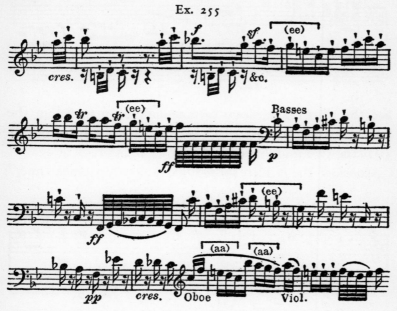

Not content with this, the *Allegretto* phrase marked (ee) closely echoes (e) of Ex. 253.

In its opening measures

Ex. 256

the Minuet is no less faithful to that same Alma Mater example (253). See how (ff) echoes (f), how (cc) copies (c), and (gg) is true to (g). While at the beginning of the Trio

Ex. 257

the (a), (b), and (e) of Ex. 253—marked here (aa), (bb), (ee)—will be found at home, though the last-named is inverted.

The first subject of the *finale*,

Ex. 258

though curiously and ingeniously disguised, gives at (hh) the first six notes of Alma Mater's opening phrase (h). The most ingenious part of the disguise consists in transposing F, the last note of (hh), surprisingly to the octave above by ascending a sixth instead of descending a third. Concealing this virtual identity of the opening themes of the *Allegro vivace* and of the *finale*—themes which are apparently in utter contrast—was one of the most consummately deft strokes of camouflage among all the brilliant feats which Beethoven performed with germ-motives. Except for F sharp instead of F, phrase (dd), Ex. 258, is an echo of (a), Ex. 253, first inverted and immediately afterwards normal. So that this first subject of the *finale* actually turns out to be the Alma mater tune (Ex. 253) rewritten, but so cleverly masqued that it has apparently escaped detection for one hundred and seventeen years. The joke-loving Master must have been immensely pleased with himself when this witty stroke of dissimulation occurred to him.

The second subject of the *finale*

Ex. 259

reminds us with its four diatonic notes (aa) of (a) (Ex. 253). And it reminds us of (i) with its drop of a fifth at (ii).

The third subject

Ex. 260

begins, (jj), with four approximate statements of (j).
The new and unauthorized melody in the coda,

Ex. 126

which we have already discussed,[20] turns out to be simply
the (k) of Alma Mater, begun on a different degree of the
scale, normal in the bassoon and simultaneously upside
down in the oboe.

Now let the reader turn back to that apparently naïve,

[20]On p. 324.

care-free, thoughtless opening tune, Ex. 253, and see with
what thoughtful but unobtrusive thrift almost every bar
of it has been used again and again in the course of the
composition. If Beethoven had written nothing but this
one symphony, such inter-movement liaison work as we
have just considered would of itself place him among the
foremost masters of construction who ever bore the name
of artist.

It is doubtful if any composer with a less prodigious and
trustworthy memory than the Master could have performed
such an exploit as this welding together of the Eighth symphony. What Beethoven told Louis Schlösser in 1823 about
his own habits of composition throws light on the power
and scope of this memory—although the Sketch Books bear
witness that the Master depended more on his pen for recording and developing ideas than the following passage
would seem to imply:

I carry my thoughts about with me long, often very long,
before I write them down. In doing this my memory stands me
in such good stead that even years afterwards I am sure not to
forget a theme that I have once grasped. I alter some things,
eliminate and try again until I am satisfied. Then begins the
mental working out of this stuff in its breadth, its narrowness,
its height and depth. And as I know what I want, the fundamental idea never deserts me. It mounts, it grows in stature, I
hear, see the picture in its whole extent standing all of a piece
before my spirit, and there remains for me only the labour of
writing it down which goes quickly whenever I have time for
it. For I sometimes have several pieces in hand at once, but am
perfectly sure not to confuse them. You will ask me where I
get my ideas. I am not able to answer that question positively.

They come directly, indirectly; I can grasp them with my hands. Out amid the freedom of nature, in the woods, on walks, in the silence of night, early in the morning, called forth by such moods as in the minds of poets translate themselves into words, but in mine into tones which ring, roar, storm until at last they stand as notes before me.[21]

After such complicated feats as he performed with the germ-motives in the *Serioso*, the *"Archduke,"* and the Eighth symphony Beethoven seems now to have reverted for a rest to easier and more overt methods of liaison. In the *Hammerklavier* sonata (Op. 106) he fell back on the simple plan for securing thematic unity which he had used in the *"Kreutzer"* and *"Appassionata"* sonatas. He began all of the four movements with the germ-motive of a rising third. An incident shows the importance he attached to the sort of initial unity thus secured. When the plates were already engraved he discovered that the *Adagio* did not conform. So he sent the present first measure posthaste to Ries for insertion.

Curiously enough this same germ-motive of a third begins all three movements of the next sonata, in E major (Op. 109),

Ex. 261

Vivace, ma non troppo. Sempre legato.

[21]Leitzmann, Vol. I, pp. 253–254.

Ex. 262

Prestissimo.

Ex. 137

Andante molto cantabile ed espressivo.

while the interval of a fourth figures prominently in the outside movements of the A flat (Op. 110), in both principal subjects of the C minor (Op. 111) and in the Ninth symphony as originally planned. The Master's taste in intervals was evidently broadening with age. If he had lived the allotted span we might have had a series of works based on the fifth.

In the *Choral* symphony complexity and subtlety of interlocking treatment returns. For here only one of several

[555]

germ-motives is represented in the device of beginning each movement with a falling fourth.

Notice it in the principal subject of the first movement.

Ex. 160

In the *scherzo* consistency is kept by beginning with the characteristic dotted figure first on D then on A, a fourth below.

Ex. 166

The main subject of the *Adagio molto* also commences with the interval of a falling fourth.[22] The *Choral finale* was an afterthought and does not conform to this scheme. But the melody of the *finale* of the A minor quartet, which Beethoven at first intended to use here,[23] begins with the same countersign as the others. Here is the curious original form in which this melody appeared in the Sketch Books.

[22]Ex. 163, p. 404.
[23]Its finished form as far surpasses Ex. 263 as Ex. 80, p. 221, surpasses Ex. 79.

Ex. 263

In the first *Allegro* there is a significant little motive at the close of the development—this time a rising fourth

Ex. 264

which is almost literally echoed near the beginning of the *Adagio's* coda.

Ex. 265

The preparation for the second subject of the *scherzo* is enough like the slow (4-bar) B major melody at bar 110 of the opening *Allegro* to help inter-movement unity.

The *Andante* part of the slow movement begins

Ex. 266

[557]

with a major version of the same melodic progression as in
that part of the *scherzo* theme marked here with a bracket,

Ex. 267

and in a motive from the first movement (see Ex. 161),
and in the Joy theme, bars 2–3.

Ex. 169

This Joy theme[24] is plainly foreshadowed in the second
subject of the first movement

Ex. 161

and at the beginning of the Trio of the *scherzo*

[24]See pp. 412–415, 524–525 and 572–573.

Ex. 155

It is more subtly hinted at in the third and fourth bars of the *scherzo's* first subject (see Ex. 267) and in the first three of its second subject.

Ex. 268

The Ninth symphony is filled with examples of Beethoven's two favourite types of melody: the scale tune and the chord-arpeggio tune. E. g. the last six themes above are all of the scale type. From which it is evident that M. D'Indy claims too much in stating[25] that "all the typical themes of the symphony present the arpeggios of the chords of D or B flat; . . . one might, therefore, consider this arpeggio as the real cyclic theme of the Ninth symphony." But this does not hold good of any of the second subjects, or of the Trio of the *scherzo*. And it is only true of the Joy theme for an expert rationalizer who gets out of it what

[25]*Beethoven*, p. 114.

he brings to it. M. D'Indy even strains to the point of treating as passing notes all those in the Joy theme which inconvenience his arpeggio theory. And he then proposes that these "secondary notes . . . might be taken to symbolize the fraternal clasp of hands united by the love of mankind"! No such extravaganza, however, is needed to demonstrate the thematic unity of the Ninth.

In the E flat quartet (Op. 127) Riemann pointed out close parallels between the closing section of the variation theme (see Ex. 173, p. 431) and the second subject of the first movement; and between the beginning of the variation theme and the *maestoso* motto which starts the quartet. This learned musicologist also felt that the first part of the *scherzo*

Ex. 228

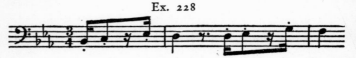

is a modification for *scherzo* purposes of this variation theme. Some analogy doubtless exists, though its apprehension requires rather more than the "bit of good-will on the hearer's part" which Riemann engagingly bespoke. It needs an alert musical imagination. But then, so does every part of this tremendous composition.

In connection with the *"Quartetto Scherzoso"* (Op. 130) the old *Sonate Pathétique* is once more brought to mind, not thematically, but in the way this quartet later on recalls its own slow Introduction. The style in which this manœuvre is accomplished in the sonata, as compared with that in the quartet, gives us a measure of Beethoven's artistic growth. There the Introduction was brought in more formally and mechanically, somewhat as themes from earlier movements are injected into the *finale* of Dvořak's *New World* symphony. Here parts of the Introduction recur again and again throughout the first movement with subtle organic inevitability. The former's opening chromatic passage

Ex. 187

is heard once more, with but little disguise, in the last bar given in Ex. 185, of the *"Beklemmt"* portion of the *Cavatina.*

Ex. 185

This begins with a faltering tune somewhat like the last three bars of Ex. 187.

The enchanting melody of the *Andante con moto, ma non troppo* pops like a fairy from a peasecod out of the lower voices of its own short Introduction. As we shall see in chapter LVI, it is nothing but a source-motive which runs through most of Beethoven's works, turned end for end.

This movement looks

> . . . before and after,
> And pines for what is not,—

and creates the little *presto* second movement out of itself, significantly enough in its own relative minor.

If we regard the first D flat of this *Andante con moto's* germ

Ex. 189

as an Introduction, and disregard the two 32ds as passing notes, and change the rhythm a bit, we have

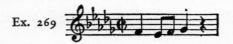

Ex. 269

which is the germ of one of the most irresistibly fetching and roguish little *scherzos* in music. It is a fair example of the subtlety and inevitability which Beethoven had, by the end of his short life, attained in the art of inter-movement thematic dovetailing.

The second subject of the first movement has two measures (marked in Ex. 270 with a bracket, the highest notes
of which echo Ex. 269)

Ex. 270

whose melodic contour resembles an important part of the
second main subject of the Great Fugue which originally
served as *finale* for this quartet.

Ex. 271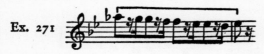

All but the final one of the last five quartets have this
trait in common. They start with either an Introduction or
a principal theme which recurs with more or less frequency
in the body of the work. The upper notes of the Introduction of the A minor (see Ex. 283, p. 573) come back in
the *Alla Breve* part of the *scherzo*,

Ex. 272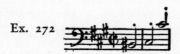

And its bass part is suggested by those sixths yearning upward in the *ritornelles* which act as preludes and postludes

to the chorale of the *Adagio*. It is suggested as well in the first two notes of the *scherzo* (see Ex. 182, p. 441).

In this quartet Beethoven seemed to rely entirely on the Introduction and on the source-motive to be studied in chapter LVI, for inter-movement liaison work.

There is space to describe only two uses as germ-motives of the fugue subject of the C sharp minor quartet (Op. 131).

Ex. 190

Adagio ma non troppo e molto espressivo.

These are two amusing anagrams. In his book on the Beethoven quartets Bargheer pointed out that if the first three notes of the first subject of the sixth movement of the C sharp minor

Ex. 198

Adagio quasi un poco Andante.

are read backwards they give the beginning of Ex. 190. While Helm discovered that by arranging the first four notes of the *finale's* second subject

[564]

Ex. 273

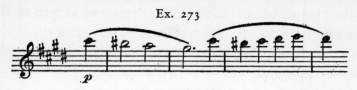

in the order 4–2–1–3 one likewise produced the beginning of Ex. 190.

One may well believe that Beethoven played these tricks deliberately. This prodigious improvisator, this demon for toiling over his material, was not the man to ignore any of its implications, no matter how finely drawn. Besides, one sets at rest any lingering doubts about the latter anagram being unconscious by seeing how the Master rewrote it in the coda:

Ex. 274

From the number of germ-motives which the writer has been fortunate enough to find in Beethoven's music within the short span of four years it may be inferred that there are large numbers awaiting discovery by more painstaking seekers.

Chapter LV

SOME SOURCE-MOTIVES

Source-Motives in Part I — Thrift and Resource — "Certain Musical Pets" — Pathétique Source-Motive — Its Modern Uses — Four Quarters and a Dotted Half — A Motive from Op. 14, No. 2 — Joy Source-Motive — Great Fugue Motive — Adelaide Motive — Triad Habit

FROM the beginning of his career Beethoven used the same source-motive in numbers of different compositions, in such a way as to produce among them a sense of thematic solidarity.

In Part I we have already considered certain small source-motives, such as the sequence of fourths[1] that joins the Fifth Lobkowitz quartet, the *Pathétique,* D major, and A flat sonatas. And we have seen the more ambitious "Fate" motive[2] of the C minor symphony connecting a larger group of compositions.

The longer one studies Beethoven's use of this device, the more he must admire the uncanny thrift and resource that could thus make a limited stock of basic ideas appear illimitable.

In saying that his stock was limited the writer would by no means imply that it was small. Here he cannot agree

---

[1]See pp. 56–57. Too late to mention in Part I, this source-motive was found in the fugue theme of the A flat sonata, (Op. 110, see Ex. 147, p. 372), and near the end of the exposition of the D major sonata (Op. 10, No. 3, first movement).

[2]See pp. 152–154.

with the late Oscar G. Sonneck, who noted on the manuscript of this book: "Isn't the real explanation of such things the fact that every composer, during his whole career, surrounds himself with certain musical pets? They become a habit, good with one composer, bad with others;—the difference between manner and mannerism. *Cum grano salis,* the baggage of every composer contains, at bottom, only a very few distinctly different ideas. These he breeds in endless variety,—or endlessly without variety."

Beethoven did not spread one idea over several compositions through poverty, but because he was actuated by the instinctive economy and constructive insight of the true artist. We shall see that his stock of basic themes which we call source-motives consisted of more than "a very few distinctly different ideas."

If one may judge from the high quality of the works for whose use he reserved it, the familiar germ-motive[3] of the *Sonate Pathétique*

Ex. 275

was also one of Beethoven's favourite source-motives. Like most of his other source-motives, this fragment of tune was not original. It had been used by many of his predecessors, notably by Johann Sebastian Bach in the subject of his A minor organ fugue.[4]

---

[3]See beginning of Ex. 7, p. 55.
[4]*"Eight Short."*

So far as the writer is aware it occurs first among Beethoven's works (as E–A–B–C) in the first subject of the *Adagio con espressione* of his C minor string trio (Op. 9, No. 3). Next, as we have seen,[5] it is found, scattered freely, in the form of the first true germ-motive, through the entire *Sonate Pathétique*.

Soon after it appears as the first four notes (A–D–E–F) of the *"Romeo and Juliet"* *Adagio affettuoso* in the F major quartet (Op. 18, No. 1).

The *Larghetto* of the Second symphony starts with this source-motive transposed to the major.[6]

Ex. 236

But the development section of this movement commences at bar 100 with the pattern in its original minor form (E–A–B–C).

The strange, morbid slow movement of the Third Rasoumowsky quartet (C major, Op. 59, No. 3) commences with the same E–A–B–C, like the scherzo of the A major violoncello sonata (Op. 69). While Part II of the first subject of the *Serioso* quartet's *finale*

---

[5] See pp. 53–55.

[6] The first four measures of Ex. 236 were destined to inspire the Trio of a much later *scherzo*—that in C sharp minor (Op. 39), by Chopin.

Ex. 248

throws off its gray-whiskered mask—and its last note—and turns out to be no other than this same germ-motive of the youthful *Pathétique*—F–B flat–C–D flat.[7]

The third theme of the *"Harp"* quartet's rondo-*Adagio*

Ex. 232

---

[7] Well-known modern uses of this motive occur in both of the Brahms *Rhapsodies* (Op. 79), at the start of the same composer's B flat sextet Variations (Op. 18) and at the words "But nevermore," in that part of Liza Lehmann's *Persian Garden* beginning "Myself when young."

gives this source-motive in its major form. So does the "*Beklemmt*" portion of the *Cavatina*

Ex. 185

from the "*Quartetto Scherzoso*" (Op. 130).
The *finale* of the A major violoncello sonata

starts with a phrase which is a source-motive more by reason of its rhythmic and harmonic scheme than through any strict melodic repetitions. It consists of four quarter notes with suspension in the tonic, followed by a dotted half. We meet it again in the first theme of the F sharp major sonata (Op. 78),

[570]

Ex. 93

and in the opening of the "*Archduke*" trio (Op. 97).

Ex. 276

This motive was taken up by Beethoven's successors, as in the famous *finale* of the César Franck violin sonata,

not to mention such minor pieces as the *finale* of Bargiel's Third trio. (See also p. 181, Ex. 59, first two bars.)

The *finale* of the C major violoncello sonata, which is the only part of opus 102 offering anything like the relief of playfulness or gaiety, starts with a bright tune

Ex. 278

which may have inspired the opening *Allegro* of an overture in the same key, written seven years later, *Die Weihe des Hauses* (Op. 124),

Ex. 279

Allegro con brio.

sf   sf   sf   sf

and may, in turn, have been inspired by memories of the *scherzo* of the G major sonata (Op. 14, No. 2).[8]

The Joy tune in the *Choral* symphony[9] represents one form of a source-motive, traces of which are found scattered through Beethoven's work over a period of thirty years. In the first part of a song, *Seufzer eines Ungeliebten und Gegenliebe* (composed about 1795) a version of this motive begins in the minor. The tune of the second part of this song, *Gegenliebe,* transposed here for convenience of comparison,

Ex. 280

Wüsst   ich,   wüsst   ich,   dass   du

mich   lieb   und   werth ein bis - chen   hiel - test,

was used, 1808, in that weak up-beat to the famous Joy *finale,* the Choral Phantasie (Op. 80).

---

[8]Note that the second full bar of Ex. 278 is identical with the first half bar of Ex. 279; and that the first six notes of 278 correspond exactly with the first six notes of the opus 14 *scherzo.*

[9]See Ex. 169, p. 413.

In 1805 a song *To Hope* (Op. 32)

Ex. 281

and in 1810 *Mit einem gemalten Band* (Op. 83)

Ex. 282

announced still more distinctly the Joy source-motive. We have seen[10] with what brilliant results it was turned into a pervasive germ-motive in the *Choral* symphony.

The A minor quartet (Op. 132) starts with an echo of the original *finale* of the "*Quartetto Scherzoso*" (Op. 130). The first four notes of the Introduction's bass melody

Ex. 283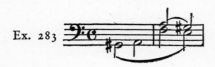

[10]See pp. 558–559.

remind one strongly of the Introduction to the *"Scherzoso's"* Great Fugue *finale*, studies for which had already been made.

Ex. 284

The writer had no sooner noted this discovery than his elation was dashed by finding that he had been long since anticipated by Nottebohm.[11] Herr Bekker points out that the first four notes of the bass tune in Ex. 283, if one transposes the F–E an octave lower, give the start of the C sharp minor fugue (transposed for comparison),

Ex. 285

minus the first note, and come with bar 1 reversed in the *finale* of that tremendous composition. Herr Bekker feels that this motive thus becomes "the leading idea of the whole group of Beethoven's three greatest quartets, and recognition of this fact throws new light on the composer's train of thought."[12] With Herr Bekker's claim that this is the leading idea of opuses 130, 131, 132 it is hard to agree, in view of the fact that a source-motive described in the following chapter of this book appears in these three great

[11]*Zweite Beethoveniana*, p. 5.
[12]*Beethoven*, p. 329.

quartets not four but twelve times.[13] Beside such emphatic iteration the Great Fugue idea seems subsidiary.

Beethoven's most popular song, *Adelaide*, contains a modest source-motive.

Ex. 286   A - de - la - i - de

This reappears in the 36th bar of the "*Harp*" quartet's *Adagio*.[14]

Ex. 287

And here it is again in the *Andante con moto* of the "*Quartetto Scherzoso*," as it suddenly winked at the author one day out of bar 29:

Ex. 288

We have already remarked Beethoven's liberal use of the triad as a germ-motive in such works as the Second, *Eroica*, and *Choral* symphonies. Beethoven lived in an age in which

---

[13]It recurs nineteen times in the last five quartets.
[14]As discovered by Miss Marion Bauer.

it was as natural for composers to use the triad and the diatonic scale for subject matter as it is for the composers of to-day to use chromaticism, polytonality, and atonality. It was natural for Beethoven to found much of his music on chord-arpeggio and scale progressions. The astonishing thing is that he could use these simple patterns over and over so often and yet be so rich and resourceful as to conceal the frequency of his essential repetitions.

All through life he had the triad tune habit. Both opus 1 and opus 2 began with chord-arpeggio tunes; and so did the last movement he ever finished, the new *finale* of the *"Quartetto Scherzoso."* The triad habit, however, was especially marked during the central part of his career, beginning with the *Entrata* of the Serenade (Op. 25), running on through the *scherzo* of the E flat Fantasia sonata (Op. 27, No. 1), the openings of the C minor violin sonata (Op. 30, No. 2), and of the first two movements of the D minor piano sonata (Op. 31, No. 2). This source-motive carries through the first *Andante* of the *Prometheus* music (Op. 43), the openings of *Adelaide* (Op. 46), the *"Kreutzer"* (Op. 47), *The Praise of God in Nature* (Op. 48, No. 4), and the *"Appassionata"* (Op. 57). The triad runs through the two middle movements of the F major and the first movement of the E minor quartet (Op. 59, Nos. 1 and 2), and the *finales* of the G major and D major concertos (Op. 58 and 61). The Fifth and Seventh symphonies, the *"Emperor"* concerto, the *"Harp"* quartet, the wind sextet, and *Fidelio* are full of it.

It is fitting that Beethoven, the heart of music, should

[576]

have built so much of his life work upon the bed rock of this compact source-motive. In so doing he also emphasized for succeeding generations the basic principle of the art—economy of material.

On the part of certain types of musician the writer has noticed a curious reluctance to believe that Beethoven consciously used the source-motive. True, they are bound to admit that he consciously used the germ-motive in such obvious places as the Fifth symphony, and that these uses were triumphs of constructive skill. But they hold that the conscious employment of the same motive in different works—no matter how subtly disguised—argues an unworthy strain of artifice. How the conscious use of a favourite motive in various movements of the same work can be artistic, while its use in various movements of different works is artificial, they do not explain.

This inconsistency is perhaps based on a conservative bias against any new light shed on the processes of the creative minds of old. The long-accepted ideas about them have crystallized almost to the rigidity of religious dogmas, and any others are branded at sight as sacrilegious. The less creative critics seldom realize clearly that not until the final stage of the composition of a work—as Beethoven's Sketch Books bear witness—does artifice flower into art. Oftentimes the more spontaneous the final product appears, the more of conscious calculation has gone to its making.[15]

---

[15]See Professor Lowes' illuminating words, p. 512.

Chapter LVI

A CHIEF SOURCE–MOTIVE OF
BEETHOVEN

"If we are rifling the urns where the dead bones of fact
have long quietly rested, it is because the unquenchable spirit
which gives beauty for ashes is there not wholly past finding
out."
—John Livingston Lowes, *The Road to Xanadu.*

*Economy of Material — Variety in Unity — Originality
and Uniqueness not Claimed for Motive — Fertility of
Creative Resources — Relative Frequency of Motive in His
Symphonies, Sonatas, Etc. — Was Its Use Conscious? —
Devices for Concealment — The Formula Stated — Traced
through Entire Life Work — Its Protean Nature — Con-
scious Employment — Beethoven as an Improvisator —
Improvises on This Motive — Inter-Resemblance of Cer-
tain Uses — Newman's Three Notes — His Theory of
Beethoven's Unconsciousness — Employment of Source-
Motive by Other Composers — Object of This Chapter
— The Anagram Idea — Implications*

We have already seen how and why Beethoven used the
source-motive. In order to realize more vividly his grasp
of two principles basic to art—economy of material, and
variety in unity—let us trace in detail through his whole
life-work one of his favourite source-motives. The writer
is far from claiming that Beethoven invented this particular
pattern of notes or from positively asserting that it was

[578]

used by him with unique frequency. The object of the present chapter is merely to demonstrate how richly fertile were his creative resources.

From long before opus 1 down through opus 135 we shall see him recurring to the pattern nearly one hundred and fifty times for main themes in most of his chief works. This motive occurs in all of his symphonies, in at least twelve out of sixteen quartets, fifteen out of thirty-two piano sonatas, seven out of ten violin sonatas, three out of five violoncello sonatas, and three out of six piano trios. Often it also appears as a germ-motive, repeated several times in the same composition, to give the work inter-movement unity.

The reader's first reaction to such a statement may perhaps be a conviction that if Beethoven actually did use a single idea to the extent described he must have done it unconsciously. For reasons to be given later, the writer holds the contrary view. But whether the Master used the formula consciously or unconsciously, and to what extent other composers may have employed it, are questions which in no way affect the interest or importance of the subject.

It is astonishing and inspiring to see how this greatest of all constructionists could continually utilize the same fairly simple design for almost half a century; yet each time make it so new that the existence of the pattern seems never to have been noticed.

With inexhaustible fertility of resource Beethoven disguised this pattern by changes of accent, rhythm, tempo, tonality, harmony, counterpoint, mode, and instrumentation; by phrasing, diminution, augmentation, turning it upside down or end for end, or both, and beginning it on each degree of the scale.

In essence this source-motive, like so many of Beethoven's themes, is a scale-tune. It consists of a fall of four consecutive notes, joined by a rise of three. In its simplest, crudest form it appears as the opening phrase of the G major sonata for violin* and piano (Op. 30, No. 3)—given twice.[1]

Ex. 289   1802

Observe that this source-motive in Ex. 289 is exactly coextensive with a figure in the first theme of the sonata. As we shall see, Beethoven seldom employed the pattern in this obvious way. Often he made of it an inconspicuous part of a motive, or made it overlap two adjacent ones. If it had been his habit always to let the formula neatly correspond with some figure or motive in his subject-matter, the device would have been instantly apparent to his contemporaries and would have resulted in an intolerable monotony.

The reader may feel that such a motive as this would

---

*Mr. Carl Engel contributes the brilliant suggestion that this source-motive is perhaps a souvenir of "Spangy's" violin-playing years; for it is the typical violin finger-exercise.

[1]For convenience of comparison all examples in this chapter are quoted in C major or A minor. The source-motive is indicated by a bracket, [⎺⎺⎺⎺⎺⎺⎺⎺] . The letter (a) shows that the motive is turned end for end; (b) that it is upside down; (c) that it is both end for end and upside down.

often inevitably be formed in the course of purely scale-wise melody-building. Perhaps; but even so, its frequent inevitability would reflect all the more lustre on the resourceful genius of any composer who hid the fact of its use so often and so successfully. Naturally, if the pattern we are considering occurred simply in passage work, it could be dismissed as merely incidental to the fall and rise of scale passages. But almost every one of the following examples shows it as some significant portion of a main subject in which every note is instinct with momentous meaning.

For the interest of following Beethoven's growing skill in devising new disguises for the formula, the examples will be given in chronological order, with dates of composition, in so far as these have been determined.

This pattern occurs in one of Beethoven's earliest compositions. For, although the second *Bagatelle* is marked opus 33, its first draught was, in all likelihood, written at the age of eleven. The first Trio of this little *scherzo* starts with the source-motive end for end—marked (a)—and followed at once by a normal version of it.

Ex. 290   1782 [?]

In an incidental way it comes into the E flat trio—the first number of Beethoven's first opus, almost as though it had been inserted as a playful afterthought. Just before the

Trio of the *scherzo*, the violoncello discovers this formula hidden in the first subject,

Ex. 291   1795

and brings it out as plainly as it was to appear in the *Lento assai* of the last quartet (see Ex. 354).

Disguised by a minor key and a repeated third note, it figures in effective contrast to Ex. 291, in the first subject of the first movement of the C minor trio (Op. 1, No. 3).

Ex. 292   1795

The beginning of the *scherzo* of the C major piano sonata (Op. 2, No. 3) starts it, though a third higher, in a manner reminiscent of the second and third measures of Ex. 291.

Ex. 293   1796

The opening of the *finale* of the C minor string trio (Op. 9, No. 3) is melodically so like Ex. 292, and rhythmically so like Ex. 293, that it seems incredible the resemblance should have escaped detection for more than a century and a quarter.

[582]

Ex. 294   1798

The *Sonate Pathétique* (Op. 13), in the second subject of
the first *Allegro*, varies the smooth design with phrasing,
shakes, and repeated notes.

Ex. 295   1799

A dotted quarter gives it a quite new complexion in the
finale of the G major string quartet (Op. 18, No. 2).

Ex. 296   1800

In the theme of the variations which open the A flat
sonata (Op. 26), compression within a single bar, a grace
note and a rapid finish constitute as effective a disguise as
any by which Sherlock Holmes astounded his faithful
Schindler, Dr. Watson.

Ex. 297   1802

The Trio of the Second symphony's *scherzo* brings to the motive a fresh rhythmical pattern.

Ex. 298   1802

The grace note worked so well in Ex. 297 that the Master used it in the theme of the *"Kreutzer"* sonata variations (Op. 47).

Ex. 299   1803

Sheer simplicity of announcement long blinded the writer of these lines to its presence in the second subject, *Allegro con brio*, of the *"Waldstein"* sonata (Op. 53).

Ex. 300   1804

In the *"Appassionata"* (Op. 57) the theme of the variations seems at first to be all harmony and no tune. Yet, when analyzed, the source-motive, cunningly oscillating between treble and bass, amounts to this:

[584]

Ex. 301   1804

And now the Master masquerader resolved on a measure too extreme for even Sherlock Holmes. In the *Leonore No. 1* overture (Op. 138) he turned the motive upside down.

Ex. 302   1805

The idea emerges uncompromisingly in the opening movement of the little known F major sonata (Op. 54), as a large part of the second subject. Compare the use of triplets with that in Ex. 294.

Ex. 303   1806

Here it is in Russian costume, claiming much space in the *Theme Russe* of the Second Rasoumowsky quartet's *Allegretto* (Op. 59, No. 2). With a touch of wit, it sounds frequently, though thrice as fast, in the second violin accompaniment.

[585]

Ex. 304   1806

The *finale* of the Third Rasoumowsky quartet in C major (Op. 59, No. 3) shows the first use of this source-motive in a fugue. It starts a degree higher in the scale than in Beethoven's greatest fugue (see Ex. 352).

Ex. 305   1806

This formula might be addressed in the words of the old song as *"Du überall!"* (Thou omnipresent one!) We meet it in the opening subject of the Violin concerto (Op. 61),

Ex. 306   1806

and near the end of the Fifth symphony (Op. 67) in the second subject of the *finale*.

Ex. 307   1808

Four times it appears, in appropriately simple rustic guise, during the first three movements of the *Pastoral* symphony (Op. 68). Ex. 308 gives two different uses of it in a single subject (the second of the *Allegro ma non troppo*).

Ex. 308   1808

Ex. 309   1808

By the Brook. *Andante molto mosso*

Ex. 310   1808

Peasants' Merry-making. *Allegro*

The last three examples offer a clear illustration of the pattern's simultaneous use as source- and germ-motive.

Nothing could well be more obvious than this motive, isolated from its context in the *Adagio* of the *"Harp"* quartet (Op. 74). Yet Beethoven has given it such perfect protective coloration that it melts into the background and almost defies detection.

Ex. 311   1809

In the first movement of the *"Emperor"* concerto (Op. 73) the motive twice becomes a compact half-measure's ornament developed out of the first subject.

Ex. 312   1809

And in the *finale* it shows affinity with Exs. 292 and 294.

Ex. 313   1809

The two following examples veil its identity with naturals in descending and sharps in ascending. The F minor quartet (Op. 95) opens thus

Ex. 314   1810

[588]

As we have seen,[2] the chief germ-motive of this quartet is the motto which ushers in the slow movement.

Ex. 315   1810

Allegretto ma non troppo

The more frequently Beethoven used this formula the harder grew the task of disguising his economy as lavishness and making the well-worn source-motive seem new each time. But his skill grew even more rapidly than the need for it. Until the end he was able to mask the old pattern with such increasingly rich variety that in our day an intelligent critic like Mr. W. H. Hadow could sincerely declare in his essay *Beethoven*: "There is no composer who repeats himself so seldom, who makes less use of the formula." Whereas the fact may be that no other composer of first rank ever made more extended use of a formula in his principal subjects than Beethoven.

This point marks the transition to his third period. Henceforth, instead of merely quoting occasional occurrences of the source-motive, all that the writer has found will be printed, in order to show the triumphant way in which Beethoven solved his increasingly difficult problems of camouflage.

The sombreness of the last two examples turns to gaiety in the *scherzo* of the "*Archduke*" trio (Op. 97), at the end of the first subject,

[2]See pp. 290, and 541-544.

Ex. 316   1811

and to yearning tenderness in the *Andante con moto,* which disguises the motive by repeating three of its notes and turning the whole end for end.

Ex. 317   1811

Immediately after, it appears in the trifling *Marcia alla Turca* from *The Ruins of Athens* (Op. 113, No. 4).

Ex. 318   1811

Now it comes end for end in the "hidden" violoncello theme at bar 39 of the Seventh symphony's dirge-like *Allegretto,*

Ex. 319   1812

and with a message of reassurance in the major part.

[590]

Ex. 320   1812

It lends its voice to the uproarious laughter at the start of the Eighth symphony's *finale*.

Ex. 321   1812

Again, beginning the *finale* of the E minor sonata (Op. 90) it stirs

> . . . the sweet forget-me-nots
> That grow for happy lovers,—

or does anything else of that general nature the hearer likes.

Ex. 322   1814

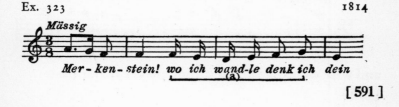

The song *Merkenstein* (Op. 100) gives the motive again end for end, but how differently from Ex. 317!

Ex. 323   1814

In the recurrent introduction of the C major violon-cello sonata (Op. 102, No. 1) Beethoven apparently threw caution aside and gave, in one even measure, as bald a statement of the formula as we have already seen in Exs. 289, 303, or 308.

Ex. 324   1815

In its D major companion sonata (Op. 102, No. 2) the motive occurs more incidentally, at the end of the first subject of the first movement.

Ex. 325   1815

And in the *Adagio* it appears so much more incidentally still that one almost wonders whether Beethoven's all-seeing musical eye had missed it here.

Ex. 326   1815

Again, as we have noticed in Ex. 308, and shall in Ex. 340, the exuberant Master used it twice in a single subject—the fugue of the A major sonata (Op. 101).

[592]

Ex. 327   1816

A slur and triplet lend it distinction in the song *To Hope*
(Op. 94).

Ex. 328   1816

Die   du   so gern in heil'gen   Näch____ ten fei-erst

A pitiable potboiler for flute and piano (Op. 105, No. 2)
reminds one, but not too much, of Exs. 292 and 294.

Ex. 329   1818

Then, in the most dramatic contrast, the source-motive
shows that, without its collaboration, the last sonata (in
C minor, Op. 111) might not have been the miracle it is.
For the familiar pattern looks out at us from a crucial part
of the principal subject of the *Allegro con brio,*

Ex. 330   1822

and from the second part of the perfect melody of the *Arietta*, with repeated notes that remind one of another supreme tune, Ex. 317.

Ex. 331   1822

Glancing back over the amazing transformations this little motive underwent in its first forty years, we see it is like Proteus in Greek mythology, who could at will become an eagle, a mountain, an elephant, roaring fire, flowing water, a mole, a dead leaf spinning down the wind, a lion, a tow-headed child, or a cloud no larger than a man's hand.

Observe the care with which Beethoven varied the pattern even in a small, frivolous song, *The Kiss* (Op. 128).

Ex. 332   1822

Compare Exs. 317, 323, and 340 with this treatment of it in *The Consecration of the House* overture (Op. 124), where it occurs once end for end and once upside down.

Ex. 333   1822

The most significant part of the fugue in the *Diabelli Variations* (Op. 120, Var. XXXII) consists of the motive disguised by repeated notes. Notice how the use of the F sharp in the ascending part is reminiscent of Exs. 314 and 315.

Ex. 334   1823

In the second *Bagatelle* (Op. 126) it appears in sixteenth notes,

Ex. 335   1823

and in the fifth it broadens out into dotted quarters. The last two measures give it upside down.

Ex. 336   1823

The *Choral* symphony is full of the motive. It occurs twice in the opening movement: in the hammer strokes

[595]

of the strong transition phrase between the first and second subjects;

Ex. 337   1823

then in the second subject itself.

Ex. 338   1823

The Trio of the *scherzo*, though notoriously taken from that of the Second symphony (see Ex. 298), makes for the motive, by means of repetition and phrasing, an entirely new rhythmical pattern.

Ex. 339   1823

The Joy theme of the *finale*, like Exs. 308 and 327, contains the motive more than once. The bracket marked (c) shows it upside down and end for end.

Ex. 340   1823

[596]

The first subject of the opening movement of the E flat quartet (Op. 127) has for the author a peculiar interest because it was here he first noticed this source-motive, through its resemblance to the end of the fugue subject of the C sharp minor quartet (Op. 131), which is given as Ex. 352.

Ex. 341   1824

At this point Beethoven performed a brilliantly daring feat. He began the motive on the fourth instead of the sixth degree of the scale, on the second instead of the third beat of the bar, and proceeded to use it undetected in the second subject as well as the first, though the time-signature remained the same. He even dared repeat in both subjects the third note of the pattern.

Ex. 342   1824

Not content with this bit of audacity he used the motive again, end for end, in the theme of the variations.

Ex. 343   1824

And in the first subject of the *finale* he let it bob up again, as impudently fresh as if it were conscious of its own entire uniqueness.

Ex. 344   1824

The Master now seemed to grow fonder and fonder of the source-motive. But, as he used it in these last five consecutive quartets, the problems of disguise accumulated rapidly. Notice how in Exs. 345–350 each employment of it resorted to some disguise of as unusual subtlety as that in Ex. 343.

The A minor quartet (Op. 132) is chronologically next in order. The germ of the opening *Allegro's* first subject is no other than the source-motive upside down and end for end.

Ex. 345   1825

As in the preceding E flat quartet (see Exs. 341 and 342), Beethoven used it in the second subject as well as the first,

here, however, not once but twice. The first time, marked
(b), it is upside down, in almost too-pointed allusion to
Ex. 345.

Ex. 346   1825

The *Molto adagio* theme of the Song of Thanksgiving
also contains it twice, and overlapping—the portion marked
(a) being end for end.

Ex. 347   1825

In this A minor quartet he was consistently topsy-turvy
in his methods of disguise. For the motive comes to light
once more at the end of the main theme of the rondo-*finale*,
upside down and end for end.

Ex. 348   1825

The next example, from the first subject of the *Andante
con moto* of the "*Quartetto Scherzoso*" (B flat, op. 130),
is also end for end.

[599]

Ex. 349   1825

In the famous *Cavatina* of this quartet Beethoven used the motive still more subtly. There is a measure's introduction by the second violin, on the last beat of which the first violin starts the melody a seventh below. The upper voice of the bracketed portion shows the second violin playing the descending notes of the source-motive and the first violin joining in with the three ascending notes. To make the motive thus overlap and bind together adjacent phrases was a truly Beethovenian stroke of camouflage! And at once he used the overlapping device again, repeating the pattern in the second and third bars, upside down and end for end.[2a]

Ex. 350   1825

After these refinements of subtlety the Master ventured out into the open. Compared with the preceding five, his next and last five uses of it were almost childishly obvious.

The Great Fugue (Op. 133) was originally composed as the *finale* of this B flat quartet. The end of the second theme lightly disguises the motive in a dotted rhythm. The F sharp

---

[2a]The motive also appears in the opening *Allegro* (see Ex. 230, p. 527).

is another reminder of the germinal motto of the *Quartett Serioso*, Ex. 315.

Ex. 351   1825

In the marvellous fugue subject of the C sharp minor quartet (Op. 131),

Ex. 352   1826

as in the prolongation of the first subject of the *scherzo*,

Ex. 353   1826

the formula begins on the second beat of a 4/4 measure.[3] But the two are completely differentiated by contrasted phrasing and tempos, and by beginning respectively or the sixth and the second degrees of the scale.

Notice how Beethoven's last use of the motive in a slow movement is reminiscent of its early undisguised statements

---

[3]Compare also Ex. 314. For a more or less similar effect see Exs. 325, 327, and 340.

in Exs. 289 and 344. This is the beginning of the *Lento assai* of the F major quartet (Op. 135).

Ex. 354   1826

What plainer revelation than this could he have made of his long-kept secret? Unless it were the literal quotation from Ex. 352, in the *finale* of this last complete work of his.[4]

---

[4]Without pretending exhaustively to complete the list, it may merely be noted that this source-motive is also to be found in the subject matter of the following compositions:

1795	*Das Liedchen von der Ruhe* (start)	Op. 52, No. 3
1796	Piano sonata F minor (Trio of *Menuetto*, bars 3–4; *finale*, episode, bars 16–17)	Op. 2, No. 1
	Violoncello Sonata G minor (*Allegro Molto*, last part 2d subject)	Op. 5, No. 2
	Adelaide (the first word *A-del-a-i-de* is the upward part of motive)	Op. 46
1797	Piano sonata E flat (1st movement, bars 20–21)	Op. 7
	Rondo C major for piano (Main theme)	Op. 51, No. 1
	Serenade for violin, viola, and violoncello (*Marcia*, 2d part; both *Adagios*; theme of variations)	Op. 8
1798	String Trio D major (*Allegretto*, 1st subject; *Menuetto*, bars 4–6)	Op. 9, No. 2
	Violin sonata A major (beginning of *Andante piu tosto Allegretto*)	Op. 12, No. 2
1800	Quartet (*Adagio*, 1st subject)	Op. 18, No. 1
	Quartet (1st movement, 2d half of 1st bar, end for end; theme of variations)	Op. 18, No. 5
	Quartet (*finale*, 1st subject)	Op. 18, No. 6
	Septet (*Adagio cantabile*, 1st subject)	Op. 20
1801	Quintet (1st movement, 2d subject)	Op. 29
	First symphony (*Andante cantabile*, 1st subject)	Op. 21
	Violin sonata A minor (*Presto*, 1st subject, upside down and end for end; *Andante scherzoso*, 1st subject, upside down; *finale*, 1st subject and simultaneously upside down in the bass)	Op. 23
	Violin sonata F major (opening *Allegro*, start of 1st subject; both subjects of *scherzo*, upside down; main subject of rondo-*finale*, upside down)	Op. 24
1802	Serenade (*Andante*, 2d half of theme; *Adagio*, 1st subject)	Op. 25
	Violin sonata A major (start of *Allegro* upside down; theme of variations)	Op. 30, No. 1
	Violin sonata C minor (*Adagio cantabile*, 1st subject)	Op. 30, No. 2

Ex. 355   1826

Allegro

More than once in the course of the present chapter the reader may have asked himself whether Beethoven used this source-motive consciously or unconsciously. The writer has already stated a belief that his use of it was conscious. Beethoven was the foremost improvisator of his age. One of his

	Piano sonata G major (*Adagio* 1st subject, bars 1–2 end for end, and 5–6; *finale*, 1st subject)	Op. 27, No. 1
	Piano sonata C sharp minor (*Adagio*, bars 12–14 from end; *Allegretto*, 1st 6 bars of 2d part end for end; *finale*, bars 10–11)	Op. 27, No. 2
	Piano sonata D minor (*finale*, 2d subject)	Op. 31, No. 2
	Piano sonata E flat (*scherzo*, bars 10–12)	Op. 31, No. 3
	"*Kreutzer*" sonata (*finale*, 2d intermediate theme)	Op. 47
1803	*Das Glück der Freundschaft*	Op. 88
	Romance G major for violin	Op. 40
1804	*Eroica* symphony (First movement, Episode, violoncello part, bar 284 ff.; Funeral March, second theme; *finale*, bars 365–366 [1st violins])	Op. 55
1805	*An Die Hoffnung* (To Hope) (Notes 4–11)	Op. 32
	Romance F major for violin	Op. 50
	Fidelio (Florestan's aria "*In des Lebens Frühlingstagen*," bars 2–4. Same in all three *Leonore* overtures; Leonora's aria "*Komm, Hoffnung*," first 8 notes, end for end)	Op. 72
1806	Fourth symphony (*Adagio*, first subject, end for end)	Op. 60
1808	Fantasie G minor (theme of variations)	Op. 77
	Fifth symphony (*scherzo*, bars 116–117)	Op. 67
	Pastoral symphony (*scherzo*, bars 95–6, end for end)	Op. 68
	Violoncello sonata A major (*scherzo*, 1st subject, upside down)	Op. 69
	Trio E flat (*Poco sostenuto*, 1st 3 bars, first upside down, then normal)	Op. 70, No. 2
	Choral Phantasie (*finale*, *Allegro*, bars 3–4; *Meno Allegro*, bars 4–6)	Op. 80
1809	"*Harp*" quartet (Second subject of opening *Allegro*; Trio of *scherzo*, bars 80–81)	Op. 74
	"*Emperor*" concerto (*Adagio*, bar 19; *finale* 1st subject, end slightly disguised by chromatic passing notes. A clever masquerade of the motive)	Op. 73
1810	*Mit einem gemalten Band* (bars 2–3)	Op. 83
1825	Canon: "Doctor, close the door to Death."	
(?)	*Rondo a capriccio* (bar 9)	Op. 129

[603]

special gifts was the power to grasp swiftly and unerringly the uttermost implications of any theme. We have seen that, at sixteen, he instantly detected the hidden melody in the subject Mozart gave him for improvisation. As a man of forty we have seen him improvising with marvellous skill from the violoncello part of Steibelt's quintet, which he snatched from the desk in passing and flung upside down upon the piano. His musical reaction period might have been measured by lightning. He was "wax to receive and marble to retain." So that he could remember and accurately reproduce his most lengthy and elaborate improvisations.

There is, indeed, a trustworthy account of his having improvised before friends upon this very source-motive. Castelli[5] relates that in 1819 he attended a banquet in Vienna given by Schlesinger the music dealer. Beethoven was present and, after a great deal of begging, consented to play if he were given a theme. Castelli, who was totally unmusical, went to the piano and with one finger bumped out the following:

Ex. 356

Beethoven laughed, sat himself down and, never once departing from the given pattern, improvised gloriously "for a full hour by the clock."

The reader will at once notice that Castelli's theme is no other than a reversible, two-way version of the source-motive treated in this chapter. One reason for Beethoven's

[5]Ignaz Franz Castelli, *Memoiren meines Lebens*, Vol. III, p. 117. Quoted in Frimmel, *Neue Beethoveniana*, 1890, p. 54.

laughter may have been his ironical recognition of an absurd situation. The tune which was being offered him as an ostensibly brand-new subject was one which he had used for the last thirty-seven years in the principal themes of scores of his works. And his intimate familiarity with this material may also account for the extraordinary length of his improvisation. Every music lover must regret that the piano on which he played that evening was not of the modern recording type.

This was the spirit who brought forth a musical cosmos from a vapid and apparently empty waltz theme, a "cobbler's patch" of Diabelli's,—who wrote the variations of the *Choral* symphony and the E flat quartet. It seems all but incredible that he could have been unconscious of the virtual melodic identity of such phrases as those marked by brackets in the following.

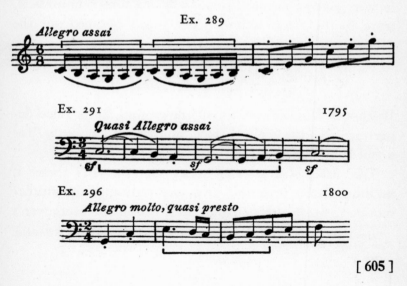

Ex. 289

[605]

It is unlikely that those who know Beethoven will seriously contend that the man who was constantly binding his larger works together by means of germ-motives, with the most subtle sort of inter-movement thematic liaison work, as in the *Eroica* and the F minor quartet, would have missed the identity of the source-motive as given in these two examples.

And if he was conscious of this identity, what more likely than that the creator of those infinitely profound variations in the C sharp minor quartet should have been luminously aware of the common source of the most apparently dissimilar examples given above? For instance, Exs. 297, 305, 307, 317, 330, 334, 340, 351, and 355. To believe that such a man could overlook the occurrence of this identical pattern more than a hundred times in the main subjects of his chief works is to strain credulity.

Such considerations, and a study of the originals of a large number of Beethoven's Sketch Books, have convinced the writer that Beethoven habitually incorporated his thematic material so fully into consciousness as to become

aware of its farthest implications and possibilities. No doubt
the original idea often sprang direct from the unconscious.
But his first thoughts were notoriously far from his best.
Customarily they were obliged to go through a long and
painful period in the *purgatorio* of his active brain before
they were ready for the *paradiso* of his perfect work.

In his charmingly written book *The Unconscious
Beethoven*[6] Mr. Ernest Newman, the dean of critics,
shows how three adjacent notes rise to the emotional climax of many of Beethoven's melodies. This is undeniable.
But Mr. Newman also states that the Master used this
formula thus, unconsciously and with unique frequency.

It is hard to comprehend how any mind so analytic and
so alertly self-critical as Beethoven's could have been unconscious of the significance of a single phrase in any of his
principal subjects.

As regards unique frequency one may find these same
notes (forming a device which the Germans call an *Anlauf*)
ascending to the emotional climax almost everywhere one
looks: whether in folk music (*Londonderry Air*); Handel
(*Angels Ever Bright and Fair, Largo, Hallelujah Chorus*);
Bach (*Air from D major Suite*); Mozart (all four movements of Twenty-second string quartet in B flat); Franck
(First movement of *Prelude, Aria and Finale; scherzo* and
finale of Violin sonata); Wagner (*Siegmund's Love Song*);
Dvořak (*Largo* and *finale* of *New World* symphony).

It took ten minutes to compile the above list—in most
cases, out of the first pieces of the first music makers that

---

[6]P. 71 ff.

came to mind. In thinking through the work of almost any composer chosen at random one seems to find Mr. Newman's phrase performing its special function, as often as in Beethoven. His study of the three ascending notes seems to the writer valuable—but valuable rather for the light it may shed on Beethoven's conscious mastery of the basic principles of art than for demonstrating the workings of his unconscious mind[7] or the uniqueness of the three notes when used as Mr. Newman describes.

The author has tried to put the subject of this chapter impartially through the same test to which he has subjected Mr. Newman's phrase. Necessarily, any pattern so fundamental to melody as this source-motive, or, for that matter, almost any other scale-tune, is often to be found outside of Beethoven; e. g. in Handel's *Largo,* in the first subject of the slow movement of Tschaikowsky's Fourth symphony and the opening phrase of the Saint-Saëns violoncello concerto in A minor. Mr. Frederick Kelsey has pointed out to the writer a powerful employment of it in the *Faith motif* from *Parsifal.*

Ex. 357

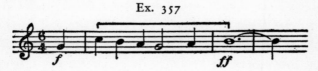

But the motive has probably not been used by other composers with the frequency of Mr. Newman's, because it is twice as long and complicated.

---

[7] In *The Musical Quarterly,* October, 1927, p. 659 ff., Mr. Carl Engel gave cogent reasons for believing that Beethoven used these three notes consciously.

Suppose, however, that the contrary were proved. Suppose that the four-down-three-up pattern occurred thick as hops in the principal themes of all other composers, ancient and modern. This would not in the least upset the argument of the present chapter, which was written to show the personal grasp of variety in unity, the characteristically opulent economy of this musical Crœsus-cum-Diogenes —quite regardless of the question whether or not other musicians have been similarly gifted.

Why did Beethoven use this pattern with such astonishing liberality? Did he perhaps read in it some private musical anagram? We know that, after his day, Joachim adopted the motto F–A–E which stood for *"Frei aber einsam"* (Free but lonely). We know that Brahms bettered his friend Joachim by adapting this into F–A–F, meaning *"Frei aber froh"* (Free but happy). And that each peppered his principal subjects freely with these anagrams.

It is doubtful if this form of notes

Ex. 358

had any such literary equivalent in the mind of the man who, in spite of the *Pastoral* and *"Battle"* symphonies, did as much as anyone to liberate music from the thralldom of literature. The source-motive formula may have had for him some sort of auspicious association. But whether it was anything which he could formulate in articulate terms, we probably shall never know.

Considering the demonstration of alchemy, economy, variety in unity, and constructive finesse which we have observed in the Master's creative processes, we may reasonably surmise that there are still at large in the sea called Beethoven greater secrets than have yet emerged.

APPENDIX

I

HOW TO KNOW BEETHOVEN
THROUGH AUTOMATIC INSTRUMENTS

THIS biography will be a failure unless it helps to interest the reader in forming a closer acquaintance with the supreme pages of Beethoven. It would be an irrelevance to set down, concerning this man's art, so many of these groping conventional symbols called words unless they should persuade men to read, hear, perform, and engrave on their minds the melodies and harmonies of the man who freed music. Thanks to the recent progress of invention it is to-day far easier and less expensive to gain an intimate and adequate knowledge of the Master's music than it was during his lifetime—or even before the Great War.

Curiously enough, Beethoven's fortunes were intimately tied up with a crude forerunner of our modern instruments for the reproduction of music. Maelzel's Panharmonicon was one of the earliest known ancestors of the present-day player-piano and phonograph. And for this pioneer invention Beethoven wrote his *"Battle"* symphony, which, despite its ghastly unworthiness, was the first piece by which he won wide popularity. In thus working with Maelzel the Master helped along that emancipation of the unskilled music lover from the necessity for technical proficiency which, a century later, was to be accomplished by automatic instruments. It is good to know that Beethoven had a hand, even though unwittingly, in the epoch-making liberation of the average man from the need for going to a concert when he wants to hear a particular piece of music.

In our own day the best of Beethoven may be played and intensively studied even by those who have never mastered the arduous and complicated craft of finger technic. They merely

[615]

need access to a good phonograph or automatic piano. In the Introduction the writer has already stated his belief that, "studying these discs and rolls, score in hand, with no limit to the repetition of any desired passage, one can discover, from dawn to dusk, more well-hidden details in a given composition than during a lifetime of casual attendance at concerts."

It is a commonplace that musical performers, from the beginning student to the supreme artist, habitually derive invaluable help from these mechanisms.

A word of counsel to those who have not yet tried mastering the best of Beethoven in this modern fashion. Play the principal themes of a symphony, sonata, or quartet over and over until you have them well in mind. Then see how Beethoven's constructive imagination developed and transfigured these few notes of subject matter.[1] More information about the forms in which Beethoven wrote will be found in the Glossary on pp. 626–635 of this volume.

An attentive use of the improved phonograph and electrically recorded discs will soon bring added enjoyment through growing familiarity with the personalities of the various instruments. Before long even the tyro will, musically speaking, come to tell a hawk from a handsaw by distinguishing the flute from the clarinet, and the bassoon from the French horn.

But do not sit in final judgment on a composition after hearing an old-style disc of it, especially if ground out upon an ancient machine. Although on the one hand the student may derive much benefit and enjoyment from the outmoded apparatus, and although, on the other hand, the latest inventions do not even yet represent the ultimate word in reproduction, it is remarkable how much new richness and how many vital parts of the music—especially the lower tones—are revealed by the

---

[1] The excellent skeleton analyses which begin the pocket scores in the Philharmonia edition point out the germinal tunes on which to concentrate.

new-style phonograph. And the electrical recordings bring out many effects unheard before, besides reproducing far more truly the characteristic tone-colours of such instruments as the oboe, clarinet, piano, and violoncello. Another advantage of the new records is that they are almost uniformly unabridged.

Two recent innovations in this field are particularly useful to those who would like to know the best of Beethoven: the lecture disc by Mr. Leopold Stokowski, introducing the Philadelphia Orchestra's reading of the Seventh symphony; and the brief review of Beethoven's life and works by Sir Alexander C. Mackenzie, printed for the eye upon the two biographical rolls for automatic piano. It is to be hoped that practical educational devices like these may soon come into general use.

The following pages offer a complete catalogue of such of Beethoven's music as has been recorded by three leading American phonograph companies and by three leading American makers of automatic pianos.[2] The first column gives the opus number (when there is one). The second names the composition; the third, the performer. The fourth gives the identifying initial of the make of phonograph record; and the last, that of the autographic piano roll.

Abbreviations Used in the Following List

A = Ampico.
acc. = accompaniment.
arr. = arranged by.
aud. = Audiographic roll.
B = Brunswick.
C = Columbia.
cond. = conducted by.

D = Duo-Art.
movt. = movement.
Orch. = Orchestra.
rec. = recorded but not yet published.
tr. = transcribed by.
V = Victor.
W = Welte-Mignon.

---

[2]All the rolls are autograph recordings by virtuosos. It is deeply to be regretted that the nonautographic rolls which allow the amateur player-pianist to project into the performance the moods and tenses of his own personality are now out of fashion and have all but disappeared from the market.

WORKS WITH OPUS NUMBERS

OPUS	COMPOSITION	PERFORMED BY	PHONO-GRAPH	PLAYER
1—No. 3	Trio, C Minor (*Piano part only*)	Adler		D
2—No. 1	Sonata, F Minor (*Piano*)	MacPherson		D
No. 2	Sonata, A (*Piano*)	Bourne (rec.)		D
	(*1st movt. only*)	Suskind		A
	(*Scherzo only*)	Scionti		W
No. 3	Sonata, C (*Piano*)	Hofmann		D
		Stewart		W
6	Sonata, D (*Piano Primo part only*) (*Piano*)	Bauer		D
7	Sonata, E Flat (*Piano*)	Bauer		D
10—No. 1	Sonata, C Minor (*Piano*)	DeGreef (rec.)		D
No. 3	Sonata, D (*Piano*)	Murdoch (rec.)		D
13	Sonate Pathétique, C Minor (*Piano*)	Murdoch	C	
		Bachaus	V	
		Adler		A
		Bauer		D
		Lamond		W
	(*1st movt. only*)	Bachaus		D
14—No. 1	Sonata, E (*Piano*)	Iturbi (rec.)		D
No. 2	Sonata, G (*Piano*)	Murdoch (rec.)		D
18—No. 2	String Quartet, G	Lener	C	
		Flonzaley	V	
No. 3	String Quartet, D	Lener	C	
	Presto (*4th movt. only*)	Flonzaley	V	
No. 4	String Quartet, C Minor	Lener	C	
	Allegro (*4th movt. only*)	Bauer		D
	Scherzo (*2d movt. only*)	Flonzaley	V	
No. 5	String Quartet, A } (*Theme and Var.*) }	Bauer		D
		Flonzaley	V	
No. 6	String Quartet, B Flat	Lener	C	
21	Symphony No. 1, C	Henschel and Royal Philharmonic Orch.	C	
22	Sonata, B Flat (*Piano*)	Doguereau (rec.)		D

[618]

WORKS WITH OPUS NUMBERS—*Continued*

OPUS	COMPOSITION	PERFORMED BY	PHONO-GRAPH	PLAYER
24	Sonata, F ("Spring") (*Piano and Violin*)	Murdoch, *Piano* } Catterall, *Violin* }	C	
26	Sonata, A Flat (*Piano*)	Landowska		D
		Deering		W
	(*last 3 movts. only*)	Georg Schumann		W
27—No. 1	Sonata, E Flat (*Piano*)	Darre (rec.)		D
27—No. 2	Sonata, C sharp minor ("Moonlight") (*Piano*)	Bauer	V	
		Friedman	C	
		Lhevinne		A
		Paderewski		W
	(*1st movt. only*)	Paderewski	V	
		Paderewski		D
		Hofmann		D
28	Sonata, D ("Pastoral") (*Piano*)	Friedman		D
31—No. 1	Sonata, G (*Piano*)	Leopold		D
No. 2	Sonata, D Minor (*Piano*)	Mero (rec.)		D
	(*1st movt. only*)	Hallet		W
No. 3	Sonata, E Flat (*Piano*)	Brailowsky		A
		Hofmann		W
34	Six Variations on Original Theme in F (*Piano*)	Kleeberg		W
36	Symphony No. 2, D	Beecham and London Symphony Orch.	C	
46	Adelaide (*arr. by Liszt*) (*Piano*)	Lamond (rec.)		D
47	Sonata, A ("Kreutzer") (*Violin and Piano*)	Menges, *Violin* } DeGreef, *Piano* }	V	
		Huberman, *Violin* Schultze, *Piano* }	B	
		Sammons, *Violin* Murdoch, *Piano* }	C	
48	*Die Ehre Gottes aus der Natur* (*Barytone*)	Schorr	B	

WORKS WITH OPUS NUMBERS—*Continued*

OPUS	COMPOSITION	PERFORMED BY	PHONO-GRAPH	PLAYER
49—No. 1	Sonata, G Minor (*Piano*)	Fryer (rec.)		D
No. 2	Sonata, G (*Piano*)	Laffitte (rec.)		D
50	Romance in F for Violin (*Piano Accompaniment*)	Thibaut Benoist	V	D
51—No. 2	Rondo, G (*Piano*)	Schnabel Howard-Jones		A W
53	Sonata C ("Waldstein")	Powell Carreño		D W
54	Sonata, F (*Piano*)	Leginska (rec.)		D
55	Symphony No. 3, E Flat ("Eroica")	Wood and New Queen's Hall Orch.	C	
		Coates and Symphony Orch. Lamond	V	
57	Sonata, F Minor ("Appassionata") (*Piano*)	Murdoch Bauer Bauer (aud.) Levitzky Schelling	C V	D D A W
59—No. 1	String Quartet, F	Lener	C	
No. 2	E Minor	Lener	C	
No. 3	C	Lener	C	
60	Symphony No. 4, B Flat	Harty and Hallé Orch.	C	
61	Violin Concerto, D	Kreisler and Berlin State Opera Orch. cond. Blech	V	
62	Coriolanus Overture, C Minor	Mengelberg and Concertgebouw Orch.	C	
		London Symphony Orch.	V	
67	Symphony No. 5, C Minor	Weingartner and Royal Philharmonic Orch.	C	

WORKS WITH OPUS NUMBERS—*Continued*

OPUS	COMPOSITION	PERFORMED BY	PHONO-GRAPH	PLAYER
		Ronald and Royal Albert Hall Orch.	V	
		Furtwaengler and Berlin Philhar-monic Orch.	B	
		Stoessel		D
	(2 *pianos*)	Suskind and Loesser, cond. Bodansky		A
		Singer		W
	(2 *pianos*)	Singer and Reichmann		W
68	Symphony No. 6, F (Pastoral)	Weingartner and Royal Philhar-monic Orch.	C	
	(2 *Pianos*)	Robinson and Singer		W
69	Sonata, A (*Violoncello and Piano*)	Salmond, *Violoncello* Rumschisky, *Piano*	C	
72a	Leonore No. 3 Over-ture	Wood and New Queen's Hall Orch.	C	
72b	Fidelio Overture	Berlin State Opera Orch.	V	
	Ha! Welch ein Au-genblick! (Act I); Hat man nicht auch Gold beineben (Act I)(Barytone)	Bohnen with Orch.	B	
73	Piano Concerto, E Flat ("Emperor")	Bachaus and Royal Albert Hall Orch. cond. Ronald	V	
74	String Quartet, E Flat ("Harp")	Lener	C	

WORKS WITH OPUS NUMBERS—*Continued*

OPUS	COMPOSITION	PERFORMED BY	PHONO-GRAPH	PLAYER
78	Sonata, F Sharp (*Piano*)	Lamond		A
		Scharrer (rec.)		D
79	Sonatina, G (*Piano*)	Hess (rec.)		D
	(*2d movt. only*)	Hess (aud.)		D
81b	Sonata, E Flat (Adieu, Absence, and Reunion) (*Piano*)	Novaes		D
84	Egmont Overture	Mengelberg and Concertgebouw Orch.	C	
		Victor Symphony Kohlberg	V	W
90	Sonata, E Minor (*Piano*)	Schwarwenka		W
92	Symphony No. 7, A	Weingartner and Royal Philharmonic Orch.	C	
		Stokowski and Philadelphia Orch. with introductory talk by Stokowski	V	
		Strauss and Berlin State Opera Orch.	B	
93	Symphony No. 8, F	Weingartner and Royal Philharmonic Orch.	C	
	(*2d movt. only*)	Stokowski and Philadelphia Orch.	V	
95	String Quartet, F Minor (Serioso)	Lener	C	
97	Trio, B Flat ("Archduke")	Murdoch, *Piano* Sammons, *Violin* Squire, *Violoncello*	C	
101	Sonata, A Major (*Piano*)	Hofmann		W

WORKS WITH OPUS NUMBERS—*Continued*

OPUS	COMPOSITION	PERFORMED BY	PHONO-GRAPH	PLAYER
106	Sonata, B Flat (Hammerklavier) (*Piano*)	Cortot (rec.)		D
109	Sonata, E (*Piano*)	Cortot		D
110	Sonata, A Flat (*Piano*)	Cortot (rec.)		D
111	Sonata, C Minor (*Piano*)	Lamond		D
113	Turkish March from "Ruins of Athens"			
	(*Violin, arr. Auer*)	Seidel	C	
	(*Piano*)	Bauer		D
	(*Piano, tr. Rubinstein*)	Hofmann	B	D
	(*Piano, tr. Rubinstein*)	Novaes		W
	(*Piano*)	Rachmaninoff	V	A
123	Missa Solemnis in D (Mass)	Orpheus Choir of Barcelona, cond. Millet	V	
125	Symphony No. 9, D Minor (Choral)	Weingartner and London Symphony Orch. with vocal soloists and chorus	C	
		Coates and Symphony Orch. with vocal soloists and chorus	V*	
129	Rondo a capriccio, G Rage Over a Lost Groschen) (*Piano*)	Ney Hofmann		A D
130	String Quartet, B Flat ("Scherzoso")	Lener	C	
131	String Quartet, C Sharp Minor	Lener	C	
132	String Quartet, A Minor	Lener	C	
135	String Quartet, F	Lener Flonzaley	C V	C

APPENDIX

WORKS WITHOUT OPUS NUMBERS

COMPOSITION	PERFORMED BY	PHONO-GRAPH	PLAYER
Andante in F ("Andante Favori") (*Piano*)	Landowska		D
	Scionti		W
Albumblatt für Elise (*Piano*)	Reisenauer		W
Farewell to the Piano	Bergere		W
Duet in E Flat (*Viola and Violon-cello*)	Paul and Rudolph Hindemith	B	
2 Bagatelles (*Piano*)	Peppercorn		W
Six Variations on Duet: "Nel cor piu non mi sento" from "La Molinara," G (*Piano*)	Buell		A
Eight Variations on theme: "Tan-deln und Scherzen," F (*Piano*)	Leginska		D
Rondino, E Flat, arr. for violin, Kreisler (*Piano acc. only*)	Charmbury		D
Rondino arr. Kreisler (*Piano*)	Danziger		W
Gavotte, Violin	Kreisler	V	
Gavotte, F (*Piano*)	Bauer	V	
	Bauer		D
Minuet, E Flat (*Piano*)	Fryer		W
	Conradi		W
Minuet, G (*Piano*)	Schnabel		A
(*Piano*)	Leginska		A
(*Piano*)	Fabre		W
(*Piano*)	Daisy Hoffman		D
(*Violin*)	Fradkin	B	
(*Violin*)	Elman	V	
Country Dance No. 1	Gordon		A
Country Dance No. 1 (tr. Seiss) (*Piano*)	Gordon		D
Contra-Danse (*Piano*)	Danziger		W
German Dance No. 1 (tr. Seiss) (*Piano*)	Wilmington		D
German Dance No. 3 (tr. Seiss) (*Piano*)	Powell		D
German Dance C (*Piano*)	Epstein		W
German Dances (*Piano*)	Danziger		W
Ecossaises, E Flat (*Arr. D'Albert*)	Levitzky		A
	Ney	B	

WORKS WITHOUT OPUS NUMBERS—*Continued*

COMPOSITION	PERFORMED BY	PHONO-GRAPH	PLAYER
Ecossaisen	Levin		W
In Questa Tomba (*Song*)	Chaliapin	V	
Ich Liebe Dich (*Song*) (*Piano*)	La Forge		D
Biographical Rolls Nos. 1 and 2	Annotated by Mackenzie (aud.)		D

GLOSSARY

Some Technical Terms Every Music Lover Should Know

APPOGGIATURA: A short note of embellishment suspending or delaying a note of melody.

ABSOLUTE MUSIC: That type of music to which no program or literary interpretation is attached by the composer. Sometimes called pure music.

ACOUSTICS: That branch of the science of physics dealing with the phenomena of sound.

ANSWER: The response to the fugue (q. v.)[1] subject. It resembles that subject but is in another key.

ARIA: One of the more ambitious instrumental forms originally used vocally in the older operas.

AUGMENTATION: Repeating a subject in notes of greater value: halves for quarters, etc. The opposite of diminution.

AUTHENTIC CADENCE: A closing formula consisting of the dominant triad (on the fifth degree) followed by the tonic triad (on the first degree).

BAGATELLE: A short simple composition, usually in song form.

BASSO OSTINATO: A bass part in which the same melodic figure obstinately recurs, as in the Rondo of the *"Pastoral"* sonata, Op. 28, bars 9–16.

BINARY FORM: Two-part form. A movement with two themes.

CADENCE: (From Latin: *cadere,* to fall.) The close (fall) or ending of a phrase, period, part, movement, or work. The harmonic formula by which a phrase or period is ended, giving a sense of temporary or complete finality. Cadences are authentic, plagal, perfect, deceptive, etc.

CADENZAS (Italian for *cadence*): An improvised florid passage usually brought in at or near the end of an instrumental

---

[1]Literally "which see."

movement or vocal aria. In the Eighteenth Century the *cadenza* was the part of the concerto best designed to exhibit the soloist's technical ability, introducing his own development of the subject matter of the movement. Later, not trusting to the powers of the artist, the composer himself wrote the *cadenza*. It is still the custom for composers or performers to compose new *cadenzas* to standard works, such as Kreisler wrote for the Beethoven violin concerto.

CANON: A composition in which a subject sung or played in one voice is imitated note for note in the others, either at the same or at a different pitch. The old-fashioned round is in canon form (e. g., Three Blind Mice).

CAVATINA: A short aria (q. v.). The term is occasionally used for a songlike instrumental piece or movement.

CHAMBER MUSIC: Music meant to be played in a small hall or room by a limited number of soloists, or a group of instrumentalists, such as wood-wind combinations, string quartet, trio, etc., with or without piano.

CHORAL: Psalm or hymn tune. A broad simple song for many voices (chorale).

CHORD: The simultaneous sounding of tones built up in thirds from a given root or fundamental. A three-voiced chord is a triad; four-voiced, a chord of the seventh, etc. To-day chords are sometimes arbitrarily built up in intervals other than the time-honoured thirds.

CHROMATIC SCALE: One which proceeds in half steps.

CODA: A concluding phrase or section added to a vocal or instrumental work, not strictly necessary for completeness, but making a more positive and effective close. It may also occur at the end of a principal section or even of a period.

CONCERTO: In Beethoven's time, an elaborate work for solo instrument and orchestra. In form it is virtually a sonata (q. v.),, usually of three movements.

[627]

CONTRAPUNTAL: Pertaining to counterpoint. Contrapuntal forms are canons (q. v.) and fugues (q. v.).

COUNTERPOINT: (Point against point. Point is an old term for note.) Two or more melodies written to sound simultaneously. Polyphonic or many-voiced style. Horizontal music as opposed to vertical or harmonic music.

CYCLICAL FORM: A composition laid out in a series of movements (as a suite or a sonata). To-day we apply the term to inter-movement thematic relation.

DEVELOPMENT: The working out of a theme, subject, or group of subjects by every device for variation, expansion, etc., at the composer's command. The second section in fugue (q. v.) and in sonata-form (q. v.). Also called free fantasia, development section, or working-out portion.

DIATONIC: A scale proceeding by consecutive tone degrees, or a melody containing no tones foreign to the key.

DIMINUTION: Repeating a subject in notes of shorter duration: e. g., quarters for halves, eighths for quarters, etc. The opposite of augmentation.

DIVERTIMENTO (DIVERTISSEMENT): An early instrumental composition usually consisting of more than four movements, and of a cheerful, entertaining character.

DOMINANT: The fifth step of the scale; dominant harmony, the triad on the fifth degree (e. g. the dominant chord of the key of G major is D–F sharp–A).

DYNAMICS: Contrasts between loud and soft, and progressions from one to the other: one of the means of producing expression in music.

ECOSSAISE: A dance of Scotch origin.

ENSEMBLE: A particular combination of instruments or voices, as chorus, string quartet, orchestra, etc. Team-work of instruments or voices. Chamber music is sometimes called ensemble music.

[628]

GLOSSARY

EXPOSITION: The thematic or subject matter set forth in the first part of a fugue or sonata.

FIGURE: A small melodic tone-group or motive.

FIGURED-BASS: A system of numeral-notation of a bass part to indicate the intended harmony. A stenographic method of writing keyboard music. Also called thoroughbass.

FINALE: The final movement of a composition in several movements.

FORM: The plan of a piece of music. The arrangement of material into symmetrical and effective order, as in the rondo, minuet, *scherzo,* sonata-form movement, etc. (q. v.).

FUGATO: A part of a composition built in the manner of a fugue (q. v.) but not carried out with its complication or completeness. The theme begins in one part and is successively imitated by the other parts.

FUGUE (From Latin: *fuga,* flight): An enlarged and elaborately developed canon (q. v.). The highest form of contrapuntal art. A fugue has a subject (q. v.), an answer (the subject repeated more or less exactly a fifth above), a counter-subject (a theme planned to dovetail contrapuntally into the answer), and episodes developed from the subject matter. Sometimes the first part, or exposition, is brought back with the subject inverted (*see* Inversion), augmented (*see* Augmentation), or diminished (*see* Diminution). The stretto (q. v.), in which the subject is shortened by telescoping in order to build up the climax of the composition, is followed by a coda (q. v.) in which there is often a long organ-point (q. v.) before the final cadence (q. v.). As it may be divided into exposition, developing portion, and recapitulation, it may be regarded as the precursor of sonata-form. Fugues are both instrumental and vocal.

GERM-MOTIVE: A musical phrase which recurs, more or less disguised, in different movements of the same composition; used as an interlocking device to lend the whole work thematic unity. (E. g., the motive G–C–D–E flat which runs through the *Sonate Pathétique. See* pp. 53–55 and 530 ff.)

HARMONY: The science which treats of chords—their construction, inter-relation, and logical progression.

IMITATION: An echoing of the theme in other voice-parts but usually higher or lower than the original statement.

INTERVAL: The distance from one tone to another; the difference in pitch between two tones.

INTRODUCTION: A passage or movement at the beginning of a work, leading up to the principal subject (q. v.) or exposition (q. v.).

INVERSION:

(a) Turning the two tones of an interval upside down.

(b) Changing the position of the tones of a chord so that some other than its root serves as bass.

(c) Reversing the intervals of a melodic line so that they go in contrary motion to their original order.

(d) In counterpoint, exchanging the position of two lines of melody so that, e. g., soprano becomes alto, and vice versa.

KEY: Any particular scale or tone series binding the triads of that scale into a unity through relation to a tonal centre which gives the key its name. "Key" and "scale" are used interchangeably. (Key of D.) (*See* Tonality.)

LEITMOTIF: A term first used by Von Wolzogen in connection with the Wagnerian music-drama. A motive intimately identified with some character, situation, or idea in opera. The lineal descendant of Beethoven's germ- and source-motive.

MASS: A choral setting, with or without accompaniment, of certain portions of the Eucharistic service in the Roman Church. Sung in Latin.

MINUET: A dance of French origin originally consisting of two eight-bar phrases in 3/4 time and of moderate pace. A second minuet was added, contrasted in feeling and usually written in three-part harmony, from which it derived the name Trio. Beethoven speeded this form up and altered it emotionally into the *scherzo* (q. v.).

MODE: A type or species of scale. To-day we have the major and minor modes in all keys, corresponding to the major and minor scales. The term was used in Hindu, Greek, and church music (Gregorian and Ambrosian modes).

MODULATION: The process of changing, in the course of a movement, from one key or tonality (q. v.) to another.

MOTIVE, MOTIF: A short melodic figure or note-group used as a structural basis for developing a composition.

MOVEMENT:

(a) Rhythmic motion.

(b) A principal division of a compound or cyclical work, such as a suite or sonata.

ORATORIO: An extended composition for solo voices, chorus, and orchestra, without stage setting or acting, usually illustrating some sacred subject.

ORGAN-POINT: A stationary bass held for a considerable time, over which other voices move freely. (*See* Beethoven's "*Moonlight*" sonata (Op. 27, No. 2), last movement, *Presto agitato*, measures 152–164. Also opus 28, first movement, measures 1–25.)

PLAGAL CADENCE: A closing formula which consists of the triad upon the fourth degree of the scale followed by the tonic triad (q. v.).

PROGRAM MUSIC: A purely instrumental composition to which a detailed poetic program is affixed by the composer.

RECAPITULATION: The restatement of a sonata or fugue exposition (q. v.). Succeeds the development (q. v.) with certain traditional changes in key relations.

[631]

RONDO: A piece derived from the old round dance in which the main theme or subject is frequently repeated, separated by secondary themes, e. g., on the model, ABACA or ABACADA.

SCALE: A definite succession of tones within an octave, written on successive staff degrees. There are many varieties, ranging from the pentatonic, or five-tone scale of the Chinese, Scotch, and many primitive races, and the modal scales of the Greeks and of the Mediæval Church, to the diatonic major and minor, and chromatic scales in use to-day, as well as the whole-tone scale of Debussy, etc.

SCHERZO: Literally the joke movement. Usually the third movement in the larger instrumental works of Beethoven. Consists of two short sections built on three-part song-form (q. v.). The second section is known as the Trio. The typical Beethoven *scherzo* usually begins fast, light, staccato, and in three-part time. Its Trio often brings in contrasting slower, smoother, and mellower music. This is followed by the more or less literal repetition of the first part.

SEQUENCE: The frequent repetition of the same melodic figure, starting on a different degree of the scale.

SONATA: (From Italian *sonare*: to sound; hence a "sound-piece".) An instrumental composition of three or four contrasting and more or less related movements. Most sonatas are for piano, or for piano and another instrument. Trios, quartets, quintets, etc., are really sonatas for groups of instruments. A symphony is a sonata for orchestra. The first movement is customarily in so-called sonata-form. The second, often a slow movement, is generally in extended three-part song-form. The third is usually in minuet or *scherzo* form. The fourth is frequently in rondo form, occasionally in sonata-form. Variation form may be used in any movement of a sonata.

SONATA-FORM: The form in which the first movement of the standard sonata is constructed. It is a development of the

[632]

three-part song form. The basic material of the typical sonata-form is found in two subjects, each of which may consist of one or more themes closely related by mood and key. The three main divisions of the form consist of:

(1) Exposition:
    (a) First subject in key of tonic, and modulation to
    (b) Second subject in complementary key which is usually dominant, or relative major if (a) is in the minor.
(2) Development: in which these subjects are worked out with much modulation (q. v.), according to the imaginative fertility and technical resource of the composer.
(3) Recapitulation: a virtual repetition of the Exposition with prescribed changes of key (second subject in tonic, etc.).

The following diagram graphically represents the typical structure of sonata-form:

1st Subject Transition 2d Subject		1st Subject 2d Subject
EXPOSITION	DEVELOPMENT	RECAPITULATION

SONG-FORM:
    (a) The small, or simple, in two or three parts;
    (b) the large, or extended, in two or three parts.

(a) is the smallest independent form in use and is so named because it is in the form of a song. Much folk music and many songs are in the small two and three part song forms. The theme from the slow movement of the E major Sonata, Op. 109, is simple, or small, two-part song-form (A+B). Many of the pieces from Schumann's *Album for the Young* and Mendelssohn's *Songs without Words* are in simple three-part song-form (A+B+A). The third part is often a repetition, more

[633]

or less exact, of the first part, and often a coda (q. v.) is added, e. g., Beethoven's Bagatelle in F major (Op. 33, No. 3).

The large two-part song-forms embrace the old dance-forms such as Allemandes, Sarabandes, also Themes for Variations, e. g., in Beethoven's A flat Sonata, Op. 26, and occasionally an entire Beethoven movement, e. g., the last of his Fourth symphony. Many minuets, *scherzos,* and slow movements are in large three-part song-form, e. g. *Adagio* of F minor sonata (Op. 2, No. 1): A+B+A+Coda.

SOURCE-MOTIVE: A musical phrase which recurs, more or less identically, in a number of distinct compositions and produces in the group an effect of thematic unity. (*See* p. 566 ff., chaps. LV and LVI.)

STRETTO: In a fugue (q. v.) a passage in which the subject and answer are introduced in close succession, so as to overlap and crowd upon each other, producing an effect of climax.

SUBDOMINANT: The fourth degree of the scale. Subdominant harmony, the triad on the fourth degree (e. g. in the key of G major, the subdominant chord is C–E–G).

SUBJECT: A melodic figure or phrase taken as a theme for treatment throughout a composition. Used specifically in a fugue and as a general term in all forms of composition. Opposed to Answer (q. v.).

SUITE: A collection of idealized dance tunes put together in contrasting tempos, rhythms, and moods. Also called partita. A precursor of the form of composition in several movements which finds its highest perfection in the Beethoven sonata. Bach, Handel, Couperin, etc., wrote suites.

SYMPHONY: A sonata for large orchestra.

SYNCOPATION: Shifting the accent to the normally weak or unaccented part of the beat or measure and holding it over the strong or accented part, thus robbing the naturally strong rhythmic position of its normal accent. This rhythmic disturbance is often carried over from one measure to another by means of tied notes. See Beethoven sonata, Op. 27, No. 1, *Adagio* bars 13–16; and *Leonore No. 3* overture, first measures of *Allegro*.

THEMATIC WORK: The development of themes (*see* Development).

THEME: A subject of a composition, or part of a subject.

THOROUGHBASS: Loosely, harmonic composition. Also Figured-bass (q. v.).

TONALITY: All relations between degrees of a scale connected with a tonal centre. A key or mode.

TONIC: The first tone of the scale (for instance, G in the scale of G).

TONIC CHORD: The chord based on the first tone of the scale, e. g., G–B–D in the scale of G.

TRIAD: A three-voiced chord, consisting of a root, third, and fifth. Triads are major, minor, augmented, and diminished.

TUTTI: Denotes the entrance of the full orchestra after passages for individual instruments.

VARIATION: The amplification or modification of a given theme. A form of composition called Theme and Variations.

III

BIBLIOGRAPHY

The literature of Beethoven is vast. This list includes the more important works published in book form.

BIOGRAPHIES

1838 WEGELER und RIES: *Biographische Notizen über Ludwig van Beethoven.* New ed. by Kalischer, 1906.

1840 SCHINDLER, ANTON: *Beethovens Biographie* (1st ed.). 3d ed., 1860. New ed. by Kalischer, 1908.

1864–77 NOHL, LUDWIG: *Beethovens Leben.* (3 vols.)

1888 WASIELEWSKI, W. J. VON: *Ludwig van Beethoven.* (2 vols.)

1899 CROWEST, F. J.: *Beethoven.*

1903 ROLLAND, ROMAIN: *Beethoven.* Eng. tr. by B. Constance Hull, 1924.

1904 MASON, DANIEL GREGORY: *Beethoven and His Forerunners.*

1907 CHANTAVOINE, JEAN: *Beethoven (Maîtres de la Musique).*

1908 DIEHL, ALICE M.: *The Life of Beethoven.*
MARX, ADOLPH BERNHARD: *Ludwig van Beethoven:* Leben und Schaffen. (2 vols.)
THAYER, ALEXANDER WHEELOCK: *Ludwig van Beethovens Leben* (Ed. by H. Deiters.) (5 vols. Vols. IV and V ed. by H. Riemann. 2d ed. of Vols. II and III and 3d of Vol. I. ed. by H. Riemann, 1919.)

1911 PAUL BEKKER: *Beethoven.* Eng. tr. by M. M. Bozman, 1925.

1911 D'INDY, VINCENT: *Beethoven.* Eng. tr. by Theodore Baker, 1913.

1913 THOMAS-SAN-GALLI, W. A.: *Ludwig van Beethoven.* 7th ed., 1920.

1920 ERNEST, GUSTAV: *Beethoven.* 3d ed., 1926.
PROD'HOMME, J. G.; *La Jeunesse de Beethoven.*

1921 THAYER, ALEXANDER WHEELOCK: *The Life of Ludwig van Beethoven.* Edited, revised, and amended from the original English manuscript and the German editions of Deiters and Riemann, concluded, and all the documents newly translated, by Henry Edward Krehbiel. (3 vols.)

1922   VON FRIMMEL, THEODOR: *Ludwig van Beethoven.* 6th ed., revised and enlarged.

1925   SCHIEDERMAIR, DR. LUDWIG: *Der junge Beethoven.*

1926   DE HEVESY, ANDRÉ: *Beethoven, Vie Intime.*

1927   GRACE, HARVEY: *Beethoven.*

LUDWIG, EMIL: "Beethoven" (essay in *Kunst und Schicksal*).

TURNER, W. J.: *Beethoven.*

(Undated)   BARTELS, BERNHARD: *Beethoven.*

LETTERS

1901   KASTNER, EMERICH: *Gesamtausgabe der Briefe Beethovens.*

1906–08   KALISCHER, ALFRED: *Gesamtausgabe der Briefe Beethovens.* (5 vols.) (2d ed. by Th. von Frimmel.)

1907–11   PRELINGER, FRITZ: *Gesamtausgabe der Briefe Beethovens.* (5 vols.)

1909   SHEDLOCK, J. S.: *Beethoven's Letters.* (2 vols.) Abridged edition (1 vol.), 1926, ed. by A. Eaglefield Hull.

1923   KASTNER-KAPP: *Ludwig van Beethovens Sämtliche Briefe.*

1927   SONNECK, OSCAR G.: *Beethoven Letters in America.*

MISCELLANEOUS WORKS

1870   WAGNER, RICHARD: *Beethoven.* Tr. by Albert R. Parsons.

1874   VON BREUNING, GERHARD: *Aus dem Schwarzspanier-hause.*

1890   TENGER, MARIAM: *Beethovens Unsterbliche Geliebte nach persönlichen Errinnerunger.* Eng. tr. by Gertrude Russell, 1893.

1891   KALISCHER, ALFRED: *Die Unsterbliche Geliebte Beethovens.*

[637]

APPENDIX

1901   KULLAK, FRANZ: *Beethoven's Piano-Playing.* Tr. by Th. Baker.

1905   VON FRIMMEL, THEODOR: *Beethovens äussere Erscheinung.*

1906   VON FRIMMEL, THEODOR: *Beethoven- Studien.* Pt. I: "Beethovens äussere Erscheinung." Pt. II: "Bausteine zu einer Lebensgeschichte des Meisters."

1908–09   LA MARA (MARIE LIPSIUS): *Beethovens Unsterbliche Geliebte: Das Geheimnis der Gräfin Brunswick und ihre Memoiren.*

      VON FRIMMEL, THEODOR: *Beethovenjahrbuch.*

1909   KALISCHER, A. C.: *Beethovens Frauenkreis.* (2 vols.)

      THOMAS-SAN-GALLI, W. A.: *Die Unsterbliche Geliebte Beethovens, Amalie Sebald.*

1911   UNGER, MAX: *Auf Spuren von Beethovens Unsterblicher Geliebten.*

1913   KERST, F., ed.: *Die Errinnerungen an Beethoven.* (2 vols.)

1919   HUSCHKE, K.: *Beethoven als Pianist und Dirigent.*

1920   LA MARA: *Beethoven und die Brunsviks.*

1921   BILANCIONI, GUGLIELMO: *La Sordità di Beethoven, Considerazioni di un otologo.*

      LEITZMANN, ALBERT: *Berichte der Zeitgenossen: Briefe und persönliche Aufzeichnungen, gesammelt und erläutert.* (2 vols.)

      OREL, ALFRED: *Ein Wiener Beethovenbuch.*

1922   SCHWEISHEIMER, DR. WALDEMAR: *Beethovens Leiden.*

1923   VON FRIMMEL, THEODOR: *Beethoven im zeitgenössischen Bildnis.*

      NOHL, W.: *Ludwig van Beethovens Konversationshefte.*

1924   SANDBERGER, ADOLPH: *Neues Beethoven-Jahrbuch.*

1925   LEY, S., ed.: *Beethovens Leben in authentischen Bildern und Texten.*

      WALDVOGEL, R. VON: *Auf der Fährte des Genius.*

1926   SONNECK, O. G., ed.: *Beethoven:* Impressions of Contemporaries.

1927   ALEXANDRE, ARSÈNE: *Les Années de Captivité de Beethoven.*

BOSSE, GUSTAV (ed.): *Beethoven Almanach der Deutschen Musikbücherei auf das Jahr 1927.*

NEWMAN, ERNEST: *The Unconscious Beethoven.*

SONNECK, OSCAR G.: *The Riddle of the Immortal Beloved.*

SONNECK, OSCAR, G.: *Beethoven Letters in America.*

SULLIVAN, J. W. N.; *Beethoven: His Spiritual Development.*

1928   CLOSSON, ERNEST: *L'Élément Flamand dans Beethoven.*

MASON, DANIEL GREGORY: *The Dilemma of American Music.*

THE MUSIC

1852   VON LENZ, WILHELM: *Beethoven et ses trois styles.* New ed., 1909.

1855   VON LENZ, WILHELM: *Beethoven eine Kunststudie.*

1857   OULIBICHEFF, ALEXANDRE: *Beethoven, ses critiques et ses glossateurs.*

1863   MARX, A. B., *Anleitung zum Vortrag Beethovenschen Klavierwerke.* New ed. by G. Behncke, 1912.

1866   NOTTEBOHM, GUSTAV: *Ein Skizzenbuch von Beethoven aus dem Jahre 1801.* New ed., 1925.

1872   NOTTEBOHM, GUSTAV: *Beethoveniana.*

1880   NOTTEBOHM, GUSTAV: *Ein Skizzenbuch von Beethoven aus dem Jahre 1803.* New ed., 1925.

1887   NOTTEBOHM, GUSTAV.: *Zweite Beethoveniana.* (Both vols. reprinted 1925.)

1890   VON FRIMMEL, THEODOR: *Neue Beethoveniana.*

1895   ELTERLEIN, ERNEST VON: *Beethovens Klaviersonaten.*

1897   COLOMBANI, ALFREDO: *Le Nove Sinfonie di Beethoven.*

WEBER, W.: *Beethovens Missa Solemnis. Eine Studie.* New ed., 1908.

1898   GROVE, SIR GEORGE: *Beethoven and His Nine Symphonies.*

1900   SHEDLOCK, J. S.: *The Pianoforte Sonatas.*

1902   MATTHEWS, J.: *The Violin Music of Beethoven.*

1905   WALKER, ERNEST: *Beethoven.* Amer. ed., abridged, 1920.

1906   DE CURZON, H.: *Les lieder et airs détachés de Beethoven.*
PROD'HOMME, J. G.: *Les Symphonies de Beethoven.* 10th ed., revised, 1926.
VON FRIMMEL, THEODOR: *Beethovenstudien.* (2 vols.)
WEINGARTNER, F.: *Ratschläge für Aufführungen klassischer Symphonien.* (Vol. I.) *Beethoven,* 2d ed., 1916. Eng. tr. by Jessie Crosland, *On the Performances of Beethoven's Symphonies,* 1907.

1910   CHOP, M.: *Ludwig van Beethovens Symphonien.*
CHOP, M.: *Ludwig van Beethoven, Fidelio.*

1912   KUFFERATH, M.: *Fidelio de L. van Beethoven.*
MARX, A. B.: *Anleitung zum Vortrag Beethovenscher Klavierwerke.* New ed. by Eugen Schmitz.

1918   SHEDLOCK, J. S.: *Beethoven's Pianoforte Sonatas.*

1918–19 RIEMANN, HUGO: *Ludwig van Beethovens sämtliche Klaviersolosonaten: Aesthetische und formal-technische Analyse mit historischen Notizen.*

1921   CHOP, M.: *Ludwig van Beethoven, Missa Solemnis.*
HELM, THEODOR: *Beethovens Streichquartette.* (3d ed.)
LOWE, C. E.: *Beethoven's Pianoforte Sonatas.*

1922   MERSMANN, H.: *Beethoven. Die Synthese der Stile.*
TOVEY, D. F.: *Beethoven's Ninth Symphony.*

1923–24 EVANS, EDWIN, Sen'r : *Beethoven's Nine Symphonies Fully Described and Annotated.*
NAGEL, WILLIBALD: *Beethoven und seine Klaviersonaten.* 2d ed. (2 vols.)
SCHMITZ, A.: *Beethovens "Zwei Prinzipi": ihre Bedeutung für Themen- und Satzbau.*

1925   MIES, P.: *Die Bedeutung der Skizzen Beethovens zur Erkenntniss seines Stiles.*
CASSIRER, FRITZ: *Beethoven und die Gestalt: ein Kommentar.*
MILNE, A. FORBES: *Beethoven: The Pianoforte Sonatas.*
WETZEL, J. H.: *Beethovens Violinsonaten.* (In progress.)
MARLIAVE, JOSEPH DE: *Les Quatuors de Beethoven.*

Introduction and notes by J. Escarra. Preface by Gabriel
Fauré. Eng. tr. by Hilda Andrews, 1928.

1926   FRIEDLÄNDER, MAX, PROF. DR.: *Beethoven an die
Ferne Geliebte.*

HADOW, W. H.: *Beethoven's Opus 18 Quartets.*

HERWEGH, M.: *Technique et interprétation . . .
sonates pour piano et violon de Beethoven.*

1927   BEHREND, WILLIAM: *Ludwig van Beethoven's Pianoforte Sonatas.* Eng. tr. by Ingeborg Lund.

(Undated) CZERNY, CHARLES: *Pianoforte Sonatas.* Pt. 4, chaps.
II and III.

KRETSCHMAR, HERMANN: *Beethovens Symphonien
im Führer durch den Konzertsaal.*

NOHL, LUDWIG: *Beethoven (Musiker-Biographien).* (2
vols.)

RIEMAN, HUGO: *Beethovens Streichquartette.*

WORKS OF REFERENCE

1865   THAYER, ALEXANDER WHEELOCK: *Chronolog-
isches Verzeichniss der Werke von Beethoven.*

1922   RIEMANN, HUGO: *Musik Lexicon.* 10th ed.

1925   NOTTEBOHM, GUSTAV: Ludwig van B., *Thematisches
Verzeichniss.* Nebst der *Bibliotheca Beethoveniana,* von
Emerich Kastner, Ergänzt von Theodor von Frimmel.

1926   VON FRIMMEL, THEODOR: *Beethoven Handbuch.* (2
vols.)

1927   GROVE, SIR GEORGE: *Dictionary of Music and Musicians.* 3d ed.

IV

A LIST OF
BEETHOVEN'S PRINTED WORKS

Abbreviations Used in Description

Acc.=Accompaniment.
Alt.=Alto.
Arrd.=Arranged.
Arrt.=Arrangement.
Bsn. = Bassoon.
C.-Bass=Contra-bass.
Cho.=Chorus.
Clar.=Clarinet.
Cor.=French horn.
Eng. H.=English horn.
Fl.=Flute.

Ob.=Oboe.
Op.=Opus.
Orch.=Orchestra.
Pf.=Pianoforte.
Sop.=Soprano.
Str.=Strings.
Ten.=Tenor.
V.=Violin.
Va.=Viola.
Vo.=Violoncello.

Abbreviations Used in Dates

ann.=announcement.
b.=before.
c. = about.
mvt.=movement.

orig. =originally.
prob.=probably.
prod.=produced.
(?) =not certain.

WORKS WITH OPUS NUMBERS

OPUS	DESCRIPTION	DEDICATED TO	COM-POSED	PUB-LISHED
1	Three Trios (E flat, G, C minor) Pf. V. Vo.	Prince Carl von Lichnowsky	1795	1795
2	Three Sonatas (F minor, A, C) Pf.	Joseph Haydn		1796
3	Trio (E flat) V. Va. Vo.		1792 (?)	1797
4	Quintet (E flat) 2 V. 2 Va. Vo.	Count M. von Fries		1797
5	Two Sonatas (F, G minor) Pf. Vo.	Frederick William II of Prussia		1797
6	Sonata (D) Pf. 4 hands			1797
7	Sonata (E flat) Pf.	Countess Babette von Keglevics		1797

[642]

WORKS WITH OPUS NUMBERS—*Continued*

OPUS	DESCRIPTION	DEDICATED TO	COM-POSED	PUB-LISHED
8	Serenade (D) V. Va. Vo.			1797 ann.
9	Three Trios (G, D, C minor) V. Va. Vo.	Count von Browne		1798 ann.
10	Three Sonatas (C minor, F, D) Pf.	Countess von Browne		1798 ann.
11	Trio (B flat) Pf. Clar. (or V.) Vo.	Countess von Thun		1798 ann.
12	Three Sonatas (D, A, E flat) Pf. V.	Anton Salieri		1799 ann.
13	Sonate Pathétique (C minor) Pf.	Prince Carl von Lichnowsky		1799
14	Two Sonatas (E, G) Pf.	Baroness von Braun		1799
15	Concerto (C) Pf. and Orch. (Really the second)	Princess Odescalchi, née Keglevics		1801
16	Quintet (E flat) Pf. Ob. Clar. Bsn. Cor. Arrd. by Beethoven as a quartet for Pf. V. Va. Vo. Also arrd. as string quartet and marked Op. 75	Prince von Schwarzenberg	b. Apr., 1797	1801
17	Sonata (F) Pf. Cor. or Vo.	Baroness von Braun	b. Apr., 1800	1801
18	Six Quartets (F, G, D, C minor, A, B flat) 2 V. Va. Vo.	Prince von Lobkowitz	1800 (1, 6)	1801
19	Concerto (B flat) Pf. and Orch. (Really the first.) (See No. 151)	Charles Nikl Edler von Niklsberg	b. Mar., 1795	1801
20	Septet (E flat) V. Va. Cor. Clar. Bsn. Vo. C-bass.	Empress Maria Theresia	b. Apr., 1800	1802
21	First Symphony (C)	Baron van Swieten	b. Apr., 1800	1801
22	Sonata (B flat) Pf.	Count von Browne	b. end of 1800	1802

WORKS WITH OPUS NUMBERS—*Continued*

OPUS	DESCRIPTION	DEDICATED TO	COM-POSED	PUB-LISHED
23	Sonata (A minor) Pf. V.	Count M. von Fries	1800 (1st 2 mvts.)	1801
24	Sonata (F) Pf. V. Orig. No. 2 in Op. 23.	Count M. von Fries		1801
25	Serenade (D) Fl. V. Va. (See Op. 41.)			1802
26	Sonata (A flat) Pf.	Prince Carl von Lichnowsky		1802
27	No. 1 Sonata quasi una Fantasia (E flat) Pf.	Princess Josephine von Liechten-stein		1802 ann.
	No. 2 Sonata quasi una Fantasia (C sharp mi-nor) "Moonlight" Pf.	Countess Giulietta Guicciardi		1802 ann.
28	Sonata (D) "Pastoral" Pf.	Joseph Edler von Sonnenfels	1801	1802
29	Quintet (C) 2 V. 2 Va. Vo.	Count M. von Fries	1801	1802
30	Three Sonatas (A, C mi-nor, G) Pf. V.	Alexander I, Em-peror of Russia	1802	1803
31	Three Sonatas (G, D minor, E flat) Pf.		1802 (1, 2)	1803 (1, 2) 1804 (3)
32	Song, "An die Hoffnung" (E flat)			1805 ann.
33	Seven Bagatelles (E flat, C, F, A, C, D, A flat) Pf.		1782– 1802	1803
34	Six Variations on an orig-inal theme (F) Pf.	Princess Odescalchi, née Keglevics	1802	1803
35	Fifteen Variations with a fugue, on theme from Prometheus (E flat) Pf.	Count M. Lichnow-sky	1802	1803
36	Second Symphony (D)	Prince Carl von Lichnowsky	1802	1804
37	Third Concerto (C minor) Pf. and Orch.	Prince Louis Ferdi-nand of Prussia	1800	1804

WORKS WITH OPUS NUMBERS—*Continued*

OPUS	DESCRIPTION	DEDICATED TO	COM-POSED	PUB-LISHED
38	Trio (E flat) Pf. Clar. or V. and Vo. Arrd. by composer from Septet, Op. 20	Prof. J. A. Schmidt		1805
39	Two Preludes, through all 12 major keys, Pf. or Organ		1789	1803
40	Romance (G) V. and Orch.		1803	1803
41	Serenade (D) Pf. Fl. or V. from Serenade, Op. 25, revised by composer			1803
42	Notturno (D) Pf. Va. Arrd. from Serenade. Op. 8			1804
43	"The Creations of Prometheus" Ballet, Nos. 1–16		Prod. 1801	1801
44	Fourteen Variations (E flat) Pf. V. Vo.			1804
45	Three Grand Marches (C, E flat, D) Pf. 4 hands	Princess Esterhazy, née Liechtenstein		1804
46	Song, "Adelaide" (B flat)	Friedrich von Matthisson	1795 (?)	1797
47	Sonata (A) "Kreutzer" Pf. V.	Rudolph Kreutzer	Lastmvt. 1802	1805
48	Six Songs by Gellert for Soprano: "Bitten," "Die Liebe des Nächsten," "Vom Tode," "Die Ehre Gottes," "Gottes Macht," "Busslied "	Count von Browne		1803
49	Two Easy Sonatas (G minor, G major) Pf.		By 1802	1805
50	Romance (F) V. and Orch.			1805
51	Two Rondos (C, G) Pf.	Countess Henriette von Lichnowsky (No. 2)		1797 (1) 1802 (2)

[645]

WORKS WITH OPUS NUMBERS—*Continued*

OPUS	DESCRIPTION	DEDICATED TO	COM-POSED	PUB-LISHED
52	Eight Songs: "Urians Reise," "Feuerfarb," "Das Liedchen v. d. Ruhe," "Mailied," "Molly's Abschied," "Die Liebe," "Marmotte," "Das Blümchen Wunderhold "		Most, possibly all, very early	1805
53	Sonata "Waldstein" (C) Pf.	Count von Waldstein	1804(?)	1805
54	Sonata (F) Pf.			1806
55	Third Symphony "Eroica" (E flat)	Prince von Lobkowitz	1804	1806
56	Triple Concerto (C) Pf. V. Vo. and Orch.	Prince von Lobkowitz	c. 1804	1807
57	Sonata, "Appassionata" (F minor) Pf.	Count F. von Brunswick	c. 1804	1807
58	Fourth Concerto (G) Pf. and Orch.	Archduke Rudolph	c. 1805	1808
59	Three Quartets (7th, 8th, and 9th) Rasoumowsky (F, E minor, C) 2 V. Va. Vo.	Count von Rasoumowsky	b. Feb., 1807	1808
60	Fourth Symphony (B flat)	Count von Oppersdorf	1806	1809
61	Concerto (D) V. and Orch. Concerto, Pf. and Orch. Arrd. by Beethoven, Op. 61	Stephan von Breuning Frau von Breuning	1806 1807	1809 1808
62	Overture to Coriolanus (C. minor)	H. J. von Collin	1807	1808
63	Arrt. of Op. 4 as Trio for Pf. and Str.			
64	Arrt. of Op. 3 for Pf. and Vo.			
65	Scena and Aria, "Ah, perfido!" Sop. and Orch.	Countess von Clary	1796	1805

WORKS WITH OPUS NUMBERS—*Continued*

OPUS	DESCRIPTION	DEDICATED TO	COM-POSED	PUB-LISHED
66	Twelve Variations on "Ein Mädchen" (Zauber-flöte) (F) Pf. Vo.			1798
67	Fifth Symphony (C minor)	Prince von Lobko-witz and Count von Rasoumow-sky	c. 1805	1809
68	Sixth symphony "Pastoral" (F)	Prince von Lobko-witz and Count von Rasoumow-sky		1809
69	Sonata (A) Pf. Vo.	Baron von Gleich-enstein		1809
70	Two Trios (D, E flat) Pf. V. Vo.	Countess Marie von Erdödy		1809
71	Sextet (E flat) 2 Clar. 2 Cor. 2 Bsn.		Early work	1810
72	Opera, "Fidelio" or "Wed-ded Love"	Archduke Rudolph	begun 1803	
73	Fifth Concerto (E flat) "Emperor" Pf. and Orch.	Archduke Rudolph	1809	1811
74	Quartet (10th), "Harp" (E flat) 2 V. Va. Vo.	Prince von Lobko-witz	1809	1810
75	Six Songs: "Kennst Du das Land," "Herz, mein Herz," "Es war einmal," "MitLiebesblick," "Einst Wohnten," "Zwar schuf das Glück," Sop. and Pf. Op. 75 is also marked to an arrt. of Op. 16 as string quartet	Princess von Kin-sky	1803 (4) 1810 (1)	1810
76	Six Variations (D) (*See* Op. 113, No. 4.) Pf.	Franz Oliva	1809 (?)	1810
77	Fantaisie (G minor) Pf.	Count F. von Brunswick	1808 (?)	1810

WORKS WITH OPUS NUMBERS—*Continued*

OPUS	DESCRIPTION	DEDICATED TO	COM-POSED	PUB-LISHED
78	Sonata (F sharp) Pf.	Countess Therese von Brunswick	1809	1810
79	Sonatina (G) Pf.		b. Dec., 1808	1810
80	Fantasia (C minor) Pf. Orch. Cho. Theme of variations is Beethoven's song, "Gegenliebe"	Maximilian Joseph, King of Bavaria	b. end of 1808	1811
81a	Sonata "Adieu, Absence, and Reunion" (E flat) Pf.	Archduke Rudolph	1809 (1st mvt.) 1810 (2, 3)	1811
81b	Sextet (E flat) 2 V. Va. Vo. 2 Cor.			1810
82	Four Ariettas and Duet for Sop. and Ten., Pf. ac-comp.: 1. "Dimmi, ben mio." 2. "T'intendo, si." 3. "Che fa, il mio bene" (*buffa*). 4. "Che fa, il mio bene" (*seria*). 5. "Odi l'aura"		1809 (4)	1811
83	Three Songs, Sop. and Pf.: "Trocknet nicht," "Was zieht mir," "Kleine Blumen"	Princess von Kin-sky	1810	1811
84	Music to Goethe's "Eg-mont." Overture. 1. Song, "Die Trommel." 2. Entracte I. 3. Entracte II. 4. Song, "Freudvoll und leidvoll." 5. En-tracte III. 6. Entracte IV. 7. Clara's Death. 8. Melodrama. 9. Sieges-symphonie		1810	Overture 1811 Rest 1812

WORKS WITH OPUS NUMBERS—*Continued*

OPUS	DESCRIPTION	DEDICATED TO	COM-POSED	PUB-LISHED
85	Oratorio, Christus am Oelberge ("Mount of Olives") Sop. Ten. Bass, Cho. Orch.		1800(?)	1811
86	Mass (C) Sop. Alt. Ten. Bass, Cho. Orch.	Prince von Kinsky	1807(?)	1812
87	Trio for 2 Ob. and Eng. H.		1794(?)	1806
88	Song, "Das Glück der Freundschaft" (A)			1803
89	Polonaise (C) Pf.	Empress Elizabeth Alexiewna of Russia	1814(?)	1815 (without op. no.)
90	Sonata (E minor) Pf.	Count M. von Lichnowsky	1814	1815
91	Orch., "Wellington's Victory, or the Battle of Vittoria"	Prince Regent of England	1813	1816
92	Seventh Symphony (A)	Count M. von Fries	1812	1816
93	Eighth Symphony (F)		1812	1816
94	Song, "An die Hoffnung"	Princess von Kinsky	1816(?)	1816
95	Quartet (11th) (F minor) 2 V. Va. Vo.	N. Zmeskall	1810	1816
96	Sonata (G) Pf .V.	Archduke Rudolph	1812	1816
97	Trio (B flat) Pf. V. Vo.	Archduke Rudolph	1811	1816
98	Song Cycle: "An die ferne Geliebte."	Prince von Lobkowitz	1816	1816
99	Song, "Der Mann von Wort"			1816
100	Duet, "Merkenstein" (F)		1814(?)	1816
101	Sonata (A) Pf.	Baroness Dorothea von Ertmann		1817
102	Two Sonatas (C, D) Pf. Vo.	Countess Marie von Erdödy	1815	1817
103	Octet, 2 Ob. 2 Clar. 2 Cor. 2 Bsn. (E flat) Original of Op. 4.			c. 1834

WORKS WITH OPUS NUMBERS—*Continued*

OPUS	DESCRIPTION	DEDICATED TO	COM-POSED	PUB-LISHED
104	Quintet (C minor) 2 Vs. 2 Vas. Vo. Arrd. Beethoven from Op. 1, No. 3.		1817	1819
105	Six very easy themes varied, Pf. Fl. or V.		1818–19	1819
106	Sonata (B flat) "Hammerklavier" Pf.	Archduke Rudolph	1818–19	1819
107	Ten national themes with variations, Pf. Fl. or V.		1818–20	1820
108	Twenty-five Scotch Songs for 1 and sometimes 2 Voices and small Cho., Pf. V. Vo.	Prince Anton Radzivil	1815–16	1821
109	Sonata (E) Pf.	Frl. Maximiliane Brentano	1820(?)	1821
110	Sonata (A flat) Pf.		1821	1822
111	Sonata (C minor) Pf.	Archduke Rudolph (by publishers)	1822	1823
112	"Calm Sea and Prosperous Voyage," Sop. Ten. Alt. Bass and Orch.	Goethe	1815	1823
113	"The Ruins of Athens." Overture and eight numbers for Cho. and Orch. For No. 4, *see* Op. 76.	King of Prussia	1811	1846
114	March and Cho. (E flat) from "The Ruins of Athens"			1824
115	Overture in C. sometimes called "Namensfeier"	Prince Anton Radzivil	1814	1825
116	Terzetto, "Tremate" (B flat) Sop. Ten. Bass		1802	1826
117	"King Stephen" Overture (E flat) and 9 numbers.		1811	1815
118	Elegiac Song (E) Sop. Alt. Ten. Bass and Str.	Baron von Pasqualati	1814	1826

WORKS WITH OPUS NUMBERS—*Continued*

OPUS	DESCRIPTION	DEDICATED TO	COM-POSED	PUB-LISHED
119	New Bagatelles (G minor, C, D, A, C minor, G, G, C, C, A minor, A, B flat, G) Pf.		1822 1–6	1821 1823 1828
120	Thirty-Three Variations on a Waltz by Diabelli (C)	Frau Antonie von Brentano	1823(?)	1823
121a	Variations on "Ich bin der Schneider Kakadu" (G) Pf. V. Vo.			1824
121b	Opferlied, Sop. with Cho. and Orch.		Orig. 1802	1825
122	Bundeslied, (B flat), Sop. Alt. Cho. and Wind		1822–23	1825
123	Mass in D, "Missa Solemnis"	Archduke Rudolph	1818 (or 19)–23	1827
124	Overture in C, "Consecration of the House"	Prince N. Galitzin	1822	1825
125	Ninth Symphony, "Choral" (D minor) Orch. Sop. Alt. Ten. Bass soli and Cho.	King of Prussia	1817–23	1826
126	Six [7] Bagatelles (G, G, minor, E flat, B minor, G, E flat, E flat) Pf.		1823	1825
127	Quartet, (12th) (E flat) 2 Vs. Va. Vo.	Prince N. Galitzin	1824	1826
128	Arietta, "The Kiss," by Weisse.		1822	1825
129	Rondo a capriccio (G) Pf. "Rage over a Lost Groschen"			1828
130	Quartet (13th) (B flat) 2 V. Va. Vo.	Prince N. Galitzin	1825–26 (Op. 133 was orig. *finale.* Present *finale* 1826)	1827

[651]

WORKS WITH OPUS NUMBERS—*Continued*

OPUS	DESCRIPTION	DEDICATED TO	COM-POSED	PUB-LISHED
131	Quartet (14th) (C sharp minor) 2 V. Va. Vo.	Baron von Stutter-heim	1826	1827
132	Quartet (15th) (A minor) 2 V. Va. Vo.	Prince N. Galitzin	1825	1827
133	Great Fugue (B flat) 2 V. Va. Vo. Originally *finale* to Op. 130.	Archduke Rudolph	1825	1827
134	Great Fugue (Op. 133) (B flat) arrd. by composer for Pf. 4 hands.	Archduke Rudolph		1827
135	Quartet (16th) (F) 2 V. Va. Vo.	Johann Wolfmayer	1826	1827
136	"Der glorreiche Augen-blick" ("The Glorious Moment"), Cantata, Sop. Alt. Ten. Bass Cho. and Orch., six numbers. Also as "Preis der Ton-kunst ("Praise of Mu-sic"), new text. F. Roch-litz.	The Sovereigns of Austria, Russia, and Prussia, etc.	1814	1836
137	Fugue (D) 2 V. 2 Va. Vo.		1817	1827
138	Overture, (C) known as "Leonore No. 1."		c. 1807	1832

WORKS WITHOUT OPUS NUMBERS

Numbers added by Grove

I. FOR ORCHESTRA OR ORCHESTRAL INSTRUMENTS

NO.	DESCRIPTION	DEDICATED TO	COM-POSED	PUB-LISHED
139	Twelve Minuets			1795
140	Twelve Deutsche Tänze			1795

[652]

WORKS WITHOUT OPUS NUMBERS—*Continued*

OPUS	DESCRIPTION	DEDICATED TO	COM-POSED	PUB-LISHED
141	Twelve Contretänze. (No. 7 is dance used in Finale of Prometheus, the "Eroica," etc. No. 11 also used in Finale of Prometheus)		1802 (2, 9, 10)	All 1803
142	Minuet of Congratulation (E flat)		1823	1835
143	Triumphal March, for Kuffner's "Tarpeia" or "Hersilia" (C)		b. Mar., 1813	1819
144	Military March (D)		1816	1827
145	Military March (F)		1809	
146	Rondino, 2 Ob. 2 Clar. 2 Cor. 2 Bsn. (E flat)		Very early	1829
147	Three Duos (C, F, B flat) Clar. Bsn.			1815 (?)
148	Allegro con Brio, V. Orch. (C) Fragment of 1st mvt. of a V. Concerto. Completed by Jos. Hell-mesberger	Dr. G. von Breun-ing	1800 (?)	1879
149	Musik zu einem Ritterbal-let		1790	1872

II. FOR PIANO, WITH AND WITHOUT ACCOMPANIMENT

NO.	DESCRIPTION	DEDICATED TO	COM-POSED	PUB-LISHED
150	Sonatina and Adagio for Mandolin and Cembalo (C minor)			
151	Rondo (B flat) Pf. and Orch. Probably finished by Czerny. Perhaps intended for Op. 19.			1829

WORKS WITHOUT OPUS NUMBERS—*Continued*

NO.	DESCRIPTION	DEDICATED TO	COM-POSED	PUB-LISHED
152	Three Quartets (E flat, D, C) Pf. V. Va. Vo. Very early. Adagio of No. 3 is employed in Op. 2 No. 1.		1785	1832
153	Trio (E flat) Pf. V. Vo.		1785(?)	1830
154	Trio in 1 movement (B flat) Pf. V. Vo.	Frl. Maximiliane Brentano	1812	1830
155	Rondo, Allegro (G) Pf. and V.		1794(?)	1808
156	Twelve Variations on "Se vuol ballare" (F) Pf. and V.	Eleonore von Breuning		1793
157	Twelve Variations on "See the Conquering Hero" (G) Pf. and Vo.	Princess von Lich-nowsky		1797
158	Seven Variations on "Bei Männern" (E flat) Pf. and Vo.	Count von Browne		1802
159	Variations on a theme by Count von Waldstein (C) Pf. 4 hands			1794
160	Air with Six Variations on "Ich denke dein" (D) Pf. 4 hands	Countess Josephine Deym and Countess Therese Brunswick	1800	1805
161	Three Sonatas (E flat, F minor, D) Pf.	Elector Maximilian Frederic of Cologne	Very early	1783
162	Sonata called Easy (C) Pf. 2 movts. only, second completed by F. Ries	Eleonore von Breuning		1830
163	Two Sonatinas (G, F) Pf. Of doubtful authenticity.			
164	Rondo, Allegretto (A) Pf.			1784
165	Menuet (E flat) Pf.		1783(?)	1805
166	Prelude (F minor) Pf.		1785(?)	1805

WORKS WITHOUT OPUS NUMBERS—*Continued*

NO.	DESCRIPTION	DEDICATED TO	COM-POSED	PUB-LISHED
167	Six Minuets (C, G, E flat, B flat, D, C) Pf. Perhaps first written for Orch.			1796
168	Seven Ländler Dances (all in D).			c. 1799
169	Six Ländler Dances (all in D except No. 4 in D minor). Also for VV. and Vo.		1802	1802
170	Andante favori (F) Pf. Orig. intended for Op. 53.		1804(?)	1806
171	Six Allemandes (F, D, F, A, D, G) Pf. and V.		1795	1814
172	Ziemlich lebhaft (B flat) Pf.		1818 By request	1824
173	Bagatelle (A minor) Pf.	"Für Elise"		
174	Andante maestoso (C) Pf. arrd. from the sketch for a Quintet and called "Beethoven's Last Musical Thought."		1826	1840
175	Ten Cadenzas to Beethoven's Pf. Concertos in C, B flat, C minor, G, D (arrt. of V. Concerto, *see* Op. 61). Also 2 to Mozart's Pf. Concerto in D minor.			1836
176	Nine Variations on a March by Dressler (C minor) Pf.	Countess von Wolf-Metternich	1780(?)	1783
177	Twenty-four Variations on Righini's air "Vieni [*sic* i.e. "Venni"] amore (D) Pf.	Countess von Hatz-feld	1790(?)	1801

WORKS WITHOUT OPUS NUMBERS—*Continued*

NO.	DESCRIPTION	DEDICATED TO	COM-POSED	PUB-LISHED
178	Thirteen Variations on Dittersdorf's air "Es war einmal" (A) Pf.		1791 (?)	1794
179	Nine Variations on Paisiello's air "Quant' è più bello" (A) Pf.	Prince Carl von Lichnowsky		1795 ann.
180	Six Variations on Paisiello's duet "Nel cor più" (G) Pf.			1796
181	Twelve Variations on minuet (a la Vigano) from Haibel's ballet "Le nozze disturbate" (C) Pf.		1795 (?)	1796
182	Twelve Variations on the Russian dance from Paul Wranizky's "Waldmädchen" (A) Pf.	Countess von Browne	1796 (?)	1797
183	Six easy Variations on a Swiss air (F) Pf. or Harp			c. 1798
184	Eight Variations on Grétry's air "Une fièvre brûlante (C) Pf.			1798
185	Ten Variations on Salieri's air, "La Stessa, la Stessissima" (B flat) Pf.	Countess Babette von Keglevics	1799	1799
186	Seven Variations on Winter's quartet, "Kind willst du" (F) Pf.			1799
187	Eight Variations on Süssmayer's trio, "Tändeln und scherzen" (F) Pf.	Countess von Browne	1799	1799
188	Six very easy Variations on an original theme (G) Pf.		c. 1800 (?)	1801
189	Seven Variations on "God Save the King" (C) Pf.			1804

WORKS WITHOUT OPUS NUMBERS—*Continued*

NO.	DESCRIPTION	DEDICATED TO	COM-POSED	PUB-LISHED
190	Five Variations on "Rule, Britannia" (D) Pf.			1804
191	Thirty-two Variations (C minor) Pf.		1806–07	1807
192	Eight Variations on "Ich hab' ein kleines Hütt- chen nur" (B flat) Pf.			c. 1831

III. WORKS FOR VOICES

NO.	DESCRIPTION	DEDICATED TO	COM-POSED	PUB-LISHED
193	Bass Solo "Germania!" Cho. Orch. *Finale* for Treitschke's Singspiel "Gute Nachricht"			1814
194	Bass Solo "Es ist voll- bracht." Cho. Orch. *Finale* to Treitschke's Singspiel "Die Ehren- pforten."			1815
195	"Misere" and "Amplius." Dirge at Beethoven's funeral 4-voiced men's chor. and 4 trombones. Adapted by Seyfried from two of three Ms. Equali for trombones.		1812	
196a	Cantata on the death of the Emperor Joseph II (Feb. 20, 1790) (C minor) Soli, Cho. Orch.		1790	
196b	Cantata (Sept. 30, 1790) "Er schlummert," on the accession of Leo- pold II.		1790	

WWWWWWWWWWWWWWWWWWWWWWWWWWWWWWW

WORKS WITHOUT OPUS NUMBERS—*Continued*

NO.	DESCRIPTION	DEDICATED TO	COM-POSED	PUB-LISHED
197	Song of the monks from Schiller's "William Tell" —"Rasch tritt der Tod." "In memory of the sudden and unexpected death of our Krumpholz" (May 3, 1817). (C minor) 2 Ten. Bass.		1817	1839
198	Chorus, "O Hoffnung" (4 bars) (G) for Archduke Rudolph		1818	1819
199	Cantata (E flat) Sop. Alt. Bass, Pf.		1823	1867
200	Cantata, "Graf, Graf, lieber Graf" (E flat) Voices and Pf.	Count M. von Lichnowsky		1865
201	Five bars (on the arrival of Herr Schlesinger of Berlin, "Glaube u. hoffe"		1819	
202	Incidental music, "Du dem sie gewunden," written for Duncker's "Leonore Prohaska" (D)		1814	1865
203–222	Many canons and small incidental pieces.			
223	Twenty-five Irish Songs, for 1 & 2 Voices with Pf. V. Vo.			1814–16
224	Twenty Irish Songs			1814–16
225	Twelve Irish Songs			1814–16
226	Twenty-six Welsh Songs			1817
227	Twelve Scottish Songs			1841
228	Twelve Songs of varied nationality, for Voice, Pf. V. Vo.		1815 (2, 6, 8, 11)	1816 (2, 6, 8, 11)
229	Song, "Schilderung eines Mädchens"		1781 (?)	1783

WORKS WITHOUT OPUS NUMBERS—*Continued*

NO.	DESCRIPTION	DEDICATED TO	COM-POSED	PUB-LISHED
230	Song, "An einen Säugling"			1784
231	Song, "Farewell to Vienna's Citizens"	Obristwacht-meister von Kövesdy	1796	1796
232	War Song of the Austrians, Solo and Cho. with Pf.		1797	1797
233	Song, "Der freie Mann"		1795 (?)	1806
234	Opferlied, "Die Flamme lodert"		1795 (?)	
235	Song, "Zärtliche Liebe"			1803
236	Song, "La Partenza"			1803
237	Song, "Der Wachtelschlag"		c. 1799	1804
238	Song, "Als die Geliebte sich trennen wollte"			1809
239	Arietta, "In questa tomba oscura" (A flat)		1807 (?)	1808
240	Song, "Andenken" (D)			1810
241	Four settings of Goethe's "Sehnsucht"			1808
242	Song, "Als mir noch"		1809	1810
243	Song, "Welch ein wunderbares Leben"			1810
244	Song, "Der Frühling entblühet"			1810
245	Song, "Des Kriegers Abschied"		1814	1815
246	Song, "Die stille Nacht"		1815 or 1816	1816
247	Song, "O das ich dir"		1811	1814
247a	Another setting of above		After Dec., 1812	c. 1840
248	Song, "Dort auf dem hohen Felsen"		1813	1814
249	Song, "Wenn ich ein Vöglein wär"		1816	1817
250	Song, "Wo blüht das Blümchen"		1815	1816

WORKS WITHOUT OPUS NUMBERS—*Continued*

NO.	DESCRIPTION	DEDICATED TO	COM-POSED	PUB-LISHED
251	Song, "Nord oder Sud!"		1817	1817
252	Song, "Lisch aus, mein Licht"		1817	1818
253	Song, "Wenn die Sonne nieder sinket"		1820	1820
254	Two songs, "Seufzer eines Ungeliebten" and "Gegenliebe." (For theme of latter see Op. 80)		1795 (?)	1837
255	Song, "Turteltaube"		1809 (?)	Prob. 1837
256	Song, "Gedenke mein! ich denke dein"		1820	1844

INDEX

Absolute music, 248.
    defined, 626.
Academies, 34.
Acoustics, defined, 626.
Adagio, mystical, the, 500.
    symphonic, 196.
Adelaide, source-motive, 575.
Adieu, Absence, and Reunion, 241.
    See also Sonata in E flat, Op.
    81a.
Æsthetic radicals, 118.
Albrechtsberger, 26, 27, 28, 29,
    321.
    BEETHOVEN takes lessons from,
    26.
Allegro, titanic, 499.
Amenda, Carl, 25, 43, 85, 332.
Amiel, 263.
An die Hoffnung, Op. 32, 160.
Anagram, B–A–C–H, 185, 186,
    400.
    idea in chief source motive?
    610.
    in Op. 131, 564–565.
"Andante Favori," 150.
Anlauf, 608.
Answer, defined, 626.
"Appassionata" sonata, *see* Sonata
    in F minor, Op. 57.
Applause *versus* tears, 42.
Appoggiatura, defined, 626.
Appropriation, genial, *versus* pla-
    giarism, 512.
Archduke Rudolph, 32, 176, 239,
    242, 291, 381.
    pupil of BEETHOVEN, 198.
"Archduke" trio, *see* Trio in B flat,
    Op. 97.

Aria, defined, 626.
Arnim, Bettina von, *see* Brentano,
    Bettina.
Artaria, 77.
Augmentation, defined, 626.
Authentic cadence, defined, 626.
Automatic instruments, BEE-
    THOVEN'S music on, 615–
    625.
Automatisms, 281.

Bach, C. P. E., 492, 514.
Bach, J. S., 16, 20, 41, 53, 79, 143,
    144, 219, 252, 369, 371, 459,
    490, 567, 608.
B–A–C–H anagram, 185, 186,
    400.
    overture, 168.
Bach's organ fugue in C minor,
    463.
    Welltempered Clavichord, 16.
Bagatelle, defined, 626.
    Op. 26, 462.
    Op. 33, 17, 18.
    source-motive in, 581.
    Op. 126, source-motive in, 581.
Baline, Israel, *see* Berlin, Irving.
Ballantine, Edward, 80.
Ballet, *The Creations of Pro-
    metheus*, Op. 43, 43, 76,
    125.
    variations on theme, 106.
Bargiel, 571.
Baryton, 30.
Bassettl, 470.
Basso ostinato, defined, 626.
Baton, BEETHOVEN'S technic, 147.
Battle of Jena, by Fuchs, 342.

[663]

Battle of Prague, by Koczwara, 342.

Battle of Vittoria, see Symphony, "*Battle,*" Op. 91.

Battle pieces, 342.

"*Battle*" symphony, *see* Symphony, "*Battle.*"

Bauer, Harold, 447, 452.

Bauer, Marion, 401 n., 524, 534, 575 n.

Beauty and truth, 395.

Beauty in the making, study of, 512.

Beckmesser, 266.

Beethoven, Johann van (father of BEETHOVEN), 2, 5, 6.
death of, 36.

Beethoven, Johann Nikolaus van (brother of BEETHOVEN), 36, 89, 206, 207, 320, 352, 469, 470, 471, 476, 479.

Beethoven, Karl van (nephew of BEETHOVEN), 445, 472, 479, 483.
attempts suicide, 468.
decides to be a soldier, 469.
friction with his uncle, 472.
goes from bad to worse, 468.
lays hands on his uncle, 468.
relations with his uncle, 385, 444, 472, 478.
steals, 468.

Beethoven, Karl Kasper van (brother of BEETHOVEN), 36, 89, 90, 181, 206, 207, 352, 353, 469, 486.

Beethoven, Ludovicus van (grandfather of BEETHOVEN), 4, 5, 12.

BEETHOVEN, LUDWIG VAN:
abolishes opening tutti, 193.
absent-mindedness of, 333.
accuses supper guests of dishonesty, 421.
address to, 416.
aids evolution of piano, 194.
alternations of mood of, 48, 49, 195.
ambition of, 38.
anagram idea in source-motive? 610.
ancestry of, 4.
appearance of, 18, 23, 378, 443.
applies for subsidy as opera composer, 200.
architectonic method of, novel, 495.
and aristocracy, 31.
and arithmetic, 480.
arrested as a vagabond, 376.
arrives in Vienna, 23.
artistic morality of, 393.
astronomy, interest in, 185.
atmosphere, early musical, 9.
his attitude towards women, 100, 101, 114, 159, 169.
attracts the young, 246.
automatic instruments, his music on, 615–625.
avarice, his growing, 351.
aviation, his interest in, 345.
baptism, date of, 8.
baton technic of, 147.
behaviour of, disconcerting, 151.
and Bettina Brentano, 4, 103, 260, 274–285, 300, 311, 315.
bibliography, 636.

BEETHOVEN, *continued*

his biographers, puritanism of, 99.

his birth, date of, 8.

place of, 8.

boisterous humor of, 312.

borrows from Haydn, 515.

from himself, 515, 516, 517, 518, 519, 520, 521.

from Mozart, 222, 514, 524.

from folk tunes, 516.

his brave wit during operation, 479.

his breadth of interests, 120.

Broadwood presents piano to, 364.

his brothers, 206.

relations with, 88.

burial of, 487.

business morality of, 393.

catastrophe and courage, 174.

cautious approach to new forms, 63.

a cembalo player, 13.

chief of many liberators, 494.

and classicism, 117, 120, 121.

a classicist, 246.

and Clementi, 204, 205.

codicil to his will, 484.

complains of neglect, 444.

composition, habits of, 3, 470, 553.

conceited? was he, 43.

concentration of, 377, 504.

as a conductor, 147, 380.

his confidence in future, 189.

confident of posterity's verdict, 480.

conscientious idealism of, 505.

BEETHOVEN, *continued*

consecutive fifths allowed by, 144, 145.

construction, a master of, 495.

contributions, his most original, 406, 499.

courage of, 51, 52, 174, 479.

Court of Cassel, offer from, 239.

Court organist, 18.

created new keyboard technic, 492.

creative freedom of, 368.

music freed from composer-executant tradition, 95.

processes of, 511, 553.

resources, fertility of his, 579.

critics of, 321.

"crown of martyrdom," 168.

cynicism of, 47.

and dancing, 25.

daydreams of, 2, 3.

deaf to applause, 420.

deafness of, 50, 52, 60, 84, 88, 94, 96, 101, 159, 358, 365, 380, 385, 395, 420, 427, 457, 467.

causes of, 96.

effects of, 94.

exaggerates his, 88.

first admission of, 84.

death of, 486.

cause of, 487.

premonition of, 445.

his deathbed, 44, 478–486.

dedication of Op. 2 to Haydn, 41.

defensive rationalization, 388.

defrauds Maelzel, 344.

his delirium, 486.

BEETHOVEN, *continued*
  democratized music, 490.
  despair of, 360.
  his detachment from earth, 382, 383.
  developed the continental concert, 490.
    forms, 496.
    mechanism of piano, 493.
    orchestra, 493.
  his difficult personality, 74.
  disciplined by Albrechtsberger, 27, 28.
  discord, unconsciousness of, 457.
  disease, nature of his, 97, 98.
  domestic troubles of, 434.
  and dramatic overture, 493.
  dramatic power of, 502.
  his dress, 25.
  early teachers of, 14.
    practice, 2.
    pupils of, 19.
  economy of, 504.
  his economy of material, 578.
  emancipator of music, 17, 489.
  embarrassing escort, an, 456.
  emotional extremes in his music, 58.
  encouraged creative listeners, 494.
  enmity of rivals, 74.
  established composer on professional basis, 489.
  euphemism for his language, 367.
  excels in *finales*, 295.
  and exhibitionism, 493.
  exposure of, 366.
  his failing health, 366.

BEETHOVEN, *continued*
  false start passages in, 330.
  fame, his growing, 287.
  family misery, 9.
  faults of, 238.
  favourite symphony, his, 359.
  feels his way with germ-motive, 532.
  fiddles, receives Cremona, 71.
  finales, excels in, 295.
  financial crises, cure for, 60.
  finding his medium, 63.
  and fish suppers at Nussdorf, 359.
  Flemish origin, influence of, 4.
  fondness for nature, 260.
    for rhythmic mottos, 191.
  and form, 492.
  forward-looking mind of, 345.
  freed music, 489, 493.
    Mass, 381, 389.
    operatic composer, 174.
  freedom of, 143.
  frees sonata-form, 138.
    music from taint of virtuosity, 96.
  frequency of a chief source-motive in his works, 579.
  and friends, 43, 47.
  friendship with Countess Erdödy, 229.
    with tavern orchestra, 266.
  and fugues, 374, 499.
  fun in his music, 62.
  a genial conjurer, 323.
  his genius unoperatic, 167.
  his germ-motives, 53–56, 498, 530, 532, 533, 534, 575, 577. *See also* Germ-motive.

BEETHOVEN, *continued*
"a gift from nature," 507.
at Gneixendorf, 469, 471.
and Goethe, 314, 315.
Grand Sourd, le, 358.
his grandparents, 4.
growing popularity of, 185.
habits, irregular, of, 366.
Handel's works, enjoys gift of, 479.
handwriting, his last, 484.
happy period of life, 177.
and harmony, 492.
and Haydn, 22, 25, 37, 41, 225, 515.
head of family, 22.
headstrong, 29.
health, failing, 366.
helplessness of, 367.
home at Von Breunings, 19.
horseplay with Abbé Stadler, 338.
humiliates the orchestra, 235.
humility of, 43, 44.
humour, sense of, 42, 267, 312, 329, 331, 332, 333, 334, 479.
hurls dish at waiter, 62.
illness of, 145, 438, 479.
  last, 478.
improvisation, ability in, 3, 18, 21, 23, 24, 42, 72, 232, 233, 285, 378, 604.
  duel with Himmel, 42.
  with Steibelt, 72.
in love, 22, 272.
inconsistency of, 318.
indebtedness to predecessors, 514.

BEETHOVEN, *continued*
indecision of, 417.
independence of, 32, 33.
inertia in starting compositions, 368.
inspiration, sources of, 225.
insults Imperial Court, 314.
  Prince Lobkowitz, 89.
interest in inventions, 345.
interests, breadth of, 120.
and interpreter-composer, 493.
and introduction forms, 307.
an introvert, 169.
invents the germ-motive, 53–56, 530.
irony of, 338.
irritability of, 98.
his Isolde, 298.
and jazz, 69.
Jekyll and Hyde in, 49, 50, 77, 210, 265, 284, 351, 390, 394, 420, 422, 505.
joint guardian of his nephew, 352.
jokes, practical, 147, 312, 330, 338, 408.
kettledrum joke, 408.
kindness to his brother, 352.
lack of sympathy with vocal music, 167.
large calibre of, 504.
largeness of outlook, 318.
last words, 485.
laughs at himself, 338.
lavish vitality of, 504.
learns from virtuosos, 59.
legends about, 80.
"Leibquartett," 447.

BEETHOVEN, *continued*

letters of. *See also* Letters of BEETHOVEN, 43, 45, 46, 47, 48, 52, 74, 85, 86, 87, 96, 101, 102, 106, 120, 144, 146, 153, 160, 205, 207, 209, 229, 230, 238, 260, 268, 272, 273, 282, 283, 286, 287, 296, 297, 298, 299, 306, 316, 317, 318, 319, 332, 333, 334, 335, 337, 338, 340, 346, 347, 351, 353, 354, 355, 360, 364, 378, 385, 392, 393, 417, 445, 446, 459, 480, 483, 502.

liberators, chief of many, 494.

and Liszt, 396.

litigation with his sister-in-law, 352.

and London Philharmonic Society, 303, 318, 360, 393, 394, 421, 480, 481, 487.

loneliness of, 444, 445.

love for his nephew, 353.

of England, 30.

of nature, 256, 258, 269.

love affairs of, 99, 103, 298, 300, 301, 302.

letter to the "Immortal Beloved," 298.

the Luther of Church music, 493.

"mad musician," 349.

makes will, 483.

making money, 36.

and the Mass, 381, 389.

matured music, 491.

BEETHOVEN, *continued*

meddles in brother's love affairs, 320.

mental climacteric, 271.

confusion, 483.

misrepresentations to Zelter, 395.

misunderstood, 238.

modernity of, 52.

modesty of, 448.

and modulation, 492.

mood, alternations of, 48, 49, 195.

moral code of, 393.

morality of, artistic and business, 393.

and Mozart, *see* Mozart.

multiplied movements, 498.

and musical parasites, 32, 33.

and musical pranks, 433.

musical tricks, 565.

witticisms of, 355.

naming his works, 321.

nature, fondness for, 260.

nephew, friction with, 472.

trouble with, 385.

love for, 353.

nervous irritability of, 98.

new forms, cautious approach to, 63.

new style, 106.

nickname, 1, 454.

not a vocal composer, 167.

and oboist, 148.

obsession of persecution, 237.

"occasional" works, 82.

operatic composer freed, 174.

operation, brave wit during, 312.

INDEX

BEETHOVEN, *continued*

and orchestra, 148, 235, 266.
origin of name, 4.
originality of, 500.
out-of-doors, passion for, 75.
overreaches the London Philharmonic Society, 303.
overtures, his best program music, 268.
and pedants, 321, 322.
personal creed of, 383.
personality, 23.
    difficult, 74.
as physician, 505.
pianist, last appearance as, 350.
piano duel with Himmel, 42.
    with Steibelt, 72.
plagiarisms by, 386, 512.
and poetic programs, 305.
popularity, his growing, 158.
posterity's verdict, confident of, 480.
poverty of, 341.
    representation of, 480.
practical jokes, 147, 312, 330, 338, 408.
praised by Mozart, 19.
precocity of, 3.
presence of mind of, 35.
priggishness of, 317, 319.
printed works, list of, 642–660.
productiveness, 270, 271.
program music, theory of, 268.
psychological insight of, 144.
and publishers, 158, 335, 337, 390, 392, 459.
and punning, 331, 332, 334.
quality, sustained, of his work, 177.

BEETHOVEN, *continued*

quarrel with Von Breuning, 145.
"raptus," 232, 280.
rebounds from misfortune, 175.
reburial of, 488.
receives annuity, 71, 239.
    Broadwood piano, 364.
    Cremona fiddles, 71.
    freedom of city of Vienna, 355.
    golden snuffbox, 41.
relations with his brothers, 88.
relics, Clementi method, 455.
religion, founder of a, 504.
relishes bad music, 266.
repels the old, 246.
resilience of, 88.
and rhythmic mottos, 191.
ripening, slow, 20.
rivals, enmity of, 74.
Robinson Crusoe costume of, 73.
and romanticism, 117, 120, 121, 141.
a romanticist, 246.
and the rondo, 499.
and Rossini, 325, 379.
rudeness to servant, 101.
Salieri, studies with, 29.
and Schenck, 26.
Schubert's visit to, 484.
self-expression in *Fidelio*, 171.
self-willed, 29.
sends for his brothers, 36.
shares rooms with Von Breuning, 145.
shocks the reactionaries, 146.
shows consideration for Rode, 340.
and singers, 148, 382.

BEETHOVEN, *continued*

sister-in-law, litigation with his, 352.

skill in selecting words, 412.

smashes bust of Lichnowsky, 200.

social rise of, 29, 30.

success of, 23.

socialistic ideas of, 45.

solicits subscriptions for *Mass in D*, 395.

and sonatas, 182, 498.

and song cycle, 357.

his source-motives, 55, 56, 153, 499, 566–611. *See also* Source-motive.

sportsman, a poor, 150.

strength of, 43.

studies harmony and counterpoint, 26.

with Albrechtsberger, 26.

with Haydn, 25.

with Schenck, 26.

subsidy as opera composer, applies for, 200.

surprises, musical, in, 330.

suspicious, 365.

and symphonies, 498.

teachers of, 15.

threatened with loss of finger, 225.

tomb of, 488.

transposition, skill in, 35.

triad habit in, 575, 576.

tributes to, 159.

trick passages in, 149.

tricks of, 433.

troubles with nephew Karl, 385.

tutti, abolishes opening, 193.

BEETHOVEN, *continued*

an unecclesiastical writer, 381.

unexpectedness of, 502.

unity and variety of, 589.

universalized the overture, 203. music, 490.

an unvocal writer, 381.

an unoperatic genius, 167.

vagabond, arrested as a, 376.

"van" in his name, 354.

variation forms, treatment of, 500.

variety in unity, 578.

and venality, 493.

and venereal disease, 97, 98.

verbal felicity of, 334.

and Vienna, 18, 23, 34, 237, 385.

Viennese loyal to, 202.

a viola player, 22.

violence of, 365.

violoncello humour, 333.

virility of, 99.

and virtuosity, 96.

vitality of, 504.

vocal music, lack of sympathy with, 167.

and Wagner, 450.

will, makes his, 483.

wit of, 313.

witticisms of, musical, 355.

works, naming his, 321.

workshop of, 509.

Beethoven concert, 233, 235, 419.

announcement of, 418.

rehearsal for, 419.

Beethoven myth, the, 61.

Beethoven program, 108.

Beethoven religion, the, 504.

Beethovenian *scherzo*, 137.

Beethovenism, 116, 118, 504.

"Beethoven's Minuet," 197.

"Beethoven's Symphony," 197.

Behrend, 102, 249, 369.

Bekker, Paul, 100, 125, 227, 229, 279, 306, 406, 410, 459, 491, 574.

Berlin, Irving, 9.

Berlin, BEETHOVEN receives snuff-box from Court at, 41.

Berlioz, 28, 56, 95, 114.

Bernard, 354.

Bettina, *see* Brentano, Bettina.

Bibliography, 636.

Binary form, defined, 626.

Biographers, puritanism of, 99.

Birchall, 304.

Bischoff, 305.

"Black Spaniard's House," the, 454.

Boehm, 433, 476.

Bolshevists and BEETHOVEN's music, 505.

Bombardment of Vienna, 232.

Bonaparte, Jerome, 238.

Bonaparte, Napoleon, 122, 124, 153, 182.

Bonn, 5, 8, 9, 11, 12, 13, 15, 19.

Bonngasse, 8, 11.

Bootjack, a musical, 365.

Boufflers, Chevalier de, 507.

Bouilly, 164.

Leonora, or Conjugal Love, 164.

Bourdelle, 4.

Brahms, 20, 35, 63, 64, 71, 112, 150, 172, 191, 194, 197, 201, 212, 232, 243, 290, 291,

Brahms, *continued*
308 n., 343, 372, 414, 433, 436, 441, 459, 569, 610.

Intermezzi, 18.

Symphony in C minor, 307.

Brauchle, Magister, 230, 334, 351.

Braun, Baron, 165.

Brentano, Antonie von, 284, 285, 352.

Brentano, Bettina, 4, 103, 260, 274–285, 300, 311, 315.

controversy about BEETHOVEN's letters to, 282.

and the "Immortal Beloved," 300.

slighted by Beethoven, 284.

Breuning, "Ariel" von, 479. *See also* Breuning, Gerhard von.

Breuning, Eleonora von, 19, 20.

Breuning, Franz von, 389.

Breuning, Frau von, 455.

Breuning, Gerhard von, 455, 486.

Breuning, Marie von, 456.

Breuning, Stephan von, 19, 145, 455.

BEETHOVEN is reconciled with, 145.

quarrels with, 145.

shares rooms with, 145.

Breunings, the Von, 19, 31, 480.

Breitkopf and Härtel, 76, 106, 229, 335.

Bridgetower, 113.

Broadwood presents piano to BEETHOVEN, 364.

Brousson, 184, 304.

Browne, Count von, 32.

Browning, Robert, 111, 141.

Brunswick, Count, 31.

INDEX

Brunswick, Countess Therese, 103, 300.

Bülow, Hans von, 145, 213, 361.

Byrd, William, *Non nobis Domine*, 401.

Cadence, defined, 626.

Cadenza, defined, 626.

Caging the Phœnix of Music, 250.

Canteloube, 516.

Canon, defined, 627.
  Es muss sein, 477.
  Signor Abbate! 337.
  To Maelzel, 326.

Casanova, 20 n.

Cassel, Court of, offer from, 239.

Castelli, 337, 604.

Cavatina, defined, 627.

Celestial music, 288, 289, 290.

Cembalo, 13.

Chamber music, defined, 627.

Cherubini, 28, 342.

Chopin, 568.
  Preludes, 18.

Choral, defined, 627.

Choral Fantasia in C minor, Op. 80, 235, 236, 572.

Choral symphony, *see* Symphony, No. 9, in D minor, Op. 125.

Chord, defined, 627.

Chronometer. Maelzel's, 334.

Christus am Ölberge, 112.

Chromatic scale, defined, 627.

Classicism and romanticism, 116, 117, 120, 121, 246.

Clemens, Joseph, 9.
  love of joke, 10.
  plagiarisms of, 10.

Clemens, Samuel (Mark Twain), 10.

Clementi, 80, 204, 205.
  relic, 455.

"Cockcrow" sonata, 340.

Coda, 627.
  development of, 307.

Codicil to BEETHOVEN's will, 484.

Coleridge, 512.

Collin, 202, 227.
  Coriolanus, 286.

Cologne, Elector of, 9, 10.

Comédie Humaine, of music, 320.

"Compliment" quartet, Op. 18, No. 1, 67.

Composer and interpreter, 493.

Composition, handicaps to, 385.

Concealment of source-motive, devices for, 579, 581.

Concert, Beethoven, 233, 235, 419.
  announcement of, 418.
  rehearsal for, 419.

Concerto, conditions in 1803, 108.
  defined, 627.
  orchestra, BEETHOVEN frees, 194.

Concerto, Violin, in D major, Op. 61, 176, 177, 190, 194, 226.
  source-motive in, 586.

—— for Piano, in C minor, 108, 112.
  first performance of, 109.

—— for Piano, in G major, Op. 58, 107, 152, 153, 176, 190, 192, 193, 194, 243.

—— for Piano, in E flat, Op. 73 (*"Emperor"* concerto), 152, 176, 191, 242.

[672]

Concerto in E flat, *continued*
Adagio un poco mosso, 243, 244.
source-motive in, 588.
—— in B flat, Op. 19, 35.
—— Triple, Op. 56, 176.
Concerts, quartet, first, 151.
Conscious use of source-motive,
577, 579, 603–608.
Consecration of the House, over-
ture, Op. 124, 594.
Consecutive fifths, 144, 145.
Contrapuntal, defined, 628.
Conversation Books, 365, 434,
469, 470, 479, 480.
Coriolanus, Collin's, 286.
Coriolanus overture, 62, 202, 268,
269.
Cortot, A., 249.
Counterpoint, defined, 628.
Cox, Catharine Morris, 46.
Cramer, J. B., 37, 44, 80.
Creations of Prometheus, The,
ballet, Op. 43, 43, 76, 106,
125.
Creative music freed from com-
poser-interpreter tradition,
95.
Creators and the golden mean, 119.
Critics, 123, 321.
Cyclical form, defined, 628.
Czerny, 36, 42, 73, 105, 130, 145,
179, 185, 215, 232, 240, 360,
409, 414.

Deafness of BEETHOVEN, 50, 52,
60, 84, 88, 94, 96, 101, 159,
358, 365, 380, 385, 395, 427,
467.
to applause, 420.

Deafness, *continued*
causes of, 96.
effects of, 94.
exaggerated, 88.
first admission of, 84.
Debussy, 212, 412.
Debussy's *Arabesques,* 18.
Deiters, Dr., 394.
Del Rio, 268.
De Marliave, 412.
De Morgan, William, 38.
Dembscher, 476.
Despairing music, 51.
Development, defined, 628.
of sonata, 633.
Devices for concealment of
source-motive, 579, 581.
Deym, Countess Josephine, 103,
300.
Diatonic, defined, 628.
Diabelli Variations, 284, 352, 397,
500, 605.
source-motive in, 595.
Die Weihe des Hauses, Op. 124,
572.
Diminution, defined, 628.
D'Indy, Vincent, 25, 99, 305, 388,
521, 559.
"Ditties of no tone," 427.
Divertimento, defined, 628.
Divertissement, defined, 628.
Domanovecz, Freiherr Nikolaus
Zmeskall von, *see* Zmeskall.
Dominant, defined, 628.
Dragonetti, 59, 60.
Dramatic music, 254.
Duet, Op. 105, source-motive in,
593.

INDEX

Duparc, Henri, 254.
Duport, 59.
Dürenberg, 305.
Dvořak, 56, 561, 608.
Dynamics, defined, 628.
Dyson, Dr. George, 503.

Ecossaise, defined, 628.
Egmont, 286.
   overture, 173, 268, 287, 524.
Ellis, Havelock, 429.
Elshemus, 163.
"Emperor" concerto, see Concerto in E flat, Op. 73.
Engel, Carl, 97 n., 401 n., 580 n., 609 n.
England, love of, 30.
   plans trip to, 423.
"English" Symphony, 400.
Ensemble, defined, 628.
Equal temperament, 65, 66 n.
Erdödy, Countess, 229, 239, 333.
   BEETHOVEN's friendship with, 229.
   suspected of murder, and banished, 230.
Ernest, 90, 119, 121, 205, 263, 300, 398, 543.
"Eroica" sonata, see Sonata in C minor, for Violin, Op. 30.
Eroica symphony, see Symphony No. 3, in E flat major, Op. 55.
Ertmann, Baroness Dorothea von, 30, 210, 266, 285, 294.
Es muss sein, canon, 477.
   theme, 528.
Esterhazy, Prince, 30, 201, 208.
Evolution of piano, 194.

Exposition, defined, 629.
   of sonata, 633.
Eybler, 74, 237.

False start, passages in, 330.
"Falstaff, Milord," 43.
Fantasia, Choral, in C minor, Op. 80, 235, 236.
Fantasia sonatas, Op. 27, 232.
Fashion in music, fluctuations in, 507.
'Fate knocking at the door,' 215.
"Fate" motive in C minor symphony, 153, 566.
Fichte, 296.
Fiction, the popularizer of music, 250.
Fiddle-neck, 12.
Fiddles, BEETHOVEN receives Cremona, 71.
Fidelio, 149, 159, 162–174.
   compressed to two acts, 165.
   failure of, 164.
   first production of, 164.
   high lights of, 169.
   influence of, 172.
   involved a loss to music, 168.
   overtures, 172, 173, 174.
   plot of, 164.
   revision of libretto, 347.
   revived, 379.
   search for libretto, 162.
   second production of, 165.
   second revision of, 166.
   self-expression in, 171.
   third production of, 166.
Figure, defined, 629.
Figured-bass, defined, 629.

Finale, defined, 629.
  BEETHOVEN excels in, 295.
Fischer, Frau, 3, 18.
Fluctuations of fashion in music, 507.
Folk tunes, French, 516.
  Slavonic, 516.
Fooling, artistic, 226.
Forecast, *"The Midway,"* 475.
Form, defined, 629.
  developed, 496.
  liberated, 492.
Formlessness as law of form, 119.
France, Anatole, 258, 304, 512.
Franck, César, 20, 56, 232, 571, 608.
  Beatitudes, The, 20.
Franz, Max, 11.
"Free Sonata," 356.
French folk tunes, 516.
Frennsen, Gustav, 473.
Friedländer, Dr. Max, 124 n., 483.
Fries, Graf von, 72, 416.
Frimmel, 48, 96, 230, 300, 313, 365.
Frohberger, 252.
Fuch's *Battle of Jena,* 342.
Fugato, defined, 629.
Fugue, defined, 629.
Fugues, 27, 372–374.
  Great, the, Op. 133, 452, 453, 600.
    source-motives, 574, 600.
  C sharp minor, 459.
  in D major sonata, 356.
  modification of, 499.
Furtwängler, Wilhelm, 372 n.

Gaertner, Louis von, 536.
"Gaieté, La," see Quartet in E flat, Op. 127.
Gál, Dr. Hans, 229.
Galitzin, Prince, orders string quartets, 423.
Galitzin quartets, No. 1, see Quartet in E flat, Op. 127.
  No. 2, see Quartet in A minor, Op. 132.
  No. 3, see Quartet in B flat, Op. 130.
Gallenberg, Count, 102.
Gallenberg, Countess, see Guicciardi.
Gegenliebe, 236.
"Geister" trio, see Trio in D major, Op. 70, No. 1.
Gellert lyrics, Op. 48, 113.
Genial appropriation *versus* plagiarism, 512.
Genius, moral sense of, 304.
George IV, King of England, 30.
"German" symphony, 400.
Germ-motive, 53–56, 498, 575.
  BEETHOVEN invents, 530.
  consciously used device, 532, 577.
  defined, 629.
  early experimentation with, 533, 534.
  feels his way with, 532.
  function of, 531.
  in late sonatas, 554.
  progenitor of leitmotif, 533.
  versus source-motive, 530.
"Ghost" trio, see Trio in D major, Op. 70, No. 1.
Gilbert, W. S., 216.

INDEX

Gilman, Lawrence, 137, 264, 319, 406, 419.

Gleichenstein, Count Ignaz von, 205, 207, 232, 260, 272, 273.

Glorious Moment, The, 346.

Glossary, 626.

Gluck's *Alceste,* 13.
Orpheus, 13.

Gneixendorf, BEETHOVEN at, 469, 471.

Goethe, 13, 20, 45, 216, 220, 250, 276, 277, 284, 367, 395, 486.
impression of BEETHOVEN, 314.
meets BEETHOVEN, 314.
resents BEETHOVEN's power, 316.

Goethe's *Egmont,* 286.

Goldberg variations of Bach, 79, 500.

Grace, Harvey, 249, 330, 331, 380, 382, 409, 467, 497.

Grands, 516.

"Great Mogul," the, 43.

Grebner, 420.

Grieg, 83.

Grove, Sir George, 94, 131, 212, 310, 369, 403.

Guicciardi, Countess Giulietta, 101, 102, 153, 300.

Gyrowetz, 74, 188, 237.

Hadow, Sir W. H., 589.

Hallelujah Chorus, Handel's, 386, 387.

Halm, Anton, 145.

"Hamburg rocket," 514.

Hammerklavier sonata, *see* Sonata in B flat, Op. 106.

Handel, 44, 45, 53, 144, 256, 386, 387, 479, 608, 609.

Hanslick, 151.

Harmonic syncopation, precursor of jazz, 441.

Harmony, defined, 630.
liberated, 492.

"Harp" quartet, *see* Quartet, *"Harp,"* in E flat, Op. 74.

Harris, T. F. Stuart, 66.

Haslinger, Tobias, 319, 355.

Hawkins, Sir John, 252.

Haydn, 12, 13, 22, 29, 31, 36, 40, 43, 44, 53, 64, 74, 78, 109, 137, 144, 180, 209, 220, 223, 246, 256, 327, 370, 371, 499.
attitude of towards BEETHOVEN's trios, Op. 1, 37.
BEETHOVEN borrows from, 515.
dedication of BEETHOVEN's Op. 2 to, 41.
encourages BEETHOVEN, 22.
honoured by BEETHOVEN, 225.
neglects BEETHOVEN, 25.
teacher of BEETHOVEN, 25.

Haydn's *Creation,* 196.
Gipsy Rondo, 515.
Seasons, 325, 326.
Sonata, No. 58, 515.

Heiligenstadt Testament, 90, 106, 261.

Helm, 476, 564.

"Hero" quartet, *see* Quartet in C major, Op. 59, No. 3 (Rasoumowsky).

Hero germ-motive, 131.
theme, 127, 130.

"*Heroic*" symphony, *see* Symphony No. 3, in E flat major, Op. 55.

Hevesy, André de, 30, 73, 300.

Hiller, J. A., 16, 17, 234.

Himmel, BEETHOVEN's improvisation duel with, 42.

Hoffmann, E. T. A., 277.

Hofmeister, 45.

Holz, Carl, 27, 65, 336, 337, 368, 374, 434, 448, 473, 476, 478, 487.

Horn sonata, Op. 17, 57.

Horsalka, Johann, 383.

Horvath, Jeannette d', 22.

Hummel, J. N., 48, 209.

Humperdinck, 401.

Hüttenbrenner, 486.

Huxley, Aldous, 398, 447.

Hymn to Joy, merits and defects of, 412–415.

Idea, new meaning of word, 531.

Iken, Dr., 304.

Imitation, defined, 630.

Imitators, 514.

"Immortal Beloved," the identity of, 300.

    letter to, 298.

        discovered in secret drawer, 487.

Improvisation, BEETHOVEN's skill in, 3, 18, 21, 23, 24, 42, 72, 232, 233, 285, 378, 604.

    duel with Himmel, 42.

    with Steilbelt, 72.

In Questa Tomba, 226.

Infinitude of music, test of, 249.

Intermovement unity, 328.

Interpreter and composer, 493.

Interval, defined, 630.

Introduction, defined, 630.

    form, development of, 307.

Inversion, defined, 630.

Jahn, 414.

Jannequin, 252

Jazz, 10, 387, 441.

    BEETHOVEN's originates, 69–70.

Jekyll and Hyde, 49, 50, 77, 210, 265, 284, 351, 390, 394, 420, 422, 505.

Joachim, 71, 448, 610.

Johannes der Laüfer, 6.

Johannes der Saüfer, 6.

Johannes der Taüfer, 6.

John the Gullet-Baptist, 6.

"Joseph Vance" type of theme, 38, 78.

Joy theme, 160, 412, 413, 524, 558, 572, 573, 596.

Junker, Carl Ludwig, 21.

Kalischer, 300.

Kanka, Dr., 347, 351, 353.

Kelsey, Frederick, 609.

Kennst du das Land, 274, 275.

Kewerich, Maria Magdalena, 6, 19.

Key, defined, 630.

Keyserling, Count, 170.

King Stephen, 303, 304.

Kinsky, Prince, 239, 284, 341.

Kiss, The, 594.

Knecht, Justin, 253, 257.

Koczwara's *Battle of Prague*, 342.

Kol Nidrei, 462.

"*Komplimentierungs*" Quartett, *see* Quartet in G major, Op. 18, No. 2.

Koninck, 246.
Koželuch, 74.
Krehbiel, 35 n., 172, 300, 391.
Krenn, Michael, 470.
Kretzschmar, 490.
Kreutzer, Rudolph, 114.
"Kreutzer" sonata, *see* Sonata in
    A major, Op. 47.
Krumpholz, 105, 367.
Kuffner, 359.
Kuhac, F. X., 516.
Kuhnau, 252.

"La gaieté," see Quartet in E flat,
    Op. 127.
La Malinconia, 70.
La Mara, 300.
Lanier, Sidney, 196.
Largo appassionato, 40.
"Leibquartett," 447.
Legrenzi, 219.
Lehmann, Liza, 569.
Leitmotif, defined, 630.
    and germ-motive, 533.
Leitzmann, A., 377, 437, 444,
    457.
Lenz, Wilhelm von, 123, 125.
Leonora, or Conjugal Love, by
    Bouilly, 164.
Leonore overtures, 149, 172, 180,
    268, 269.
    source-motive in No. 1, Op. 138,
    585.
Lessing, 13,
Letters of BEETHOVEN. *See also*
    BEETHOVEN.
    to Amenda, Carl, 85, 332.
    to Bettina Brentano, 282, 283.
    to Brauchle, 334, 351.

Letters of BEETHOVEN, *continued*
    to Breitkopf and Härtel, 335.
    to Breuning, Stephan von, 146.
    to Del Rio, 268.
    to little Emily, 316.
    to Erdödy, Countess, 230.
    to Gleichenstein, 207, 260, 272.
    to Haslinger, 319, 335.
    to Hofmeister, 45.
    to Hummel, 48.
    to the "Immortal Beloved," 298,
    299.
    to Johann (brother), 238.
    to Kanka, 351, 353.
    to Karl (nephew), 445, 446.
    to Lichnowsky, 417.
    to Nägeli, 319.
    to Neate, Charles, 96, 351.
    to Peters, 392, 393, 395.
    to Piuk, 354.
    to Ries, 351.
    to Schindler, 335, 417, 483, 502.
    to Schott, 319, 459.
    to Schuppanzigh, 417.
    to Sebald, Amalie, 297, 306, 480.
    to Streicher, 318, 385.
    to Varena, 317.
    to Wegeler, 52, 86, 87, 107, 272,
    273.
    to Zmeskall, 205, 286, 287, 333,
    338, 360.
Libretto, search for, 162.
Lichnowsky, Prince, 30, 33, 37,
    71, 109, 150, 165, 199, 346,
    416, 417.
    bust of, smashed by BEE-
    THOVEN, 200.
Lichnowsky, Princess, 102, 165,
    178.

Lichnowskys, the, 30.

Linke, 179, 433.

Listener, and Fifth symphony, 224.
and last quartets, 424–429.

Liszt, 351, 372, 396.

Literature and music, relation of,
17, 81, 213–217, 248–254,
269.

Lobkowitz, Prince, 30, 31, 45, 46,
89, 147, 200, 201, 209, 233,
239, 341.
insulted by BEETHOVEN, 89.

Lobkowitz quartets, Op. 18, 66,
70, 88, 179.

Logic and music, correspondence
between, 141.

London Philharmonic Society, 318,
360, 393, 394, 421, 480, 487.
gift from, to BEETHOVEN, 480–
482.
overreached by BEETHOVEN,
303, 480–482.

Love, rôle of, in BEETHOVEN's life,
99, 103, 272, 298, 300, 301,
302.

Lowes, J. L., 512, 578.

Ludwig, Emil, 305, 439.

Lydian mode, 438.

Lyrics, Gellert, Op. 48, 113.

Macbeth, projected opera, 227.

Macco, 153.

Maelzel, canon to, 326.
chronometer, 326, 334.
defrauded by BEETHOVEN, 344.
metronome, 326.
Panharmonicon, 341, 615.

Mähler, 135, 261.

Mahlerey, 264.

Malfatti, Dr., 296.

Malfatti, Therese, 103, 272, 300,
304.

"Man, help thyself," 13.

"Mannheim rocket," the, 39, 222,
514, 534.

Marginalia, 348, 358.

Mark Twain, 10.

Marx, 305.

Mason, Daniel Gregory, 80, 116.

Mass, defined, 630.
BEETHOVEN frees, 381, 389.

Mass in C major, Op. 86, 208, 209.
Credo, 266.

Mass in D major (Missa Solemnis),
Op. 123, 229, 381–389.
Agnus Dei, 386, 387.
begun as an occasional work,
381, 384, 385.
Benedictus, 386.
Credo, 385, 386.
Et vitam venturi, 407.
Gloria, 385.
Incarnatus, 229.
Kyrie, 385.
plagiarism in, 386.
Sanctus, 386.
subscriptions solicited for, by
BEETHOVEN, 395.
value of, 388.

"Meaning" of music, 17.

Meier, Sebastian, 149.

Melodies, Russian, 179.

"Memory" sonata, 369.

Mencken, H. L., 496.

Mendelssohn, 144, 210, 212, 294.
Midsummer Night's Dream
overture, 20.

Merkenstein, Op. 100, 591.

Metronome, Maelzel's, 326.

Meyerbeer, 344.

"*Midway*" forecast, the, 475.

Milder, Frau, 235.

Millay, Edna St. Vincent, 505.

"Milord Falstaff," 43.

Minerva and the sow, 436.

Minuet, 327.

   defined, 630.

"Minuet, Beethoven's," 197.

Minuets, piano, 197.

Missa Solemnis, see Mass in D, Op. 123.

Mit einen gemalten Band, Op. 83, 573.

Mode, defined, 631.

Modulation, defined, 631.

   emancipation of, 492.

"Mogul, the Great," 43.

Mollo, 77.

Montagnarde, 517.

"*Moonlight*" sonata, *see* Sonata in C sharp minor, Op. 27, No. 2.

Moral sense of genius, 304.

Moscheles, 32, 349, 480, 481, 487.

Motif, defined, 631.

Motive, defined, 631.

   concealment of source-, 579, 581.

Mount of Olives, The, Op. 85, 112.

Moussorgsky, 59, 438.

   Boris Godounov, 179.

Movement, defined, 631.

Mozart, 13, 14, 16, 18, 19, 22, 36, 39, 40, 44, 53, 63, 64, 67, 78, 109, 130, 144, 169, 209, 222, 223, 342, 371, 535, 608.

   Abduction from the Seraglio, 13.

Mozart, *continued*

   Bastien et Bastienne, 130.

   BEETHOVEN's borrowings from, 222, 514, 524.

   Divertimento in E flat, 12.

   Don Juan overture, 515.

   G minor symphony, 514, 515.

   "*Haffner*" symphony, 524, 525.

   Hero theme, resemblance, 130.

   La Finta Giardiniera, 19, 525 n.

   praises BEETHOVEN, 19.

   Sonata, *Fantasie,* in C minor, 463.

Müller, Wilhelm, 366, 367.

Murry, J. M., 74, 501.

Music, absolute, 248.

   defined, 626.

   cannot be "explained," 249.

   and literature, 17, 248, 269.

   and logic, 141.

   made more self-contained, 494.

   matured, 491.

   and meaning, 17, 249.

   philosophy of, 16, 278.

   and poetry, 250.

   popularized by fiction, 250.

   program, 5, 248, 251, 252, 253, 255, 256, 268.

   pure, defined, 626.

   with a purpose, 385.

   realism in, 256.

   therapeutic, 176.

"Music Count," the, 333.

Musical anagram, 185, 564–565.

   blasphemy, 577.

   parody, 80.

   pets, 567.

   sketches, 27.

   witticisms, BEETHOVEN's, 355.

Muss es sein? origin of, 475.

Mystical *Adagio*, the, 500.

Nägeli, 319.

Napoleon, 122, 124, 153, 182.

Neate, Charles, 96, 258, 304, 351.

Neefe, Christian Gottlob, 15, 17.

Nephew, *see* Beethoven, Karl van (nephew).

Neufeldt, 523.

New forms, cautious approach to, 63.

Newman, Ernest, 97, 229, 496, 608, 609.

Nickname, BEETHOVEN'S, 1, 454.
Schuppanzigh's, 43.

Nietzsche, 43.

Nohl, 300.

Nottebohm, 26, 172, 222, 403, 574.

Nuance, cultivation of, 490.

Obermeyer, Therese, 320.

Oboist, joke on, 148.

Ode to Joy, 412.

Oldman, C. B., 53.

Operatic composer, freed by BEE-THOVEN, 174.

Oppersdorf, Count, 209, 318.

Oratorio, defined, 631.
Mount of Olives, The, Op. 85, 112.

Orchestra, BEETHOVEN develops, 493.
BEETHOVEN frees, 194.
BEETHOVEN humiliates, 235.
BEETHOVEN'S joke on, 148.

Organ-point, defined, 631.

Ortigue, 305.

Oulibischeff, A., 123, 125, 305, 324.

Overture, B–A–C–H, the projected, 168.
in C major, Op. 115, 304.
Consecration of the House, The, Op. 124, 594.
Coriolanus, 62, 202, 268, 269.
Egmont, 173, 268, 287, 524.
Fidelio and *Leonore Nos. 1, 2, and 3*, 172, 173, 174.

Overture, BEETHOVEN universalizes and vitalizes the, 203, 268.

Paer, 79.

Palffy, Count von, 32.

Panharmonicon, Maelzel's, 341, 615.

Parody, musical, 80.

Parry, Sir H. H., 496, 497, 531.

Passedel, 470, 476.

"Pastoral" sonata, *see* Sonata in D major, Op. 28.

Pastoral symphony, *see* Symphony No. 6 in F major, Op. 68.

"Peasants' Merrymaking" *scherzo*, 266, 267.

Pedants, 321.

"Per aspera ad astra" pattern, 213.

Peters, 392, 393.

Pets, musical, 567.

Pfeiffer, 14.

Phantasie, G minor, Op. 77, 232.

Philosophy of music, 16, 278.

Phonograph, BEETHOVEN'S music on, 616.

Piano, automatic, BEETHOVEN's music on, 616.

Piano, BEETHOVEN develops mechanism of, 493.

Piano minuets, 197.

Piuk, 354.

Plagal cadence, defined, 631.

Plagiarism, 10.
  versus genial appropriation, 512.
  in Mass in D, 386.

Pleyel, Ignatz, 232.
  quartet, BEETHOVEN improvises on second violin part, 233.

Poetic programs, 305.

Poetry and music, 250.

Political revolution and romanticism, 118.

Poll, Maria Josepha, 5,

Polonaise, Op. 89, 303, 346.

Praise of God in Nature, The, Op. 48, 113.

Printed works, BEETHOVEN's, list of, 642–660.

Program music, 5, 248, 251, 252, 253, 255, 256, 268.
  defined, 631.
  theory of, 255–257, 268.

Program question, 406.

Programs, 438.
  poetic, 305.

Prometheus theme in *Eroica* symphony, 129, 131, 133, 539.

Prospecting adventures in BEETHOVEN, 511.

Proust, Marcel, 425, 505.

Publishers and BEETHOVEN, 158, 335, 337, 390, 392, 459.

Pückler-Muskau, Prince, 276.

Pun in C sharp minor, 336.

Pure music, defined, 626.

Quartet, "Compliment," *see* Quartet in G major, Op. 18, No. 2.

—— in F major, Op. 18, No. 1, 67, 568.

Adagio, 70, 179.

—— in G major, Op. 18, No. 2, 67, 70, 461, 473.

source-motive in, 583.

—— in D major, Op. 18, No. 3, 153.

—— in C minor, Op. 18, No. 4, 57, 68–69.

Allegro, 68–69, 516.

Finale, 515.

germ-motive in, 534, 535.

—— in A major, Op. 18, No. 5, 56–57, 163.

Finale, 56, 153.

Trio of Minuet, 515.

—— in B flat, Op. 18, No. 6, 69, 70.

—— in F major, Op. 59, No. 1 (Rasoumowsky), 67, 176, 179, 181, 183, 192, 521.

—— in E minor, Op. 59, No. 2 (Rasoumowsky), 176 185, 186, 585, 586.

—— in C major, Op. 59, No. 3 (Rasoumowsky) ("*Hero*"), 187, 190, 568, 586.

—— in E flat, Op. 74 ("*Harp*"), 154, 244, 245, 527.

Adagio molto e mesto, 190, 196, 246, 569, 575.

source-motive in, 587, 588.

Presto, 246.

Quartet in F minor, Op. 95 (*Quartett Serioso*), 274, 288, 289, 290, 321.
Allegretto ma non troppo, 288–289, 541.
Allegro assai vivace ma serioso, 289–290, 542.
Allegro con brio, 290, 541.
Finale, 520, 542, 543, 568.
interlocking device, 541, 543.
germ-motive in, 290, 541–544.
source-motive in, 588, 589.
—— in E flat, Op. 127 ("*La gaieté*") (First Galitzin), 430, 560.
Adagio, ma non troppo e molto cantabile, 431.
emotional unity of, 431.
Finale, 433.
inspires Schumann and Brahms, 431, 433.
Scherzo, 430, 526.
source-motive in, 597–598.
suggestion of the *Missa*, 431.
of the *Pathétique*, 431.
—— in B flat, Op. 130 ("*Quartetto Scherzoso*") (Third Galitzin), 195, 446, 447, 560.
Alla Danza Tedesca, 154, 446.
Allegro, 448, 527.
contrapuntal part-writing in, 448, 449, 450.
Andante con moto, 447, 451, 575.
Cavatina, 38, 293, 447, 448, 528, 561, 570, 600.
Finale, 452, 573, 574.
Fugue in (afterwards published

Quartet in B flat, *continued* separately as the "*Great Fugue*," Op. 133), 447, 451–453.
Presto, 447.
Scherzo, 446, 447.
source-motive in, 599–601.
—— in C sharp minor, Op. 131, 407, 454, 525, 527.
Adagio quasi un poco andante, 462, 564.
Adagio ma non troppo e molto espressivo, 459, 463, 564.
Allegretto, 156, 461, 466.
Allegro, 460.
Andante moderato, 460.
BEETHOVEN's masterpiece, 459.
completed, 459.
"cribbed" yet new, 459.
Finale, 462.
Fugue in, 459, 462.
germ-motive in, 564.
preëminence of, 458.
Scherzo, 461, 464.
sketches for, 506.
source-motive in, 597, 598, 601.
—— in A minor, Op. 132 (Second Galitzin), 195, 229, 438, 460, 525, 573.
Allegro, 440, 525, 526, 527, 557.
Allegro assai, 558.
Allegro ma non tanto, 439, 440–441, 460.
Andante, 526.
Finale, 442, 526, 556, 557.
Molto adagio, 438.
motto of slow movement, 438.
source-motive in, 598, 599.

Quartet in F major, Op. 135, 67, 528.
brevity of, reason for, 473.
Finale, 475, 477.
finished, 473.
Lento assai, 474.
Muss es sein? 475, 476.
retrospect, 474.
source-motive in, 602.
Vivace, 474.
Quartets, string, 62, 65, 175, 427.
first, concerts, 151.
how to approach, 424–429.
last, 424.
germ-motive in, 556.
preparation necessary for hearing, 424.
and the listener, 424–429.
new forms, 428.
Quartets, six, Op. 18 (Lobkowitz), 51, 66, 67, 70, 88, 179.
"Queen of the Night," 353, 358.
Quintet in E flat major, Op. 16, 57.
Quintet in C major, Op. 29, 76.

Radicals, æsthetic, 118.
Radicati, 189.
Ramm, 147, 148.
Rau, 481.
Raugel, Felix, 209.
Ravel, 95.
Rasoumowsky, Count, 209, 423.
commissions three string quartets, 178.
Rasoumowsky quartets, 107, 179, 180, 188.

Rasoumowsky quartets, *continued*
First, in F major, Op. 59, 67, 176, 179, 181, 183, 192, 521.
Second, in E minor, Op. 59, 176, 185, 186, 585, 586.
Third, in C major, Op. 59, 187, 190, 568, 586.
Recapitulation, defined, 631.
of sonata, 633.
"Recitative" piano sonata, *see* Sonata in D minor, Op. 31, No. 2.
Reese, Gustave, 463.
Rehearsals, 109.
Reicha, Joseph, 131.
Reichardt, J. F., 194, 234, 239, 437.
Reinitz, Max, 482.
Reiss, Theresa Johanna, 469, 486.
Religion, BEETHOVEN founder of a, 504.
Rellstab, 81, 443, 456, 457.
word portrait of BEETHOVEN, 443.
Remenyi, 35.
Researches into BEETHOVEN's works, 511.
Respighi, 264.
Ridotto balls, 527.
Riemann, 300, 370, 463, 541, 543, 560.
Ries, Ferdinand, 29, 32, 37, 72, 76, 100, 109, 144, 147, 148, 150, 157, 159, 198, 239, 301, 318, 351.
Rieses, the, 12.
Rochlitz, Ferdinand, 405, 422.

Rode, 340.

Roeckel, 165.

Roentgen, Julius, 539.

Rolland, Romain, 312, 316.

Romanticism, 141.
and classicism, 116, 117, 120, 121, 246.
and poetical revolution, 118.

Romberg, B., 59, 188, 293.

Rondo, defined, 632.
modified by BEETHOVEN, 499.

Rondo in G major, for Piano, Op. 51, No. 2, 102.

Rossini, 173.
calls on BEETHOVEN, 379.
inspired by BEETHOVEN, 325.

Rossini's *The Barber of Seville*, 325.

Rudolph, Archduke, 32, 176, 198, 239, 242, 291, 381.

Ruins of Athens, The, 303, 304.
source-motive in, 590.

Russell, Sir John, his description of BEETHOVEN, 378.

Russian melodies, 179.

Rust, T. W., 521.

Rust imposture, the, 521.

Rzewiska, Countess, 226.

Sakadas, 252.

Salieri, 29, 74, 237.

Salomon, Franz, 12.

Salomon, Johann, 12.

Salomons, the, 11.

San-Galli, 300.

Scale, defined, 632.
chromatic, defined, 627.

Schall, Count Marshall von, 36.

Schenck, Johann, 26, 29.

Scherzo, 110, 499.
Beethovenian, 137.
defined, 632.
new kind of, 183.

Schiedermair, Professor Ludwig, 6 n., 20 n.

Schiller, 13.

Schiller's "Ode to Joy," 412.

Schindler, 101, 102, 107, 154, 209, 214, 216, 218, 258, 264, 267, 294, 300, 318, 319, 335, 354, 368, 375, 380, 383, 396, 417, 420, 421, 478, 480, 483, 485, 502.

Schlesinger, 473, 604.

Schlösser, 553.

Schopenhauer, 429.

Schott, 319, 336, 458, 486.

Schubert, Franz, 83, 396, 414, 525.
visit to BEETHOVEN, 484.

Schubert's *Gretchen at the Spinning Wheel*, 20.
Impromptu, 18.

Schumann, Clara, 436.

Schumann, Eugenie, 436.

Schumann, Robert, 95, 112, 184, 194, 212, 305, 307, 525.

Schumann's *Kinderscenen*, 18.

Schuppanzigh, Ignaz, 43, 48 n., 71, 151, 180, 188, 319, 341, 365 n., 417, 420, 433, 434, 476, 480.

Schuppanzigh's quartet, 71, 178.

"Scratch according to the notes," 2.

Sebald, Amalie, 296, 300, 301, 306, 480.

Second-violin trouble, 12.

Secret drawer, finding the, 487.

Segur, Nicolas, 513.

Seibert, Dr., 479.

Septet, Op. 20, 64.

Sequence, defined, 632.

Seufzer eines Ungeliebten, und Gegenliebe, 572.

Sex, appeal of, to BEETHOVEN, 99.

Sexual obsessions of BEETHOVEN, 98, 206.

Seyfried, Ignaz von, 48, 377.

Shakespeare's *Tempest,* 154, 155.

Simrock, Peter, 12, 365.

"Sinfonia Giocosa," 321.

Sister-in-law, litigation with, 352.

Skeletons, musical, 27.

Sketch Books, 24, 38, 75, 100, 159, 175, 178, 201, 221, 226, 253, 255, 263, 318, 348, 353, 358, 381, 403, 607.

Slavonic folk tunes, 516.

Smart, Sir George, 480.

Sonata, 368.

   defined, 632.

   lengthened, 498.

   liberated, 182.

Sonata, in F minor, Op. 2, No. 1, 39.

   Finale, 39.

   germ motive in, 534.

   opening theme, 222, 514.

—— in A major, p. 2, No. 2, 40.

   Largo Appassionato, 40.

   Scherzo, 40.

—— in C major, Op. 2, No. 3, 40.

   Scherzo, 40.

   source-motive in, 582.

—— in F major, for Violoncello and Piano, Op. 5, No. 1, 41.

Sonata in G minor, for Violoncello and Piano, Op. 5, No. 2, 41, 59.

—— for four hands, Op. 6, 153.

—— in E flat, Op. 7, 42.

—— in C minor, Op. 10, No. 1, 52.

   Finale, 153.

—— in F major, Op. 10, No. 2, 81.

   Finale, 87.

—— in D major, Op. 10, No. 3, 88, 517, 518, 520.

   Largo e mesto, 51, 106.

—— Three for Violin, Op. 12, 58.

—— in C minor (*Sonate Pathétique*), Op. 13, 38, 51, 52, 53, 54, 56, 58, 69, 560.

   Adagio cantabile, 52, 54, 403.

   Allegro di molto, 54, 88.

   germ-motive in, 53, 54, 55, 534, 567.

   Grave, 88.

   Rondo, 56.

   source-motive in, 567, 583.

—— in E major, Op. 14, No. 1, 58.

—— in G major, Op. 14, No. 2, 58.

   Scherzo, 572.

——, Horn, Op. 17, 57.

—— in B flat, Op. 22, 74.

—— in A minor, for Violin, Op. 23, 83.

   germ-motive in, 534.

—— in F major for Violin, Op. 24 (*"Spring"* sonata), 81, 82, 83, 88.

Sonata in F major, *continued*
germ-motive in, 535.
Scherzo, 62, 332.
—— in A flat major, Op. 26, 78, 88.
Funeral march, 79.
Minuet, 80.
source-motive in, 583.
variations, 79.
—— in E flat, Op. 27, No. 1, 78, 88.
—— in C sharp minor, Op. 27, No. 2 (*"Moonlight"* sonata), 40, 78, 88, 101, 180, 232, 240.
many possible interpretations of, 81.
Finale, 153.
legends about, 80.
—— in D major, Op. 28 (*"Pastoral"* sonata), 75.
—— in A major, for Violin, Op. 30, No. 1, 113.
—— in C minor, for Violin, Op. 30, No. 2 (*"Eroica"* sonata), 82, 83, 295.
Allegro con brio, 83.
—— in G major, for Violin, Op. 30, No. 3, 580.
—— in G major, Op. 31, No. 1, 105.
—— in D minor, Op. 31, No. 2 (*"Recitative"*), 105, 153, 226.
—— in E flat, Op. 31, No. 3, 52, 106, 107, 229, 519, 520.
Finale, 106.
Menuetto, 520.
Scherzo, 106.

Sonata in A, for Violin, Op. 47, (*"Kreutzer"* sonata), 82, 83, 113, 114, 152, 158, 180, 316.
Finale, 113.
interlocking device, 536.
source-motive, 584.
—— in C major, Op. 53 (*"Waldstein"* sonata), 38, 40, 106, 150, 152.
source-motive in, 584.
—— in F major, Op. 54, 585.
—— in F minor, Op. 57 (*"Appassionata"* sonata), 38, 40, 42, 106, 107, 152, 154, 156, 157, 158, 176, 180.
Allegro assai, 539.
Finale, 156, 157, 176.
germ-motive in, 539.
source-motive in, 584–585.
—— in A major, for Violoncello, Op. 69, 230, 231, 568.
Finale, 570.
—— in F sharp major, Op. 78, 240, 570.
Allegro, 241, 571.
—— in E flat, Op. 81a (*Adieu, Absence, and Reunion*), 241.
—— in E minor, Op. 90, 346.
program of, 347.
source-motive in, 591.
—— in G major, for Violin, Op. 96 (*"Cockcrow"* sonata), 82, 340.
Adagio, 340.
—— in A major, Op. 101, 356, 461, 525.
source-motive in, 592.
—— in C major, for Violoncello, Op. 102, 355, 356.

Sonata in C major, *continued*
  Allegro con brio, 526.
  Andante, 356.
  Finale, 571.
  source-motive in, 592.
—— in D major, for Violoncello,
  Op. 102.
  *Adagio con molto sentimento
    d'affetto,* 356.
  Finale, 356.
  Fugue, 356.
  source-motive in, 592.
—— in B flat, Op. 106 (*Hammer-
  klavier* sonata), 229, 399.
  Adagio sostenuto, 361.
  Fugue, 362.
  germ-motive in, 554.
—— in E major, Op. 109, 369.
  *Andante molto cantabile ed
    espressivo,* 369, 555.
  germ-motive in, 554.
  Prestissimo, 555.
  Vivace ma non troppo, 554.
—— in A flat, Op. 110 ("*Memory*" sonata), 369, 400,
  527.
  Allegretto molto, 372.
  Arioso dolente, 373, 440.
  echoes of other works in, 370,
    371.
  Finale, 372, 373.
  Fugue, 374, 529.
—— in C minor, Op. 111.
  Allegro con brio ed appassionato,
    374.
Arietta, 374, 375.
  difficulties of, for listener, 375.
  source-motive in, 593.

Sonatas:
  "*Appassionata,*" *see* Sonata in
    F minor, Op. 57.
  "*Cockcrow,*" *see* Sonata in G for
    Violin, Op. 96.
  "*Eroica,*" *see* Sonata in C minor,
    Op. 30.
  Free, see Sonata in C major,
    Op. 102.
  Hammerklavier, see Sonata in B
    flat, Op. 106.
  "*Kreutzer,*" *see* Sonata in A for
    Violin, Op. 47.
  "*Memory,*" *see* Sonata in A flat,
    Op. 110.
  "*Moonlight,*" *see* Sonata in C
    sharp minor, Op. 27, No. 2.
  "*Pastoral,*" *see* Sonata in D
    major, Op. 28.
  Pathétique, see Sonata in C
    minor, Op. 13.
  "*Spring,*" *see* Sonata in F, for
    Violin, Op. 24.
  "*Waldstein,*" *see* Sonata in C
    major, Op. 53.
Sonata-form, defined, 632.
  BEETHOVEN frees, 138.
Sonate Pathétique, see Sonata in C
  minor, Op. 13.
Song of Penitence, Op. 48, 113.
Song-cycle, 357.
Song-form, defined, 633.
Sonneck, Oscar G., 127 n., 148 n.,
  301, 452, 481, 482, 532,
  567.
Sonnleithner, 164.
Source-motive, 55, 56, 153, 499,
  566, 577.
  a chief, 578–611.

Source-motive, *continued*
    conscious use of, 577, 579, 603–608.
    devices for concealment of, 579, 581.
    defined, 634.
    protean nature of, 594.
    use of, 608.
    versus germ-motive, 530.
Spaeth, Sigmund, 80.
Spandrell, 439.
"*Spangol, der,*" 1, 454.
"*Spangy,*" 1, 2, 454.
Spanish Castle tunes, 15.
Spohr, 32, 147, 321, 350, 540.
Stadler, Abbé, 338.
Steibelt, 24.
    his piano duel with BEETHOVEN, 72.
Steiner, 335, 355.
Strauss, Richard, 80, 247, 251, 262, 322.
Stravinsky, 95, 266.
Streicher, Andreas, 194, 385.
Streicher, Nanette, 318, 337, 341.
Stretto, defined, 634.
Stumpff, 479, 480.
Stutterheim, Baron von, 469.
Subdominant, defined, 634.
Subject, defined, 634.
Suite, defined, 634.
Sullivan, J. W. N., 167, 362, 393, 394, 424, 465.
Surprise symphony, 332.
Symphonic *adagios*, 196.
Symphony, defined, 634.
    BEETHOVEN lengthened the, 498.
    BEETHOVEN's favourite, 359.

Symphony, *continued*
    comparative qualities of symphonies, 506.
    unification of, 142.
    "unproblematic," 306.
Symphony, "*Battle,*" Op. 91, 174, 265, 268, 341, 342, 345, 615.
    first performance of, 343.
    popular success of, 344.
—— "Beethoven's," 197.
—— *Choral,* see Symphony No. 9, in D minor, Op. 125.
—— "*English,*" 400.
—— *Eroica,* see Symphony No. 3, in E flat major, Op. 55.
—— "*German,*" 400.
—— *Pastoral,* see Symphony No. 6 in F major, op. 68.
—— "*Spring,*" see Symphony No. 4, in B flat major, Op. 60.
—— *Surprise,* 332.
Symphony, No. 1, in C major, Op. 21, 63, 88, 146.
    Allegro, 515.
    Andante cantabile con moto, 515.
    Finale, 62.
—— No. 2, in D major, Op. 36, 109, 111, 112, 179.
    Finale, 109.
    Germ-motive in, 110, 111, 535.
    Larghetto, 110, 535, 568.
    Scherzo, 110, 536, 584.
    source-motive in, 584, 596.
—— No. 3, in E flat major, Op. 55 (*Eroica*), 69, 76, 122 to 142, 144, 147, 148, 179, 180,

Symphony, No. 3, *continued*
212, 243, 266, 268, 302, 372, 407, 521.
criticism of, 142.
Episode, 139.
Finale, 125, 126, 129, 136, 138.
Funeral March, 127, 134, 309, 372, 515.
germ-motive in, 538.
Hero theme in, 130.
interlocking of movements in, 133.
liberation of sonata-form in, 138.
momentousness of, 126.
novelty of, 136.
Prometheus theme in, 129, 131, 133, 539.
Scherzo, 124, 128, 131, 137.
sonata-form in, 141.
liberation of, in, 138.
variations, a gigantic set of, 126.
—— No. 4, in B flat major, Op. 60 ("*Spring*"), 107, 176, 194, 195, 197.
Adagio, 196, 197.
Allegro Vivace, 196.
—— No. 5, in C minor, Op. 67, 69, 83, 110, 152, 153, 176, 183, 187, 191, 211, 213, 216, 229, 234, 246.
Andante con moto, 220, 221.
compared with *Eroica*, 212.
criticisms of, 234.
"*Fate*" motive of, as germ-motive, 540, 566.
Finale, 227.
germ-motive in, 539–540.

Symphony, No. 5, *continued*
possible interpretations of, 216, 217, 219.
music of, 221.
plagiarisms in, 222.
Scherzo, 39, 60, 229, 331.
source-motive, 152–154, 587.
—— No. 6, in F major, Op. 68 (*Pastoral*), 62, 176, 215, 216, 218, 252, 255, 248, 251, 253, 295, 402, 403.
Allegro ma non troppo, 262.
Bird-like figures, 263, 264.
Bird notes in, 214.
Brook Scene in, 263, 264.
Finale, 265.
first movement, 261.
harmonic effect, daring, 265.
opening, 516.
Scherzo, 62, 265, 266, 267, 516.
source-motive in, 587.
Storm, 265.
Trio, 516.
—— No. 7, in A major, Op. 92, 156, 307–312.
Allegretto, 156, 308, 309, 404.
Allegro con brio, 311.
Coda, 312.
Finale, 311.
illusion of vastness in, 313.
introduction, *Poco sostenuto*, 307.
outside interpretation of, 305.
Scherzo, 310.
source-motive in, 590.
Vivace, 307, 524.
—— No. 8, in F major, Op. 93, 62, 83, 88, 320.

Symphony, No. 8, *continued*
   Allegretto scherzando, 324, 325, 326, 549.
   Allegro vivace, 547, 551.
      opening, 321, 331, 547.
      second subject, 322.
   Finale, 324, 327, 329, 331, 447, 550, 551.
   germ-motives in, 547.
   interlocking devices, 546, 553.
   a masterpiece of camouflage, 551.
   Minuet, 327.
   source-motive in, 591.
   Trio, 550.
—— No. 9, in D minor, Op. 125 (*Choral*), 160, 164, 211, 295, 400, 526.
   Adagio, 38, 403–405, 410–411, 556.
   Allegro ma non troppo, 402.
   Finale, 412, 538.
      Andante Maestoso, 414.
      Joy theme in, 160, 413, 558, 572, 573.
   first movement, 405, 407, 556.
   fusion of two schemes in, 404.
   interlocking devices in, 555.
   long incubation period of, 399.
   melodies in, types of, 559.
   memorandum for, 399.
   memories in, 400.
   Presto, 537.
   Scherzo, 331, 400, 401, 407, 408, 409, 536, 556.
   source-motives in, 572, 595.
—— No. 10 (unpublished), 312.
   memorandum for, 399.

Syncopation, defined, 634.
   harmonic, 441.

Tears *versus* applause, 42.
Temperament, equal, 66.
Tennyson's lack of musical knowledge, 25 n.
Thalberg, 420.
Thayer, 26, 35 n., 89, 99, 172, 177, 206, 207, 271, 279, 300, 341, 351, 391, 420, 456, 476, 478, 479, 527.
Theme, defined, 635.
   B–A–C–H, 185, 186, 400.
Thematic work, defined, 635.
Therapeutic music, 176.
Thoroughbass, defined, 635.
"Three blind mice," 242.
Thürheim, Countess, Lulu, 20.
Tieck, 119.
To the Distant Beloved, Op. 98, 357, 358.
To Hope, Op. 32, 160, 573.
   Op. 94, source-motive in, 593.
Tolstoi, 316.
Tonality, defined, 635.
Tonic, defined, 635.
Tonic chord, defined, 635.
Toscanini, 220.
Tovey, Donald, 409.
Transposition, BEETHOVEN's skill in, 35.
Treitschke, 347.
Triad, 111.
   defined, 635.
   as a germ-motive, 111, 575.
   as a source-motive, 576.
Triad habit, 575, 576.

Trio in E flat, Op. 1, No. 1,
36–37.
source-motive in, 581, 582.
—— in D major, Op. 1, No. 2,
37–38.
—— in C minor, Op. 1, No. 3, 36–
37, 74.
source-motive in, 582.
—— in E flat, for strings, Op. 3,
11, 12.
—— in C minor, for strings, Op.
9, No. 3.
Adagio con espressivo, 568.
Allegro molto e vivace, 520.
source-motive in, 582.
—— in B flat major, Op. 11,
(Clarinet trio), 58, 62, 72.
—— in D major, Op. 70, No. 1
(*"Ghost"* trio, or *"Geister"*
trio), 226, 228, 229, 517,
518.
Largo, 226, 229.
—— in E flat, Op. 70, No. 2,
226, 228, 229, 519, 520.
Allegretto ma non troppo, 519.
—— in C, Op. 87 (for 2 oboes
and English horn), 77.
—— in B flat, Op. 97 (*"Archduke"* trio), 290–296, 521,
571.
Allegro moderato, 291, 544.
Andante con moto, 38, 522,
546.
Finale, 295, 546.
germ-motive in, 544, 546.
scherzo, 102, 292, 544, 545.
source-motive in, 589, 590.
Trio, 292.
Trios Op. 1, 11, 12, 36.

Triple concerto, Op. 56, 176.
Truth and beauty, 395.
Tschaikowsky, 56, 212, 308 n.,
609.
Türkheim, Baron von, 46.
Turner, W. J., 501.
Tutti, defined, 635.
Beethoven abolishes opening,
193.

Umlauf, 420, 421.
Unger, 300, 420.
"Unproblematic" symphony, 306.

"Van" in Beethoven's name, 354.
Van den Eeden, 14.
Varena, 296, 318.
Variation, defined, 635.
form, 79.
treatment of, 500.
Variations, Bach's Goldberg, 79,
500.
Variations Diabelli, 284, 352, 397,
500, 605.
source-motive in, 595.
Variations on theme from *Prometheus*, 106.
Verdi, 28.
Victory, Wellington's, see Symphony, *"Battle,"* Op. 91.
Vielhorsky, Count, 234.
Vienna, an appropriate home for
Beethoven, 237.
Beethoven arrives in, 23.
bombardment of, 232.
first appearance of Beethoven
in, 34.
freedom of, bestowed on Beethoven, 355.

INDEX

Vienna, *continued*
  intelligence of police in, 376.
  musical conditions in, 34.
  visited by BEETHOVEN, 18.
Viennese loyal to BEETHOVEN, 202.
Vigano, Salvatore, 76.
Violoncello humour, 333.
Virtuosity, BEETHOVEN frees music from, 96.
Virtuosos, BEETHOVEN learns from, 59.
Vivaldi, 53, 252.
Vocal composer, BEETHOVEN not, 167.
Vogler, Abt, 21.
Voltaire, 506.

Wagner, Richard, 20, 95, 124, 140, 351, 413, 450, 464, 465, 466, 491, 608.
Wagner's *The Flying Dutchman*, 20.
Waldstein, Count Ferdinand von, 20, 22, 23, 31.
"Waldstein" sonata, *see* Sonata in C major, Op. 53.
Waldvogel, Dr. Richard von, 271.
Walker, Ernest, 414, 452, 491, 500.
Warner, Waldo, 184.
Wawruch, Dr., 478.
Weber, Carl Maria von, 172, 296, 307, 321.

Wegeler, Dr. Franz, 20, 35, 99, 101, 146, 272, 273.
  letter of, 86, 87.
Weigl, 74.
Weingartner, Felix, 420.
Weiss, 178.
Weissenbach, Dr., 96.
Wellington's Victory, see Symphony, *"Battle,"* Op. 91.
Westerhold, Marie, 22.
Whitman, Walt, 31, 75, 258.
Will, BEETHOVEN makes his, 483.
  codicil to, 484.
Willmann, Magdalena, 102, 300.
Winter, Dr. Helmuth, 163.
Wolanek, 435.
Women, BEETHOVEN's attitude towards, 100, 101, 114, 159, 169.
Wood, Dr. Charles, 127, 403.
Works, BEETHOVEN's printed, list of, 642–660.
  naming BEETHOVEN's, 321.
  researches into BEETHOVEN's, 511.
Wyzewa, T. de, 220, 524.

Zelter, 220, 367, 395.
Zmeskall, Freiherr Nikolaus, von Domanovecz, 43, 46, 205, 286, 287, 330, 333, 334, 360, 361, 367, 416.
Zulehner, 158.